40

Books by Elizabeth Bishop

The Collected Prose

Elizabeth Bishop

The Collected Prose

EDITED, WITH AN INTRODUCTION,

BY ROBERT GIROUX

Farrar · Straus · Giroux

NEW YORK

Library of Congress Cataloging in Publication Data
Bishop, Elizabeth, 1911–1979.
The collected prose.
Includes bibliographical references.
I. Giroux, Robert. II. Title.
PS3503.I785A15   1984   818'.5408   83–16418

Contents

❧

Introduction

BY ROBERT GIROUX

It was Elizabeth Bishop's prose, rather than her poems, that brought us together. In November 1956 her literary agent—the late, and greatly missed, Bernice Baumgarten—told me that Elizabeth had completed a prose work which the publisher of her poems had declined. Would I be interested in seeing her translation of the diary of a girl who had lived at the turn of the century in a diamond-mining town in Brazil? My initial response was, I admit, tepid. A childhood diary in translation seemed spectacularly unpromising, and I was mainly interested in Elizabeth Bishop as a poet. The book, I suggested to Bernice, sounded like a project undertaken as a labor of love and perhaps as a respite from poems—poems that Elizabeth's regular publisher would have the right to publish in the future. It *was* a labor of love, Bernice replied, and in Elizabeth's eyes a work of importance: she had spent three years rendering the diary from Portuguese into English, with the help of her friend Lota de Macedo Soares; she had sought out and met the author, now elderly and still living in Brazil; she had written an excellent introduction giving the background and genesis of the diary, about which Georges Bernanos had sent the author a letter praising its "genius"; and she would offer her next book of poems only to the publisher of the diary. I asked at once to see the manuscript. Elizabeth at that time called the book *Black Beans and Diamonds*, and it was fascinating. We were delighted to sign it up, we published it under her new title, *The Diary of "Helena Morley,"* and at this writing it is still in print. (We had to wait eight years—they were worth it—for Elizabeth's poems, *Questions of Travel*.)

At our first meeting, which took place when she signed the contract early in 1957, I found Elizabeth attractive and rather shy, and noted her excellent manners and shrewd glance. She was an extremely attentive listener, but scarcely spoke until I told her of my experience escorting Marianne Moore to the New York première of T. S. Eliot's *The Cocktail Party*, at his request (he was unable to leave London). After the performance, we had been caught in the aisle behind the Duke of Windsor, and heard him say (at which point Marianne gently poked me in the ribs): "They tell me Mr. Eliot wrote this play in verse, but I must say you'd *never* know it!" This made Elizabeth laugh, and she responded with an amusing account of Miss Moore's careful arrangement for their first meeting, when Elizabeth was a Vassar undergraduate—on the right-hand bench outside the doorway of the reading room of the New York Public Library. (The full story is told in "Efforts of Affection," Elizabeth's memoir of the poet and her mother, the ninth piece in this book.) Thus began my publishing relationship with Elizabeth Bishop, which soon deepened into a friendship that lasted until her death, twenty-two years later.

"Yes, all my life I have lived and behaved very much like that sandpiper [in her poem]—just running along the edges of different countries, 'looking for something,' " Elizabeth said in her acceptance speech at the University of Oklahoma in 1976, on receiving the *Books Abroad*/Neustadt International Prize for

Literature. Perhaps her early uprootedness made her a traveler, at first by necessity and later by choice: she lived in Nova Scotia and Paris, Ouro Preto and Worcester, London and Key West, Poughkeepsie and Cape Cod, Petrópolis and San Francisco, Mexico and Boston, North Haven and Greenwich Village, Seattle and Rio de Janeiro; and she chose geographical titles for her books—*North & South, Questions of Travel, Geography III.*

Her life almost from its beginning was marked by losses, which makes it all the more admirable that there is not a trace of self-pity in her writing. "The art of losing isn't hard to master" is the refrain of her villanelle "One Art." She lost her father, William Thomas Bishop, eight months after her birth on February 8, 1911, in Worcester, Massachusetts. He died of Bright's disease. Her mother, Gertrude Bulmer Bishop, seriously affected by her husband's death, still wore black five years later, and was hospitalized several times for treatment of a mental disorder. The color black figures in one of Elizabeth's earliest memories, of a ride with her mother in a swan boat in the Boston Public Garden. This occurred, wrote Elizabeth, "at the age of three and is chiefly memorable for the fact that one of the live swans paddling around us bit my mother's finger when she offered it a peanut. I remember the hole in the black glove and a drop of blood." The mother's final breakdown occurred in 1916, when her five-year-old daughter saw her for the last time. Mrs. Bishop died in a sanatorium in 1934.

The first real home Elizabeth knew was in the coastal town of Great Village, Nova Scotia, where her widowed mother returned in order to be with her parents, the Bulmers. The grandmother, who came from the seafaring Hutchinson family, was the daughter of the master and part owner of a sailing vessel lost at sea off Cape Sable Island. Elizabeth's portrait of the Bulmer grandparents in her poems and prose is that of unpretentious country people, whom she deeply loved. "Primer Class," the memoir which opens this book, reveals that when Elizabeth left their house each morning to go to her one-room village school, she used to "ask Grandmother . . . to promise me not to die before I came home." The story with which this book ends, "In the Village," a prose-poem about an idyllic yet fearful childhood, records her terror at her mother's scream and the solace and refuge she sought, and found, in the "beautiful pure" sound—*clang*—that Nate the blacksmith made on his anvil. There seems to be general agreement that this story is a masterpiece.

Elizabeth's peremptory removal from Nova Scotia by her wealthy Bishop grandparents was a jolt and displacement. It happened when she was six, and she describes it in "The Country Mouse": "I felt as if I were being kidnapped, even if I wasn't." John Wilson Bishop, her paternal grandfather, who came originally from Prince Edward Island just north of Nova Scotia, had emigrated to Worcester, Massachusetts, founded a successful business, and in 1870 married Sarah A. Foster. (This grandmother's maiden name served as a pen name for Elizabeth when she wrote "The Housekeeper" in 1948.) By the turn of the century, the J. W. Bishop Company, building contractors, had become one of the leading construction firms in the East, known for the government buildings they had erected at West Point; halls of learning at Harvard, Princeton, and Andover; libraries at Boston and Providence; palatial residences at Newport, Lenox, and New York; and many other business and institutional buildings in New England. Elizabeth's father had been a principal executive in the firm until his untimely death at thirty-nine. Elizabeth's brief stay—nine months—as a "country mouse" in the big Bishop house in Worcester was unhappy:

> I had been brought back unconsulted and against
> my wishes to the house my father had been born

in, to be saved from a life of poverty and provin-
cialism, bare feet, suet puddings, unsanitary
school slates, perhaps even from the inverted *r*'s
of my mother's family. With this surprising extra
set of grandparents, until a few weeks ago no
more than names, a new life was about to begin.

This experiment (as it appears to have been) was terminated by
illness. During her months there Elizabeth contracted asthma,
and suffered from eczema, bronchitis, and other ailments. Her
account of this ordeal is, like all her writing, precise and objec-
tive. Her grandparents were acting generously by their lights
toward their son's only child, but the kind of imagination shown
in her grandfather's gift of three Golden Bantams, which de-
lighted her, was offset by the family's humorless rigidity. When
Elizabeth felt disloyal to Canada at saluting the stars and stripes
in the classroom, her grandmother insisted she learn *all* the
verses of "The Star-Spangled Banner" at her feet. After the
warmth, acceptance, and *unselfconsciousness* of Great Village,
these new circumstances were such that "I . . . never felt at all
secure about my status." She equated herself as being "on the
same terms in the house" as the Boston bull terrier Beppo.

At this crucial juncture, her Aunt Maude, her mother's elder
sister, living in South Boston with her husband "in the top tene-
ment of a small, shabby, wooden two-tenement house," took
her in and provided the care she needed. She has left no
finished piece of writing about this period of her life. (An
uncompleted story about those years, "Mrs. Sullivan Down-
stairs," is concerned with an Irish immigrant neighbor of theirs
who fascinated Elizabeth: "She sang nice mournful songs in
Celtic.") Her health seems to have been improved by this move,
and by the summer holidays Aunt Maude arranged for her
with the Bulmers in Nova Scotia.

When Elizabeth turned twelve, she also spent two months each year on Cape Cod at Camp Chequesset or, as she preferred to call it, the Nautical School for Girls. An inveterate reader by the time she was fourteen, she had discovered the poems of George Herbert in a Provincetown shop that sold secondhand books. She relates that she picked up "this little volume of Herbert. I had never heard of him at that point. I liked him so much I bought the book." His naturalness of tone combined with his uncommon themes made him one of her favorite poets for life. In her interview at the Academy of American Poets in 1974 she also said of "Love Unknown," one of her favorite Herbert poems: "I like the purity of language, which manages to express a very deep emotion without straining; he doesn't even capitalize when he is obviously referring to Christ (at least in my edition)."

Elizabeth always maintained that she received little formal early schooling because of illness, but her formative Canadian primer class, her innate, precocious gifts, and an inheritance from her father's estate stood her in good stead, and she was accepted in 1927 by the Walnut Hill boarding school at Natick, Massachusetts. One of her closest friends at school and college, Frani Muser, has given us a vivid glimpse of Elizabeth at sixteen:

> When I arrived at the Walnut Hill School in Natick in 1927, I met a most remarkable girl. She looked remarkable, with tightly curly hair that stood straight up, while the rest of us all had straight hair that hung down. And she was remarkable in many ways besides. She had read more widely and deeply than we had. But she carried her learning lightly. She was very funny. She had a big repertory of stories she could *tell*, not read, and of wonderful songs she could sing,

like ballads and sea chanteys. And if some school occasion called for a new song, or a skit, it would appear overnight like magic in her hands. Her name was Elizabeth Bishop. We called her "Bishop," spoke of her as "the Bishop," and we all knew with no doubt whatsoever that she was a genius.

Walnut Hill was a very serious school with one purpose, to get its girls into college, a good college. . . . We sang two hymns a day for three or four years. They were Congregational hymns, not high church, or low, but vigorous American songs, rugged as good New England granite. Singing them with gusto released our pent-up feelings. And on a rainy day, when outdoor exercise was canceled, Elizabeth and I would often repair to the practice room, set up the hymnal, improvise a stirring four-hand accompaniment, and sing.

This addiction to hymns and hymn singing had more to do with the arts of poetry and music than religion; Elizabeth Bishop, like Emily Dickinson, was an unbeliever (see her marvelous poem "The Unbeliever," inspired by Bunyan's words "He sleeps on the top of a mast"). As she explained in the interview, "Where I lived in Canada, people used to sing hymns in the evening. They liked to play on the piano and organ, and they'd sing and sing and sing. My grandfather [Bulmer] went to two churches— one Presbyterian, one Baptist—one in the morning and one in the afternoon. So I'm full of hymns." On one occasion in 1972— at the memorial service for Marianne Moore which we attended at a Presbyterian church in Brooklyn—I was a witness to Elizabeth's unselfconscious pleasure in the singing of hymns. In one of her last letters to Frani Muser, written in August 1979 from her summer house in North Haven, Maine, she wrote that she had "attended a fine hymn-sing at Mrs. Thacher's. We sang a lot of nice hymns but . . . either the piano was tuned an octave too high—or I can't get any higher than a middle C any more." It was fitting that at her memorial service held at Agassiz House, Harvard, on October 21, 1979, her friends sang "Rock of Ages," "We Gather Together," "A Mighty Fortress," and "There Is a Balm in Gilead."

The details of her years at Vassar and her friendship with Marianne Moore; her first trip abroad (to Paris) in 1935; her nine years of residence in Key West, Florida, where her friend Loren MacIver encouraged her to pursue her gifts as a painter, where she discovered the primitive painter described in "Gregorio Valdes," and where (as she relates in "Mercedes Hospital") she encountered a suspect saint; as well as her later friendships with Randall Jarrell and Robert Lowell—all these are well documented. So is her literary history: the publication in 1946 of her first book, *North & South,* and the subsequent works that earned her ever greater acclaim over the next thirty years. What is not so well known is that she became a resident of Brazil almost by accident, from illness. Her condensed notes, in the chronology she prepared for *World Literature Today* (previously *Books Abroad*), tell the story:

> 1951. In November [I] started to travel around South America; stopped over to visit Brazilian friends. In Rio de Janeiro, because of a violent allergic reaction to the fruit of the cashew, gave up [my] dream trip to the Straits of Magellan, et cetera. After recovering, decided to stay in Brazil. For some fifteen years, with occasional visits to New York, shared a house in the mountains near

Petrópolis and an apartment in Rio de Janeiro
with a Brazilian friend met in New York in 1942,
Lota Costellat de Macedo Soares. . . .

1961.   Trip down the Amazon. Also trips to the
"interior," to Minas Gerais and, with Aldous
Huxley, to Matto Grosso to see Indian tribes. . . .

1967.   Stern-wheeler trip down the Rio São Fran-
cisco. . . . Rio de Janeiro and Ouro Preto, Minas
Gerais, where [I] restored a colonial house (built
in the 1690s) bought in 1965.

I have always regretted not being able to accept her invitation
to visit the unusual house at Ouro Preto, called Casa Mariana
after (a) Marianne Moore and (b) the fact that it was on the road
to the town of Mariana. Her letter described the house as having
"five bedrooms, two *salas,* a spectacular view across the valley,
fruit trees, a walled garden, a waterfall, a panorama of seven
baroque churches, and just about everything except a tele-
phone." This lack of a telephone led to a bizarre experience
when she won the National Book Award for Poetry in 1970. I
prepared myself to follow her instructions to phone the little
post office at Ouro Preto, and ask them to send a messenger for
her, after having cabled her some weeks earlier that I was certain
she would win the award. The acceptance ceremony would take
place forty-eight hours after the judges met, and I wanted her to
arrange to fly to New York on twenty-four-hours notice. As soon
as I learned that the prize was hers, I put through the call, ex-
pecting a long delay before it reached Ouro Preto and finally
Elizabeth, but the English-speaking operator in Rio rang through
at once to the post office, and suddenly I heard Elizabeth's voice:
"Why, Bob, this is amazing! I've just come to the post office to
put through a call to you, when I heard another operator speak

my name." Her letter, which came a week later, explained what
had happened:

> I can't get over the coincidence of our meeting in
> mid-air like that. Perhaps it wouldn't strike you
> as so strange, in New York, but if you could see
> the circumstances here: the dismal little office I
> just happened to go to at that time, and the two
> very stupid telephone girls with whom I'd been
> arguing for ten minutes to put through my call to
> you. They informed me that Oregon was a state
> [the office telephone exchange at that time was
> Oregon 5], and what city in Oregon did I want,
> and they had to be taught to pronounce Dr.
> Roberto's last name, and so on—until finally
> when I got into booth No. 1, they abandoned me
> to talk to two boy friends, very loudly. But then
> I heard an English-speaking operator, I suppose
> in Rio, using my full name, though on this end
> I'd given 'Dona Elizabeth,' as the custom is—and
> I realized right away that you were calling me,
> and also that I had probably received the award.
> It was very nice. Roxanne [Cumming] and I, with
> two ex-Peace Corps workers visiting us, all went
> out to dinner that evening at the best (that's not
> very good) restaurant here to celebrate.
>
> After I left the post office the Brazilian cultural
> attaché called me, via a neighbor, and was disap-
> pointed that I already knew of the award. He
> said, "Oh, you've taken the wind from my sails,"
> and he had a car ready to send for me to make it
> to the plane for Rio, and reservations on a night
> plane to New York—all very nice of him. . . . Oh,

I toyed for several hours with the idea of going,
but it really would have been extremely compli-
cated and very expensive, even with the plane
fare paid for me. . . . I gave the attaché my cable
asking Cal [Lowell] to accept for me—safer than
sending it from here. I thought of several witty (I
thought) things to say, but then decided it was
probably better to be strictly conventional. I'd
love to hear about the goings-on at Philharmonic
Hall [where the ceremony was held].

When I began to compile this book, I came across a single
typed sheet among Elizabeth's papers, headed "In the Village &
Other Stories." This was corrected in her handwriting to "In the
Village: Stories & Essays (?)." Under this, above the tentative
contents, she added "with dates and intro." It was a relief and
great help to have this record of her first thoughts about a collec-
tion of her prose. I am happy to say that *The Collected Prose,*
which we decided to publish as a companion volume to her
poems, contains every available piece she had intended to collect,
with the exception of the short prose-poem "The Hanging of
the Mouse." This had two question marks written beside it, in-
dicating her doubts, and it is of course preserved in *The Com-
plete Poems, 1927–1979.* (Its source, which she revealed in a
1937 letter to Marianne Moore, is worth recording: "I once
hung Minnow's artificial mouse on a string to a chair back, with-
out thinking what I was doing—it looked very sad.") There were
only two items in her list that it was impossible to include. One
was the unfinished story "Lulu & His Wife, or the Golden
Glasses," set in Brazil, of which only three or four promising
pages, and her notes, could be found. The other was the essay
"Mexico, 1943," of which no trace could be discovered. Ap-

parently it was to be an account of the nine months she spent in Mexico, during which her chance meeting with the Chilean poet Pablo Neruda led to their friendship. (Neruda recorded the lofty circumstances of this meeting in "Notebook V" in his *Passions and Impressions* (1983): "Vinícius de Moraes drives me to . . . Ouro Preto, colonial and calcareous, with the clearest air in South America . . . Elizabeth Bishop lives here—the great North American poet I met several years ago on the summit of a pyramid in Chichén Itzá. She wasn't in Brazil, so I wrote her a little poem in English.")

Among Elizabeth's unpublished papers in the Manuscript Collection of the Vassar College Library, I was surprised to find as many as seven pieces which, with very few changes, she might readily have published in her lifetime, and only four of these— the ones in italics—were in her contemplated table of contents: "The U.S.A. School of Writing," *"Mercedes Hospital,"* "A Trip to Vigia," *"To the Botequim & Back,"* *"Primer Class,"* "The Country Mouse," and *"Efforts of Affection."* Perhaps the most important was her memoir of Marianne Moore, of which she left a number of versions with only slight variations. Those numerous drafts struck me very much as that bushel basketful of rejects in Marianne Moore's kitchen struck her. One of the reasons Elizabeth's poems seem to remain ever fresh is that she, too, was a perfectionist.

I have asked myself why she did not publish, or even put on her list, a piece as humorous and evocative as "The U.S.A. School of Writing," the account of her first job after leaving Vassar. Or a piece as subtle and delicate as "A Trip to Vigia," a study in the contrasts between a country's poverty and its people's fine manners. Its form is perfect, unlike that of "To the Botequim & Back," which, while it conveys perfectly the reality —natural beauty amid human squalor—of Ouro Preto, was apparently intended for further development. And why did she not indicate publication for "The Country Mouse," which she had worked over and reworked, and which is central to an understanding of her biography? There are several possible answers, the most obvious being her highly developed sense of privacy, illustrated by her remark on confessional poetry: "You just wish they'd keep some of those things to themselves." But perhaps the best answer is that she had not got around to releasing any of these prose pieces because she wanted to make all seven of them better. I recall Lloyd Schwartz's remark at the reading held in her memory in Boston, the sad one she had been scheduled to read at herself: "Elizabeth worked fastidiously. Sometimes she'd spend years thinking about a phrase or a word." Robert Lowell also recorded this sense of perfectionism in his poem "For Elizabeth Bishop 4": "Do / you still hang your words in air, ten years / unfinished, glued to your notice board, with gaps / or empties for the unimaginable phrase— / unerring Muse who makes the casual perfect?"

We are fortunate to have these lately discovered prose works, for themselves, and for the light they shed on her life and work. In "Primer Class" her interest in the classroom wall maps reveals that one of the major themes of her poems entered into her consciousness when she was five years old. We also now know that the strange moment of self-awareness described in her poem "In the Waiting Room" had as background the unhappy period of her childhood recounted in "The Country Mouse," the conclusion of which is another version of the same moment, in prose. And how could one have known, before "The U.S.A. School of Writing" became available, that one of the scraps of paper found on the beach in her story "The Sea & Its Shore" is taken from a letter her elderly pupil Mr. Jimmy O'Shea addressed to her—in the persona of "Mr. Margolies"—just before she decided to break with the shady correspondence school? It is also worth noting that the hero of this early (1935) story is named Edwin Boomer, a phonetic equivalent of Bulmer. (This family name actually appears as "Boomer" in printed accounts of Bishop funerals.)

The setting of most of her published stories is a rural and maritime community like (and sometimes in fact) Great Village. "Gwendolyn," her story of a child's death and funeral as observed by a child, involves not only Great Village but her Bulmer grandmother and her mother's younger sister, Aunt Mary, who also figures in "Primer Class." Elizabeth's first published story, "The Baptism," a study in religious mania, occurs in a setting like Great Village, though the place is not named. "The Housekeeper," which has Cape Cod and Boston as backgrounds, is an exception as to setting but not as to theme—the unselfish devotion of an older woman for orphan children. "Memories of Uncle Neddy" is wholly concerned with the author's recollections of a member of her mother's family in their Nova Scotia village. (This Neddy is not to be confused with Uncle Ned in "The Country Mouse," her father's younger brother, whose real name was John Bishop. It was usual but not absolutely consistent for Elizabeth to change the names of relatives in her writing: Aunt Consuelo in "In the Waiting Room" is Aunt Jenny in "The Country Mouse," and in life Aunt Florence.) Elizabeth's two most fanciful stories, "The Sea & Its Shore" and "In Prison," which she described to Marianne Moore as "these horrible 'fable' ideas that seem to obsess me," have a common theme of refuge and retreat from the world. In the former, Edwin Boomer has taken up his strange and isolated existence in the course of his pursuit of "the life of letters." On the other hand, the Poe-like narrator of "In Prison," an inveterate reader, regards the prospect of incarceration as a kind of equivalent of Henry James's "the great good place."

There are two pieces in this book which she omitted from her list and yet published in her lifetime—her introduction to *The*

Diary of "Helena Morley" and her story "The Farmer's Children." She considered the latter "a very bad story" (see page 130); perhaps it is more conventional and sentimental than anything else she wrote, yet its rural setting, the defenseless orphan children who are its protagonists, and their gratuitous suffering and death are themes familiar to her fiction. The fact that it was chosen as one of the "Best American Short Stories" for the year in which it was published is less an irony than a tribute to its professional competence. I take the responsibility for its inclusion here, as I do also for the introduction to the Brazilian diary. Marianne Moore singled this out in her review of the diary in *Poetry* by referring to the "exactness of observation in the introduction which is an extension, in manner, of Miss Bishop's verse and other writing." Perhaps Elizabeth's omission of it can be explained by the fact that she never thought of it as a separate prose work that could be disconnected from the diary for which it was written. But it, too, belongs with the body of her prose work.

Let me close by paraphrasing a notice to readers written in an earlier era: "It had been a thing worthy to have been wished that the Author herself had lived to have set forth and overseen her own writings. But since it hath been ordained otherwise, and she by death departed from that right, I pray you do not envy her Friend the office of his care and pain to have collected and published them."

I have been greatly helped by others in preparing *The Collected Prose of Elizabeth Bishop,* and wish to thank Alice Methfessel, literary executor, for asking me to edit the book, for editorial advice and help in locating and preparing manuscripts and in dating them as accurately as possible, and for granting me permission to quote from Elizabeth's unpublished letters and other writing; Lisa Browar, Curator of Rare Books and

Manuscripts at Vassar College, who has been unfailingly responsive with copies of much needed documents and bibliographical information; Nicholas Basbanes, literary editor of the Worcester *Telegram* and *Evening Gazette,* for help on the genealogy of the Bishop family and the history of the J. W. Bishop Company; Henri Cole, executive director of the Academy of American Poets, for the transcript of the interview with Elizabeth Bishop which contained her statements about hymn-singing in Great Village and her discovery of the poems of George Herbert; Frani Muser, who allowed me to quote from her memoir of her fellow student, which she originally read at the memorial service at Harvard in 1979; her daughter, Cynthia Krupat, who designed this book and chose the watercolor by Elizabeth Bishop reproduced on the dust jacket; and last but not least poets Frank Bidart and Lloyd Schwartz, close friends of the author, for their editorial suggestions. Three books have been invaluable— Candace W. MacMahon's *Elizabeth Bishop: A Bibliography, 1927–1979* (University of Virginia Press); the anthology edited by Lloyd Schwartz and Sybil P. Estess, *Elizabeth Bishop and Her Art* (University of Michigan Press); and John Unterecker's fine study of Elizabeth Bishop in *American Writers: A Collection of Literary Biographies* (Charles Scribner's Sons).

MEMORY:

PERSONS & PLACES

Primer Class

🎜

Every time I see long columns of numbers, handwritten in a certain way, a strange sensation or shudder, partly aesthetic, partly painful, goes through my diaphragm. It is like seeing the dorsal fin of a large fish suddenly cut through the surface of the water—not a frightening fish like a shark, more like a sail-fish. The numbers have to be only up to but under a hundred, rather large and clumsily written, and the columns squeezed together, with long vertical lines between them, drawn by hand, long and crooked. They are usually in pencil, these numbers that affect me so, but I've seen them in blue crayon or blurred ink, and they produce the same effect. One morning our newspaper delivery man, an old Italian named Tony, whom I'd seen over and over again, threw back the pages of his limp, black, oilcloth-covered account book to my page, and there, up and down, at right angles to the pages' blue lines, he had kept track of my newspapers in pencil, in columns of ones and ones, twos and threes. My diaphragm contracted and froze. Or Faustina, the old black lottery-ticket seller, and *her* limp school notebook with a penciled-off half-inch column waveringly drawn for each customer. Or my glimpse of a barkeeper's apparently homemade, home-stitched pad, as he consulted long thin numbers referring to heaven knows what (how many drinks each of his customers had had?), and then put the pad away again, under the bar.

The real name of this sensation is memory. It is a memory I do not even have to try to remember, or reconstruct; it is always right there, clear and complete. The mysterious numbers, the columns, that impressed me so much—a mystery I never solved when I went to Primer Class in Nova Scotia!

Primer Class was a sort of Canadian equivalent of kinder-garten; it was the year you went to school before you went to "First Grade." But we didn't sit about sociably and build things, or crayon, or play, or quarrel. We sat one behind the other in a line of small, bolted-down desks and chairs, in the same room with grades one, two, three, and four. We were at the left, facing the teacher, and I think there were seven or eight of us. We were taught reading and writing and arithmetic, or enough of them to prepare us for the "First Grade"; also, how to behave in school. This meant to sit up straight, not to scrape your feet on the floor, never to whisper, to raise your hand when you had to go out, and to stand up when you were asked a question. We used slates; only the real grades could buy scribblers, beautiful, fat writing pads, with colored pictures of horses and kittens on the covers, and pale tan paper with blue lines. They could also go up front to sharpen their pencils into the waste-basket.

I was five. My grandmother had already taught me to write on a slate my name and my family's names and the names of the dog and the two cats. Earlier she had taught me my letters, and at first I could not get past the letter *g*, which for some time I felt was far enough to go. *My* alphabet made a satisfying short song, and I didn't want to spoil it. Then a visitor called on my grandmother and asked me if I knew my letters. I said I did and, accenting the rhythm, gave him my version. He teased me so about stopping at *g* that I was finally convinced one must go on with the other nineteen letters. Once past *g,* it was plain sailing. By the time school started, I could read almost all my primer, printed in both handwriting and type, and I loved every word. First, as a frontispiece, it had the flag in full color, with "One Flag, One King, One Crown" under it. I colored in the black-and-white illustrations that looked old-fashioned, even to me, using mostly red and green crayons. On the end pages I had tried to copy the round cancellation marks from old envelopes: "Brooklyn, N.Y. Sept. 1914," "Halifax, Aug. 1916," and so on, but they had not turned out well, a set of lopsided crumbling wheels.

The summer before school began was the summer of numbers, chiefly number eight. I learned their shapes from the kitchen calendar and the clock in the sitting room, though I couldn't yet tell time. Four and five were hard enough, but I think I was in love with eight. One began writing it just to the right of the top, and drew an S downwards. This wasn't too difficult, but the hardest part was to hit the bottom line (ruled on the slate by my grandmother) and come up again, against the grain, that is, against the desire of one's painfully cramped fingers, and at the same time not make it a straight line, but a sort of upside down and backwards S, and all this in *curves.* Eights also made the worst noise on the slate. My grandmother would send me outside to practice, sitting on the back steps. The skreeking was slow and awful.

The slate pencils came two for a penny, with thin white paper, diagonally striped in pale blue or red, glued around them except for an inch left bare at one end. I loved the slate and the pencils almost as much as the primer. What I liked best about the slate was washing it off at the kitchen sink, or in the watering trough, and then watching it dry. It dried like clouds, and then the very last wet streak would grow tinier and tinier, and thinner and thinner; then suddenly it was gone and the slate was pale gray again and dry, dry, dry.

I had an aunt, Mary, eleven or twelve years older than me, who was in the last, or next-to-last, year of the same school. She was very pretty. She wore white middy blouses with red or blue silk ties, and her brown hair in a braid down her back. In the mornings I always got up earlier than Aunt Mary and ate my porridge at the kitchen table, wishing that she would hurry and get up too. We ate porridge from bowls, with a cup of cream at the side. You took a spoonful of porridge, dipped it into the cream, then ate it; this was to keep the porridge hot. We also had cups of tea, with cream and sugar; mine was called "cambric tea." All during breakfast I listened for the school bell, and wished my aunt would hurry up; she rarely appeared before the bell started ringing, over on the other side of the river that divided the village in two. Then she would arrive in the kitchen braiding her hair, and say, "That's just the *first* bell!" while I was dying to be out the door and off. But first I had to pat Betsy, our little dog, and then kiss Grandmother goodbye. (My grandfather would have been up and out for hours already.)

My grandmother had a glass eye, blue, almost like her other one, and this made her especially vulnerable and precious to me. My father was dead and my mother was away in a sanatorium. Until I was teased out of it, I used to ask Grandmother, when I said goodbye, to promise me not to die before I came home. A year earlier I had privately asked other relatives if they thought my grandmother could go to heaven with a glass eye. (Years later I found out that one of my aunts had asked the same question when she'd been my age.) Betsy was also included in this deep but intermittent concern with the hereafter; I was told that of course she'd go to heaven, she was such a good little dog, and not to worry. Wasn't our minister awfully fond of her, and hadn't she even surprised us by trotting right into church one summer Sunday, when the doors were open?

Although I don't remember having been told it was a serious offense, I was very afraid of being late, so most mornings I left Mary at her breakfast and ran out the back door, around the house, past the blacksmith's shop, and was well across the iron bridge before she caught up with me. Sometimes I had almost reached the school when the second bell, the one that meant to come in immediately from the schoolyard, would be clanging away in the cupola. The school was high, bare and white-clapboarded, dark-red-roofed, and the four-sided cupola had white louvers. Two white outhouses were set farther back, but visible, on either side. I carried my slate, a rag to wash it with, and a small medicine bottle filled with water. Everyone was supposed to bring a bottle of water and a clean rag; spitting on the slates and wiping them off with the hand was a crime. Only the bad boys did it, and if she caught them the teacher hit them on the top of the head with her pointer. I don't imagine that wet slate, by itself, had a smell; perhaps slate pencils do; sour, wet rags do, of course, and perhaps that is what I remember. Miss Morash would pick one up at arm's length and order the owner to take it outside at once, saying *Phaaagh*, or something like that.

That was our teacher's name, Georgie Morash. To me she seemed very tall and stout, straight up and down, with a white starched shirtwaist, a dark straight skirt, and a tight, wide belt that she often pushed down, in front, with both hands. Everything, back and front, looked smooth and hard; maybe it was corsets. But close to, what I mostly remember about Miss Morash, and mostly looked at, were her very white shoes, Oxford shoes, surprisingly white, white like flour, and large, with neatly tied white laces. On my first day at school my Aunt Mary had taken me into the room for the lower grades and presented me to Miss Morash. She bent way over, spoke to me kindly, even patted my head and, although told to look up, I could not take my eyes from those silent, independent-looking, powdery-white shoes.

Miss Morash almost always carried her pointer. As she walked up and down the aisles, looking over shoulders at the scribblers or slates, rapping heads, or occasionally boxing an ear, she talked steadily, in a loud, clear voice. This voice had a certain fame in the village. At dinner my grandfather would quote what he said he had heard Miss Morash saying to us (or even to me) as he drove by that morning, even though the schoolhouse was set well back from the road. Sometimes when my grandmother would tell me to stop shouting, or to speak more softly, she would add, "That Georgie!" I don't remember anything Miss Morash ever said. Once when the Primer Class was gathered in a semicircle before one of the blackboards, while she showed us (sweepingly) how to write the capital *C*, and I was considering, rather, the blue sky beyond the windows, I too received a painful rap on the head with the pointer.

There was another little girl in the Primer Class, besides me, and one awful day she wet her pants, right in the front seat, and was sent home. There were two little Micmac Indian boys, Jimmy and Johnny Crow, who had dark little faces and shiny black hair and eyes, just alike. They both wore shirts of blue cotton, some days patterned with little white sprigs, on others with little white anchors. I couldn't take my eyes off these shirts or the boys' dark bare feet. Almost everyone went barefoot to school, but I had to wear brown sandals with buckles, against my will. When I went home the first day and was asked who was in Primer Class with me, I replied, "Manure MacLaughlin," as his name had sounded to me. I was familiar with manure—there was a great pile of it beside the barn—but of course his

real name was Muir, and everyone laughed. Muir wore a navy-
blue cap, with a red-and-yellow maple leaf embroidered above
the visor.

There was a poor boy, named Roustain, the dirtiest and
raggediest of us all, who was really too big for Primer Class and
had to walk a long way to school, when he came at all. I heard
thrilling stories about him and his brother, how their father
whipped them all the time, *horsewhipped* them. We were still
horse-and-buggy-minded (though there were a few automobiles
in the village), and one of the darkest, most sinister symbols in
our imaginations was the horsewhip. It *looked* sinister: long,
black, flexible at a point after the handle, sometimes even with
lead in it, tasseled. It made a swish *whissh*ing sound and some-
times figured in nightmares. There was even a song about the
Roustains:

> *I'm a Roustain from the mountain,*
> *I'm a Roustain, don't you see,*
> *I'm a Roustain from the mountain,*
> *You can smell the fir on me.*

Not only did their father whip them, but their mother didn't
take care of them at all. There were no real beds in their house
and no food, except for a big barrel of molasses, which often
swarmed with flies. They'd dip pieces of bread in the molasses,
when they had bread, and that was all they had for dinner.

The schoolroom windows, those autumn days, seemed very
high and bright. On one window ledge, on the Primer Class
side, there were beans sprouting up in jars of water. Their
presence in school puzzled me, since at home I'd already grown
"horse bean" to an amazing height and size in my own garden
(eighteen inches square), as well as some radishes and small,
crooked carrots. Beyond, above the sprouting beans, the big

autumn clouds went grandly by, silver and dazzling in the deep blue. I would keep turning my head to follow them, until Miss Morash came along and gave it a small push back in the right direction. I loved to hear the other grades read aloud, unless they hesitated too much on words or phrases you could guess ahead. Their stories were better, and longer, than those in my primer. I already knew by heart "The Gingerbread Boy" and "Henny Penny," in my primer, and had turned against them. I was much more interested when the third grade read about Bruce watching the spider spin his web. Every morning school began with the Lord's Prayer, sitting down, then we stood up and sang "O maple leaf, our emblem dear." Then sometimes —and not very well, because it was so much harder—we sang "God save our gracious king," but usually stopped with the first verse.

Only the third and fourth grades studied geography. On their side of the room, over the blackboard, were two rolled-up maps, one of Canada and one of the whole world. When they had a geography lesson, Miss Morash pulled down one or both of these maps, like window shades. They were on cloth, very limp, with a shiny surface, and in pale colors—tan, pink, yellow, and green—surrounded by the blue that was the ocean. The light coming in from their windows, falling on the glazed, crackly surface, made it hard for me to see them properly from where I sat. On the world map, all of Canada was pink; on the Canadian, the provinces were different colors. I was so taken with the pull-down maps that I wanted to snap them up, and pull them down again, and touch all the countries and provinces with my own hands. Only dimly did I hear the pupils' recitations of capital cities and islands and bays. But I got the general impression that Canada was the same size as the world, which somehow or other fitted into it, or the other way around, and that in the world and Canada the sun was always shining and everything was dry and glittering. At the same time, I knew perfectly well that this was not true.

One morning Aunt Mary was even later than usual at breakfast, and for some reason I decided to wait for her to finish her porridge. Before we got to the bridge the second bell—the bell that really meant it—started ringing. I was terrified because up to this time I had never actually been late, so I began to run as fast as I possibly could. I could hear my aunt behind, laughing at me. Because her legs were longer than mine, she caught up to me, rushed into the schoolyard and up the steps ahead of me. I ran into the classroom and threw myself, howling, against Miss Morash's upright form. The class had their hands folded on the desks, heads bowed, and had reached "Thy kingdom come." I clutched the teacher's long, stiff skirt and sobbed. Behind me, my awful aunt was still *laughing*. Miss Morash stopped everyone in mid-prayer, and propelled us all three out into the cloakroom, holding me tightly by the shoulder. There, surrounded by all the japanned hooks, which held only two or three caps, we were private, though loud giggles and whispering reached us from the schoolroom. First Miss Morash in stern tones told Mary she was *very* late for the class she attended overhead, and ordered her to go upstairs at once. Then she tried to calm me. She said in a very kindly way, not at all in her usual penetrating voice, that being only a few minutes late wasn't really worth tears, that everything was quite all right, and I must go into the classroom now and join in the usual morning songs. She wiped off my face with a folded white handkerchief she kept tucked in her belt, patted my head, and even kissed me two or three times. I was overcome by all this, almost to the point of crying all over again, but keeping my eyes fixed firmly on her two large, impersonal, flour-white shoes, I managed not to give way. I had to face my snickering classmates, and I found I could. And that was that, although I was cross with Aunt Mary for a long time because it was all her fault.

For me this was the most dramatic incident of Primer Class, and I was never late again. My initial experiences of formal education were on the whole pleasurable. Reading and writing caused me no suffering. I found the first easier, but the second was enjoyable—I mean *artistically* enjoyable—and I came to admire my own handwriting in pencil, when I got to that stage, perhaps as a youthful Chinese student might admire his own brushstrokes. It was wonderful to see that the letters each had different expressions, and that the same letter had different expressions at different times. Sometimes the two capitals of my name looked miserable, slumped down and sulky, but at others they turned fat and cheerful, almost with roses in their cheeks. I also had the "First Grade" to look forward to, as well as geography, the maps, and longer and much better stories. The one subject that baffled me was arithmetic. I knew all the numbers of course, and liked to write them—I finally mastered the eight—but when I watched the older grades at arithmetic class, in front of the blackboard with their columns of figures, it was utterly incomprehensible. Those mysterious numbers!

c. 1960

The Country Mouse

❧

"My grandfather's clock was too tall for the shelf . . ." I knew
that song very well, having been sung it many times by my
other grandfather. But this grandfather himself seemed too tall
—at any rate, too tall for this train we were on, the old Boston
and Maine, gritting, grinding, occasionally shrieking, bearing
us west and south, from Halifax to Boston, through a black,
seemingly endless night. This grandfather snapped on the over-
head light again.

He had taken off his boots. They stood on the floor, to the
left. His coat and vest and necktie were hanging up on a hanger
to the right, jiggling. He had kept his other clothes on, just
unfastening his braces. He had been trying to sleep in the upper
berth of our "drawing room." Now he descended, god-like and
swearing, swept Grandma out of the way, and wedged himself
into the lower berth. His thick silver hair and short silver beard
glittered, and so did the whites of his eyes, rolled up as if in
agony. (He was walleyed. At least, one eye turned the wrong
way, which made him endlessly interesting to me. The walleye
seemed only right and natural, because my grandmother on the
other side in Canada had a glass eye.) His shoulders were up at
an odd angle, a little frosted lamp shining over one of them.

This grandma, jiggling too, stood by helplessly, watching him writhe and grunt. She wore a long purple dressing gown and her curly white hair was partly pulled back into a small pigtail.

"Sarah! Get in the other way around!" She turned off the overhead light once more, and obeyed.

From where I lay, across the room, stretching my tiny bones on what they had called a "sofa," I peered at them in dumb wonder as they reclined, head-to-foot, in their dramatically lit, mysterious, dark-green-curtained niche. I can look back on them now, many years and train trips later, and clearly see them looking like a Bernini fountain, or a Cellini saltcellar: a powerful but aging Poseidon with a small, elderly, curly Nereid. But that night I was dazed, almost scandalized. I had never seen either of them *en déshabillé* before, not even in bed. In fact, I scarcely knew them.

The little light blinked out. We were off again (not that we had ever stopped, of course) through the night: *unk-etty, unk-etty, unk-etty*, doubtless still going through some black hairy forest I had watched out the window before the porter had made the beds. I felt as if I were being kidnapped, even if I wasn't. My sofa smelled of coal dust and tobacco, and its stiff green velour pricked right through the sheet. The train went into a long curve and tried to bend its stiff joints; my sofa tried to throw me off. The walls creaked. *Ee-eee-eee* went our whistle, miles ahead, and I held on for dear life. It was awful, but almost a relief, to hear from time to time, above the other noises, my grandfather growling savagely to himself in the pitch dark.

In the morning I was sick, and Grandma rushed me into the strange, solid tin (as I thought) bathroom just in time. I threw up, yellow, into something I referred to—probably thinking of the farm accoutrements I was more familiar with than bathrooms—as a "hopper." Grandpa, who was brushing his white hair with *two* brushes, like a trick, laughed loudly, displaying his many gold teeth. Grandma produced soda crackers from somewhere for me to chew. I got better. We went on with our complicated, embarrassing dressing and the porter arrived to do *his* tricks with our beds.

Yesterday's white socks were very dirty. "And she only has one pair, John," said Grandma. More embarrassment. Grandpa stopped buffeting his head. I soon learned that he had a way of suggesting an immediate and practical solution to almost any problem, after just a moment's thought, like (one gathers) the Duke of Wellington. "Turn them inside out," he commanded. This was done, but then white threads hung at my heels. However, they would be concealed, more or less, my grandparents agreed, by my black patent-leather slippers. Putting his watch in his vest pocket, Grandpa finally left us to get his breakfast. Grandma and I sat opposite each other on the two green seats, nibbling soda crackers for ours, and studying each other in the strong dust-filled sunlight.

Outside there were more woods, but no longer firs, and among the greens there were some yellows because it was September. We clanked over several bridges above little blue brooks. There were some birches. Three crows flew wildly off, sideways, cawing silently. I was beginning to enjoy this trip, a little.

Grandma was dressed in gray silk, with her hat on and her veil pushed up. She was very neat and tight and fitted. The neck of the dress was filled in with fine white net, and a small structure of the net stretched on little bones, around her neck, like a miniature fish weir. On the left of her bosom was a small round gold case that held a fine gold chain to her pince-nez coiled up tight, on a spring. One could pull it out and it would snap back—not that anyone was allowed to do this, but one was aware of it. She had blue eyes and a small, rather snub, nose, and the curling white hair was parted in the middle. She was very pretty, in a doll-like way, and she had already told me that she wore a size 3 shoe. The strongest exclamation I had heard her use was "Pshaw," and occasionally, "Drat."

Yes, I was beginning to enjoy myself a little, if only Grandma hadn't had such a confusing way of talking. It was almost as if we were playing house. She would speak of "grandma" and "little girls" and "fathers" and "being good"—things I had never before considered in the abstract, or rarely in the third person. In particular, there seemed to be much, much more to being a "little girl" than I had realized: the prospect was beginning to depress me. And now she said, "Where's your doll? Where's *Drusilla?*"

Oh dear. I had dolls, back home in Nova Scotia; I was even quite fond of one or two of them. But Grandma had found them all in no condition to go traveling in Pullmans. She had bought me the best our country store could provide, and made her a checked dress herself. And when I had been reluctant to name her, she had even given her that unappealing name. The doll (I couldn't say that name) was totally uninteresting, with embossed yellow-brown hair that smelled like stale biscuits, bright blue eyes, and pink cheeks, and I could scarcely conceal my real feelings about her. But that seemed to be one of Grandma's ideas: a "little girl" should carry a doll when she went traveling. I meekly dug out the horror from under a pillow and held her on my knee until we got to Boston.

It was 1917. When the chauffeur, Ronald, met us at North Station in his dark uniform, black leather puttees, and cap with a black visor, I thought at first he was a new kind of soldier. But he was too old to be a soldier; he was married and had four grown children. (Later we were to become good friends and I would ride in front with him in the Cadillac limousine, and he would tell me about his son in the army and, inevitably, how much his back ached.) Now Grandma and I were immediately driven to Stern's to buy me some decent clothes. Everything we bought was brown: a brown tweed coat, a brown beaver hat with streamers, two pairs of brown laced boots, long brown stockings. I hated them all but tactfully said nothing. Then we met Grandpa at the Touraine for lunch and I ate creamed chicken and was given an ice cream like nothing I had ever seen on earth—*meringue glacée*, it must have been.

After lunch we drove to Worcester. I think I must have fallen asleep, but I do remember arriving at a driveway lined with huge maple trees. To my slight resentment (after all, hadn't I been singing "O maple leaf, our emblem dear" for years?), they were pointed out and named to me. The front of the house looked fairly familiar, very much the same kind of white clapboards and green shutters that I was accustomed to, only this house was on a much larger scale, twice as large, with two windows for each of the Nova Scotia ones and a higher roof. As we drove up and around it, wings stuck out here and there; at one side was a quite incongruous curved porch, and at the other a glass-enclosed box on another porch, the "conservatory." Grandma and I went into the house through this.

I had been brought back unconsulted and against my wishes to the house my father had been born in, to be saved from a life of poverty and provincialism, bare feet, suet puddings, unsanitary school slates, perhaps even from the inverted *r*'s of my mother's family. With this surprising extra set of grandparents, until a few weeks ago no more than names, a new life was about to begin. It was a day that seemed to include months in it, or even years, a whole unknown past I was made to feel I should have known about, and a strange, unpredictable future.

The house was gloomy, there was no denying it, and everyone seemed nervous and unsettled. There was something ominous, threatening, lowering in the air. My father had been the oldest

of eight children. All of them were dead, except for three—
Aunt Marian, who was married and lived in Providence; Aunt
Jenny, unmarried and the next-to-oldest after my father; and
Uncle Neddy, the youngest. The latter two and my grand-
parents made up the family, though Aunt Jenny and Uncle
Neddy were away a good deal of the nine months I lived there.

The old white house had long ago been a farmhouse out in
the country. The city had crept out and past it; now there were
houses all around and a trolley line went past the front lawn
with its white picket fence. There was no doubt but what the
neighborhood, compared to the old days, was deteriorating.
The Catholics had been trying to buy the house for years; they
wanted to build a church there. All the time I was there the
subject was under debate—to sell or not to sell. However, there
were still fifteen acres of land, an old apple orchard behind the
house, and tall chestnut trees up on the hill. The life my grand-
parents still led was partly country, partly city. There were hens
and two cows, and a large barn also up on the hill. They had
their own cottage cheese and sometimes butter. There was a
large vegetable garden, the greater part of which was planted
in celery and asparagus. There were a Bartlett pear tree, a
crab-apple tree, a dark green "summer house" with old robins'
nests in it, and two tremendous horse-chestnut trees and under
them two wonderful swings with broad seats and thick ropes.
The trees had been cared for and cemented and propped up,
very old and spreading. We could easily climb into many of
them and hang on by bars rather than branches. They were
preserved at all costs, like Grandpa's teeth.

There were also a weeping birch, a large bed of cannas, lilacs
along one fence, lilies of the valley under them, and violets.
Back of the house the lawn was graded in a long green wave,
but a spring kept coming up there and in the next season the
grading was soiled again at great expense. The house, Grandma

said, was "a hundred and fifty years old." There were awful rats in the attic and they could be heard fighting and scuttling at night. The cats were ugly, orange and white; they lived in the barn and ran away from me—not like my black Nanny in Nova Scotia.

Later that same day I met Aunt Jenny for the first time, although she kept insisting she had known me before as a baby. She didn't seem particularly glad to see me. She was very tall, as so many people in the "States" seemed to be. She suggested that I walk up to the barn with her to get her car. As she turned to go and I saw her edgewise, I was amazed how tall and flat, like a paper doll, she looked. I tagged along slightly behind her. She had on a long jumper-like blue jersey garment, around whose middle was a wonderful chatelaine belt, all little chains, boxes, and medals that clinked as she moved her long legs. I wanted to examine it or ask her about it, but didn't dare. We walked out through the conservatory and, farther up the drive-way, up a small hill. The barn was on two levels: on the ground floor there were three cows; on the upper floor, which opened on the other side onto the hillside, there was a large garage. On its big swinging doors were nailed rows and rows of old license plates because all the family had been early motoring enthusiasts. In fact, Uncle Neddy had driven in one of the first auto races from Boston to New York.

In the barn stood the limousine we had recently arrived in, and a blue, rather high, lady-like car, Aunt Jenny's Buick. She opened the screw top on the tank at the back and measured the gasoline with a yardstick. This was all fascinating, but what had caught my eye was a carriage sitting at the back of the garage, under the noses of the two cars. "Yes," said Aunt Jenny, "that's your grandma's carriage. It hasn't been used for many years now." It was dark green. I climbed inside by the two little steps. There were black lamps on either side; inside was dark brown leather, musty-smelling. It made the most beautiful little house imaginable. I wanted to stay in it forever, but Aunt Jenny had finished her checking up and invited me to ride down as far as the house with her, so I had to go.

She had also been an early driver, but always a very bad one. Uncle Neddy later pointed out the exact spot where "Jenny tipped Papa over." It was when she had her first car, a Ford, and had offered to show Grandpa how she could drive, and within two minutes of his getting into it, she had rounded the canna bed too fast and tipped over. They had landed inelegantly among the red and yellow cannas, squashing them flat. Grandpa had never driven with her again.

In the household there was a cook, a maid named Agnes, a gardener named Ed, and his son. A laundress came in once a week. Except for Ronald the chauffeur, they were all Swedish and spoke Swedish among themselves. I became very fond of Agnes, perhaps because Grandma fought with her constantly. When Agnes would polish the beautiful mahogany dining-room table, Grandma kept after her: "*With* the grain, Agnes, *with* the grain." Ed, the gardener, in blue denim overalls and jacket, also fought regularly with Grandma, I don't know what about—once, I think, about the correct way of banking celery. Anyway, every so often he would lay down his rake or hoe or stop milking a cow, and announce that he was through. His young son would immediately take over where Ed had left off. This had been going on for thirty years. The next morning at seven o'clock, Ed would be back on the job again. He had been the driver for Grandma's horse-drawn carriage, but had refused flatly to learn to drive a car. One day the cook left dramatically, by the front door, out into a snowstorm. For four days Grandma cooked for us, very badly, and Grandpa had dinner at the hotel. Then another cook arrived, a very nice one this time, Swedish, fat, and cheerful. She and my dear Agnes hit it off immediately.

Even dour Ed joined in the kitchen coffee parties. She made wonderful hard yellow coffee cakes, braided and frosted.

There was a dog, a Boston bull terrier nominally belonging to Aunt Jenny, and oddly named Beppo. At first I was afraid of him, but he immediately adopted me, perhaps as being on the same terms in the house as himself, and we became very attached. He was a clever dog; he wore a wide collar with brass studs, which was taken off every night before he went to bed. Every morning at eight o'clock he would come to my door with the collar in his mouth, and bang it against the door, meaning for us to get up and dressed and start the day together. Like most Boston terriers he had a delicate stomach; he vomited frequently. He jumped nervously at imaginary dangers, and barked another high hysterical bark. His hyperthyroid eyes glistened, and begged for sympathy and understanding. When he was "bad," he was punished by being put in a large closet off the sewing room and left there, out of things, for half an hour. Once when I was playing with him, he disappeared and would not answer my calls. Finally he was found, seated gloomily by himself in the closet, facing the wall. He was punishing *himself*. We later found a smallish puddle of vomit in the conservatory. No one had ever before punished him for his attacks of gastritis, naturally; it was all his own idea, his peculiar Bostonian sense of guilt.

Next door—that is, just across the maple-lined driveway— stood another large white house in the sort of "bungalow" style of the early part of the century. Grandpa had built it for Aunt Marian when she married, but she had moved away for good and it was now rented to a family named Barton. Mr. Barton was a banker, wore a derby, and drove about in a shiny black car. They had a very young chauffeur, Richard, who wore a dashing greenish uniform—again, not a soldier's. (I heard he was not fighting in Flanders because of some ailment whose nature I could not learn, eavesdrop though I tried.)

The day after our arrival, Grandma took me to call on the Bartons to meet Emma, who was to be my playmate. The mother was out and I met Emma's grandmother, an old old lady who sat in a wheelchair all day, knitting for the soldier boys. She had knitted ninety-two helmets and over two hundred "wristers," and let me try on one of each. She was deaf and had a sort of black box beside her to hear with. Emma's grandmother was much older than either of mine, who were old enough. Her daughter was a Christian Scientist, but apparently she permitted her old mother to be lame and deaf if she wanted to.

Emma appeared. She was five and a half, a year younger than me. She was a very pretty child. I immediately felt the aura of wealth surrounding her, like a young Scott Fitzgerald. Her hair was in a "Dutch cut" (so was mine), but hers was sleek and smooth and black. It even had blue highlights in it, but I suspect someone may have pointed that out to me. Her eyes were gray and her skin very white. She was a little plump, and was wearing a beautiful pair of "rompers," made of some spongy kind of crepe, deep rose red. She always wore rompers of the same material but in different colors, with a white ruff at the neck. I think I thought they were possibly a Christian Science costume.

Emma's grandmother said, "Aren't you going to show your new friend your playroom and your toys?" Emma looked put out. She said, ungraciously, "I've just put everything in *apple-pie order*." It was the first time I had heard that expression and it baffled me. However, her grandmother finally persuaded her to show off her possessions and we went upstairs together, to a small white-walled room at the head of the stairs, with shelves around the walls and a bay window with a window seat in it. Outside a shop, I had never seen so many toys in my life; the display of dolls was overpowering. What I liked best was a milk can that wound up, played a little tune and, with his long ears first, up came a white woolly rabbit, who looked around him and sank down again. Emma was allowed to read the funny papers, which I was not. Now it seems to me that "Mutt and Jeff" and "Buster Brown and His Dog Tige" were rather highbrow fare for a little girl.

Naturally, Emma and I became very close friends. Often her mother came over to argue with Grandpa about Christian Science in the evenings. She was tall, with blue eyes and black hair like her daughter, and very high coloring. She got nowhere with Grandpa of course, who never even went to church, but he loved to argue with her and would pretend to give in on certain points just to be able to point his cigar at her and demolish her logic. All this I understood, like Beppo, by tone of voice rather than by words, but I listened and listened while pretending to play cards and to read the *Literary Digest* myself.

Outside their house the Bartons had a catalpa tree. I don't know why this tree, or perhaps its name, fascinated me. I rather disliked its big hanging pale green leaves and those long beans, but every day Emma or I would say, "After lunch we'll meet under the catalpa tree." Once we had a fight, I don't remember what about. I pulled her shiny black hair, and she screamed. Agnes came running from our house and Emma's mother's maid from theirs, and they pulled us apart and we were not allowed to play together for three days.

At school the teacher's name was actually Miss Woodhead. She had bright red hair and was very pretty. We loved her so much we didn't even make fun of her name. We sat in alternate rows of boys and girls, and began every morning by singing "Good morning to you, good morning to you," bowing to either side. At my left sat a beautiful boy named Royal Something. His name made him doubly attractive to me, stuffed as I was with the English royal family, although I realized he wasn't really royal. He had dark eyes and shiny dark brown hair cut rather long. At the end of the day we helped each other on with our coats and once, when he helped me buckle my arctics, as I looked at his long shiny hair, neat starched collar, and red necktie, I felt a wonderful, powerful thrill go through my stomach.

I did stay on at school through Thanksgiving, I suppose, because there was the business of the Pilgrim Fathers. Miss Woodhead made a model of "The Landing of the Pilgrims" on a large tabletop. The Rock was the only real thing. Miss Woodhead made the ocean in a spectacular way: she took large sheets of bright blue paper, crumpled them up, and stretched them out over the table. Then, with the blackboard chalk, she made glaring whitecaps of all the points: an ocean grew right before our eyes. There were some little ships, some doll people, and we also helped make log cabins. (Twenty years later I learned the Pilgrim Fathers had no log cabins when they landed.) But I felt closely related to them all: *"Land where my father died / Land of the pilgrims' pride"*—for a long time I took the first line personally. Miss Woodhead asked us to bring anything we had at home to contribute to Plymouth and Thanksgiving, and in my conceit I said (to the wonder and admiration of the class, I hoped) that we had some real little trees, just the right size, with snow on them. So I contributed four trees from the toy village my grandparents let me play with, and from then on the village was half deforested when set up at home.

Whenever I could, I explored the house like a cat. It was an old colonial pre-Revolutionary house, but wings had been added and porches built on with no regard for period style. The front room was rarely used. Once in a while Grandma entertained a friend there in the afternoon. Yet it was my favorite. This was before the days when people were conscious of preserving the character of old houses. Perhaps because this room was so little used, it had been preserved by accident. The antique furniture was upholstered in gray blue, the walls were papered, and it all went together. There were even some paintings I now realize were primitives, in gold frames on the walls, done by an ancestress. It was a quiet room, and I could sit on the carpet there undisturbed and think. On both porches the floors were set with thick green panes of glass, frosted over and scratched, I suppose to give light to the cellar underneath. To me they were as beautiful as slabs of jade or malachite. Grandma's sitting room on the front, with a fireplace and bay windows onto the lawn, was called the "sewing room," but I never saw Grandma sew. In the dining room I studied each and every plate and cup on display in two glass cases, and the silver on the sideboard.

In the wing at the back, the largest room had once held a billiard table when the sons were alive; now it was used as a living room, but it was always referred to as the "billiard room." It had layers and layers of curtains, the innermost of brickish red velvet. The Oriental carpet was a slightly lighter red. In the middle there was a large square table with a lamp on it, and layers of magazines were laid out on the front. There were some black leather sofas and armchairs. At the back was an enormous rubber plant in a gigantic brass pot; Grandma was quite proud of it. There was an upright piano, a fireplace with magnificent brass fenders and fire tongs, and high on the mantel was a tiny pair of top boots that had belonged to my father.

In the evenings Grandpa sat in the billiard room in a leather chair, smoking cigars and reading the newspapers. He smoked thirteen or fourteen cigars a day and the room reeked of them. Occasionally, to my delight, he varied the cigars by smoking a long church-warden pipe. There was a rack of pipes on the wall at his side, and a plaster plaque of Dante's head. I sat under the big table, and pretended it was a ship, wheezing slightly. One of the table's large bulging legs became a sturdy mast. (I had once been taken aboard a docked sailing vessel, to my intense delight.) Grandma read the *Literary Digest* under the red lamp; then she played solitaire.

In the library there were some bookcases filled with dark leatherbound books, but I was the only one who ever used it. After two months or so of my sojourn, I got up my courage and slid open the glass doors. The carpet was a deep rich blue. There was a mahogany desk in the middle of the room, with a brass desk set and a paperweight in the form of three lifelike bronze cigars. It was heavy, but I picked it up many times and found it smelled of metal, not cigars.

I frequently had indirect questions aimed at me, like "Wouldn't some little girl like to take piano lessons?" So Miss Darling arrived. I was supposed to practice fifteen minutes at a time. The staves were enormous and I wrote notes in them as large as watermelons. I couldn't touch the pedals, of course. But how I loved the sound of the wide yellow piano keys!

The War was on. In school at recess we were marched into the central hall, class by class, to the music of an upright piano, a clumping march that has haunted me all my life and I have never yet placed. There we pledged allegiance to the flag and sang war songs: "Joan of Arc, they are ca-alllll-ing you." I hated the songs, and most of all I hated saluting the flag. I would have refused if I had dared. In my Canadian schooling the year before, we had started every day with "God Save the King" and "The Maple Leaf Forever." Now I felt like a traitor. I wanted us to win the War, of course, but I didn't want to be an American. When I went home to lunch, I said so. Grandma

was horrified; she almost wept. Shortly after, I was presented
with a white card with an American flag in color at the top.
All the stanzas of "Oh, say, can you see" were printed on it in
dark blue letters. Every day I sat at Grandma's feet and at-
tempted to recite this endless poem. We didn't sing because she
couldn't stay in tune, she said. Most of the words made no
sense at all. *"Between his loved home and the war's desolation"*
made me think of my dead father, and conjured up strange
pictures in my mind.

Aunt Jenny gave a "War Party" to raise money for some
organization, perhaps the Red Cross. I was allowed to help set
the table. All I remember were the red, white, and blue bonbons
and the red, white, and blue flowers. Mrs. Barton's mother
continued to knit helmets and wristers and Grandma decided
that I, too, should learn to knit. On a pair of needles that
seemed awfully long I began to knit and purl some small squares
to make an afghan, but I hated it. I cherish the memory of the
colors, half bright pink and half pea-green, but knitting I
thought almost as bad as the "numbers" game. It reached such
a point that I would actually drop stitches when Grandma left
the room, and so most of the afghan was finally knitted by her.
She decided I wasn't any good with my hands. I have never
knitted since.

There were the war cartoons, several big books of them:
German helmets and cut-off hands haunted us. Aunt Jenny
spoke of such things and was shushed. Because of the "Belgians,"
I ate my mashed potatoes. We were hoarders; in the closet under
the front stairs were four barrels of sugar, which hardened like
rock. In the kitchen one evening the cook hammered it with a
rolling pin with all her might, redder than ever. There was
something conspiratorial about the scene, which I associated
with Aunt Jenny. Since she was rarely at home, I got the idea
that her "War Work" was some kind of full-time profession. In

Nova Scotia the soldiers, some of whom I actually knew, wore beautiful tam-o'-shanters with thistles and other insignia on them. When they got dressed up, they wore kilts and sporrans. One of them had come courting my young aunt in this superb costume, carrying a swagger stick, and let me examine him all over. The Johnny-get-your-gun type of soldier in Worcester seemed very drab to me. I missed black Nanny and the little gray cat, Tippy, named after the song. I liked "Tipperary" and "The long, long trail" and "Every nice girl loves a sailor" much better than the Worcester songs. I particularly hated "Joan of Arc, they are ca-alllll-ing you."

They talked about high prices at the table; I heard that eggs were five cents apiece. And the price of clothes! I rarely spoke, but this time I felt I had something to contribute. I said, "The last time my aunt in Nova Scotia bought a pair of shoes, they cost three dollars." Everyone laughed. I lost my courage about making conversation at the dinner table and I have never regained it.

Sunday morning there was always oyster stew and muffins. Afterwards Grandma and Uncle Neddy would argue; it seemed a Sunday-morning ritual. They always argued until it was time for Grandma to put on her high black satin hat and be driven to the Pilgrim Congregational Church. I was frightened; I thought they were really fighting and were about to come to blows. They would walk up and down together, round and round the billiard room, even out and around the house. Grandpa meanwhile would be reading the Sunday-morning papers, but would chip in a loud comment once in a while: "I told you that stock was no good, Ned. You're throwing your money away." "Jenny has no brains; never had. That woman is a damn fool." Sometimes he'd snort: "Why don't you two do your fighting someplace else? I swear I'll go down to the hotel." Finally I realized the sessions always ended with Uncle Neddy kissing Grandma, looking pleased with himself, and helping her into her black coat.

The dressmaker came. Her name, oddly, was Miss Cotton. Grandma was fond of her and she ate her lunch on a tray, while the fat orange canary shrieked overhead. She made me four hideous dresses, too long, too dark, and with decorations made from leftovers of Grandma's dresses. (Forty-three years later I can scarcely bear to think of those dresses.) Even Grandpa said, "Aren't that child's skirts too long?" Blue serge, large pockets, everything outlined with a silver braid that had a thread of red running through it. Then Grandma decided I should have long hair and braids, like "nice little girls." Emma had short hair, but that didn't seem to count in my favor.

Grandpa once asked me to get his eyeglasses from his bedroom, which I had never been in. It was mostly white and gold, surprisingly feminine for him. The carpet was gold-colored, the bed was fanciful, brass and white, and the furniture was gold and white too. There was a high chest of drawers, a white bedspread, muslin curtains, a set of black leatherbound books near the bed, photographs of Grandma and my aunts and uncles at various ages, and two large black bottles (of whiskey, I realized years later). There were also medicine bottles and the "machines." There were two of them in black boxes, with electric batteries attached to things like stethoscopes—some sort of vibrator or massager perhaps. What he did with them I could not imagine. The boxes were open and looked dangerous. I reached gingerly over one to get his eyeglasses, and saw myself in the long mirror: my ugly serge dress, my too long hair, my gloomy and frightened expression.

Then I became ill. First came eczema, and then asthma. At nights Beppo and I scratched together, I in my bed and he outside my door. Roll and scratch, scratch and roll. No one realized that the thick carpets, the weeping birch, the milk toast, and Beppo were all innocently adding to my disorders. By then I was so sick that I had my breakfast in bed. Sometimes, around ten o'clock, I would get out of bed from boredom and go downstairs to watch Uncle Neddy having his breakfast. His hair was parted in the middle, his face was shiny and lightly freckled, his shirt was dazzling white, and his cuff-links glittered. I loved and hated him at the same time. He'd say things like, "At your age I'd be out and up the hill picking up all the nuts," and "What *you* need, young lady . . ." I wanted to be on good terms with everyone, but he would insist on making jokes I couldn't understand, and talking about spankings and other horrors.

One night something marvelous did happen. I was asleep when Grandma came in and said, "Grandpa wants you to come downstairs and see the present he's brought you from Providence." The lights in the kitchen were very bright. On the white enameled table, dazed and blinking, stood three little hens—no, two little hens and one rooster. They were Golden Bantams, for me. When one hen pecked at some cornmeal on the enamel table, and made miniature but hen-like sounds, I could have cried with pleasure. Where to put them for the night? The problem was solved by using one of the "set tubs" in the laundry off the kitchen. But hens and roosters have to perch, and Grandma found a bleached stick that the laundress used for stirring her wash. It was stuck into one stone tub and the three tiny fowl immediately and obligingly hopped on and clung to it. They were reddish, speckled, with tiny doll-like red combs; the rooster had long tail feathers. They were *mine*, and they were to live in a special henhouse Ed would fix in the morning. I could scarcely bear to leave my little poultry.

One night I was taken to the window in the upstairs front hall to see the ice on the trees, lit by the street lamp at the end of our drive. All the maple trees were bent by the weight of the ice. Branches had cracked off, the telephone wires were covered with ice, and so was the row of thin elms that grew along the street—a great pale blaze of ice filling the vision completely, seeming to circle and circle if one squinted a bit. My grandfather, wearing his nightshirt and red dressing gown, held me up to the window. "Squint your eyes, Grandpa," I said, "tight!" and he did. It was one of the few unselfconscious moments of that whole dismal time.

Then Agnes left. She was going back to Sweden to get married. I wept and clung to her skirts and large suitcase when she kissed me goodbye. After that, things went from bad to worse. First came constipation, then eczema again, and finally asthma. I felt myself aging, even dying. I was *bored* and lonely with Grandma, my silent grandpa, the dinners alone, bored with Emma and Beppo, all of them. At night I lay blinking my flashlight off and on, and crying. As Louise Bogan has so well put it:

> *At midnight tears*
> *Run into your ears.*

Three great truths came home to me during this stretch of my life, all hard to describe and equally important. Emma and I were sitting under the chestnut trees, making conversation in the way both children and adults do. She asked me about my parents. I said my father was dead; I didn't ever remember seeing him. What about my mother? I thought for a moment and then I said in a *sentimental* voice: "She went away and left me . . . She died, too." Emma was impressed and sympathetic, and I loathed myself. It was the first time I had lied deliberately and consciously, and the first time I was aware of falsity and the great power of sentimentality—although I didn't know the word. My mother was not dead. She was in a sanatorium, in another prolonged "nervous breakdown." I didn't know then, and still don't, whether it was from shame I lied, or from a hideous craving for sympathy, playing up my sad romantic plight. But the feeling of self-distaste, whatever it came from, was only too real. I jumped up, to get away from my monstrous self that I could not keep from lying.

I learned a second lesson when Grandma insisted I bring another little girl home from school to play with. I picked out an inoffensive small blonde whose name and features I can't remember. It was a winter afternoon and the lights were already lit in the kitchen. We were sitting on the dining-room floor, looking at magazines, and I felt bored bored bored. The cook was starting dinner, talking to Agnes, who was still with us. Light showed around the swinging kitchen door, and my ostensible playmate asked, "Who lives in that part of the house?" Social consciousness had struck its first blow: I realized this pallid nameless child lived in a poorer world than I (at this moment, at least, for I had never felt at all secure about my status), and that she thought we were in an apartment house. Fairly quickly, I think, I said tactfully, "Oh, a *family* . . ." and since the servants were all speaking Swedish, this was safe enough.

After New Year's, Aunt Jenny had to go to the dentist, and asked me to go with her. She left me in the waiting room, and gave me a copy of the *National Geographic* to look at. It was still getting dark early, and the room had grown very dark. There was a big yellow lamp in one corner, a table with magazines, and an overhead chandelier of sorts. There were others waiting, two men and a plump middle-aged lady, all bundled up. I looked at the magazine cover—I could read most of the words—shiny, glazed, yellow and white. The black letters said: FEBRUARY 1918. A feeling of absolute and utter desolation came over me. I felt . . . *myself*. In a few days it would be my seventh birthday. I felt *I, I, I*, and looked at the three strangers in panic. I was *one* of them too, inside my scabby body and wheezing lungs. "You're in for it now," something said. How had I got tricked into such a false position? I would be like that woman opposite who smiled at me so falsely every once in a while. The awful sensation passed, then it came back again. "You are you," something said. "How strange you are, inside looking out. You are not Beppo, or the chestnut tree, or Emma, you are *you* and you are going to be *you* forever." It was like coasting downhill, this thought, only much worse, and it quickly smashed into a tree. *Why* was I a human being?

1961

The U.S.A. School

of Writing

When I was graduated from Vassar in 1934, during the Great
Depression, jobs were still hard to find and very badly paid.
Perhaps for those very reasons it seemed incumbent on me and
many of my classmates to find them, whether we had to or not.
The spirit of the times and, of course, of my college class was
radical; we were puritanically pink. Perhaps there seemed to
be something virtuous in working for much less a year than our
educations had been costing our families. It was a combination
of this motive, real need for a little more money than I had,
idle curiosity, and, I'm afraid, pure masochism that led me to
answer an advertisement in the Sunday *Times* and take a job.
It was with a correspondence school, the U.S.A. School of
Writing.

First I had an interview at the school with its head, or presi-
dent, as he described himself, Mr. Black. His opening remark
was that the U.S.A. School of Writing stood for "The United
States of America School of Writing," and my pleasure in that
explanation trapped me immediately. But I can see now that I
was just made to order for Mr. Black, and he must have been
mentally rubbing his hands and licking his chops over me all
during our little talk. I couldn't type—properly, that is; I

wanted to smoke while I worked, which was against the fire laws; and I had had no experience at anything at all. But I was from Vassar and I had had a story and three poems published in magazines. I hadn't the faintest idea of my own strength; he would have taken me, probably, even if I had asked for twenty-five dollars a week instead of the fifteen dollars he was offering, but of course such an idea never occurred to me. No doubt he was already plotting how my high-class education and my career in print could be incorporated into his newest circulars.

However, there was a slight catch to that. For a while, at least, I would have to fulfill my duties at the school under the name of Fred G. Margolies, which had been the name, not of my predecessor, but of the one before the one before that. It developed that some of Mr. Margolies's students were still taking the course and had to receive their corrected lessons signed by him, and I would have to be Mr. Margolies until they had all graduated. Then I could turn into myself again, and steer new students. I felt I'd probably like to keep on being Mr. Margolies, if I could. He had had something published, too, although I never succeeded in delving deep enough into the history of the school to find out what it was. And he or they must have been good letter writers, or even fuller of idle curiosity than I was, or just very kindhearted men, to judge by the tone of the letters I received in our name. In fact, for a long time afterwards I used to feel that the neurotically "kind" facet of my personality *was* Mr. Margolies.

The school was on the fourth floor, the top floor, of an old tumble-down building near Columbus Circle. There was no elevator. I had accepted—although "accept" cannot be the right word—the job in the late fall, and it seems to me now that it was always either raining or snowing when I emerged mornings from the subway into Columbus Circle, and that I was always wearing a black wool dress, a trench coat, and galoshes, and carrying an umbrella. In the dark hallway there were three flights of steps, which sagged and smelled of things like hot iron, cigars, rubber boots, or peach pits—the last gasps of whatever industries were dying behind the lettered doors.

The U.S.A. School consisted of four rooms: a tiny lobby where one girl sat alone, typing—typing exactly what her colleagues were typing in the big room behind her, I discovered, but I suppose she was placed there to stave off any unexpected pupils who might decide to come to the school in person. The lobby had a few photos on the wall: pictures of Sinclair Lewis and other non-graduates. Then came the big room, lit grayly by several soot-and-snow-laden skylights, lights going all the time, with six to a dozen girls. Their number varied daily, and they sat at very old-model typewriters, typing the school's "lessons." At the other end of this room, overlooking the street, were two more tiny rooms, one of which was Mr. Black's office and the other Mr. Margolies and Mr. Hearn's office.

Mr. Hearn was a tall, very heavy, handsome woman, about thirty years old, named Rachel, with black horn-rimmed glasses, and a black mole on one cheek. Rachel and I were somewhat cramped in our quarters. She smoked furiously all the time, and I smoked moderately, and we were not allowed to keep our door open because of the poor transient typists, who were not allowed to smoke and might see us and go on strike, or report us to the nearest fire station. What with the rain and fog and snow outside and the smoke inside, we lived in a suffocating, woolly gray isolation, as if in a cocoon. It smelled like a day coach at the end of a long train trip. We worked back to back, but we had swivel chairs and spent quite a bit of our time swung around to each other, with our knees almost bumping, the two cigarettes under each other's nose, talking.

At first she was horrid to me. Again in my innocence I didn't realize it was, of course, because of my Vassar stigmata and my literary career, but her manner soon improved and we even got to like each other, moderately. Rachel did most of the talking. She had a great deal to say; she wanted to correct all the mistakes in my education and, as so many people did in those days, she wanted to get me to join the Party. In order to avoid making the trip to headquarters with her, to get my "card," something we could have done easily during any lunch hour, once I'd put an end to my nonsense and made the decision, I told her I was an anarchist. But it didn't help much. In spite of my principles, I found myself cornered into defending Berkman's attempt to assassinate Andrew Carnegie's partner, Henry Frick, and after that, I spent evenings at the Forty-second Street Library taking out books under *"An,"* in desperate attempts to shut Rachel up. For a while I was in touch with an anarchist organization (they are hard to locate, I found) in New Jersey, and received pamphlets from them, and invitations to meetings, every day in my mail.

Sometimes we went out to lunch together at a mammoth Stewart's Cafeteria. I liked cafeterias well enough, but they afflict one with indecision: what to eat, what table to sit at, what chair at the table, whether to remove the food from the tray or eat it on the tray, where to put the tray, whether to take off one's coat or keep it on, whether to abandon everything to one's fellow diners, and go for the forgotten glass of water, or to lug it all along. But Rachel swept me ahead of her, like a leaf from the enchanter fleeing, toward the sandwich counter. The variety of sandwiches that could be made to order like lightning was staggering, and she always ate three: lox and cream cheese on a bun, corned beef and pickle relish on rye, pastrami and mustard on something-or-other. She *shouted* her order. It didn't matter much, I found, after a few days of trying to state my three terms loudly and clearly; the sandwiches all tasted alike. I began settling for large, quite unreal baked apples and coffee.

Rachel, with her three sandwiches and three cups of black coffee simultaneously, and I would seat ourselves in our wet raincoats and galoshes, our lunches overlapping between us, and she would harangue me about literature.

She never attempted politics at lunch, I don't know why. She had read a lot and had what I, the English major, condescendingly considered rather pathetic taste. She liked big books, with lots of ego and emotion in them, and Whitman was her favorite poet. She liked the translations of Merezhkovski, all of Thomas Wolfe that had then appeared, all of Theodore Dreiser, the Studs Lonigan series of James Farrell, and best of all she liked Vardis Fisher. She almost knew by heart his entire works to date. A feeling of nightmare comes over me as I remember those luncheons: the food; the wet, gritty floor under my hot feet; the wet, feeding, roaring crowd of people beneath the neon lights; and Rachel's inexorable shout across the table, telling me every detail of Vardis Fisher's endless and harrowing autobiography. She may have worked in some details from her own, I'm not sure; I made up my mind then never to read the books, which she offered to loan me, and I never have. I remember her quoting the line and a half from "Modern Love" from which Fisher had taken three titles in a row: *"In tragic life, God wot, | No villain need be! Passions spin the plot . . ."* and my wondering dazedly in all the hubbub why he had neglected the possibilities of "God wot," or if he'd still get around to it. I had recently come from a line analysis of *The Waste Land*, and this bit of literary collage failed to impress me.

"Realism" and only "realism" impressed *her*. But if I tried to imply, in my old classroom manner, that there was "realism" and "realism," or ask her what she *meant* by "realism," she would glare at me savagely, her eyes glittering under Stewart's lighting fixtures, and silently stretch her large mouth over the bulging tiers of a sandwich. Her mole moved up and down as she chewed. At first I was afraid of those slap-like glares, but I grew used to them. And when one day, back in our office, she asked me to read one of her sentences to see if the grammar was right, I knew that she had begun to like me in spite of my bourgeois decadence and an ignorance of reality that took refuge in the childishness of anarchism. I also knew she had already sensed something fishy about my alleged political views.

Overbearing, dishonest, unattractive, proud of being "tough," touchy, insensitive, yet capable of being kind or amused when anything penetrated, Rachel was something new to me. She had one rare trait that kept me interested: she never spoke of herself at all. Her salary was twenty-five dollars a week. Her clothes were shabby, even for Stewart's in those days, and dirty as well. The only thing I learned about her was that she had a sister in a state tuberculosis sanatorium whom she went to see once a month, but whom she didn't particularly like; the reason seemed to be because she was sick, and therefore "no good." Rachel herself had tremendous strength and I soon realized that she inspired fear, almost physical fear, in everyone at the so-called school, including President Black. I also soon realized that she was the entire brains of the place, and afterwards I even suspected that in her power and duplicity perhaps it was she who really owned it, and was using Mr. Black as a front. Probably not, but I never knew the truth about anything that went on there.

Her cigarettes were stolen for her somewhere by a "man" she knew—how, or who the man was, I never discovered. From time to time other objects appeared—a new bag, a fountain pen, a lighter—from the same source or perhaps a different "man," but she never spoke of love or romance, except Vardis Fisher's. She should have hated me; my constant gentle acquiescence or hesitant corrections must have been hard to take; but I don't think she did. I think we felt sorry for each other. I think she felt that I was one of the doomed, enjoying my little grass-hopper existence, my "sense of humor," my "culture," while I could, and that perhaps at some not very future date, when the chips were down, she might even put in a good word for me if she felt like it. I think that later she may well have become a great business success—probably a shady business, like the writing school, but on a much larger scale. She seemed drawn toward the dark and crooked, as if, since she believed that people were forced into being underhanded by economic cir-cumstances in the first place, it would have been dishonest of her not to be dishonest. "Property is theft" was one of her favorite sayings.

Poor Rachel! I often disliked her; she gave me a *frisson*, and yet at the same time I liked her, and I certainly couldn't help listening to every word she said. For several weeks she was my own private Columbus Circle orator. Her lack of a "past," of any definable setting at all, the impression she gave of power and of something biding its time, even if it was false or silly, fascinated me. Talking with her was like holding a snapshot negative up to the light and wondering how its murks and trans-parencies were actually going to develop.

The course we offered on "How to Write" was advertised in the cheapest farm magazines, movie and Western magazines. It was one of those "You, too, can earn money by your pen" advertisements, glowingly but carefully worded. We could in-struct anyone, no matter what his or her education, in any branch of the writing art, from newspaper reporting to adver-tising, to the novel, and every student would receive the personal attention and expert advice of successful, money-making authors like Mr. Hearn and Mr. Margolies. There were eight lessons, and the complete course, payable in advance, cost forty dollars. At the time I worked there, the school had only about a hundred and fifty "students" going, but there had been a period, just before, when it had had many, many more, and more were expected again, I gathered, as soon as the courses had been "revised." There had been a big upheaval in the recent past, entailing the loss of most of the student body, and for some reason, everything, all the circulars, contract blanks, and "lessons," had to be revised immediately and printed all over again. That was why, off and on, so many typists were employed.

All these revisions, including the eight new lessons, were being done by Rachel. She sat with the school's former "literature" cut into narrow strips, and clipped together in piles around her. There were also stacks of circulars from rival correspondence schools, and a few odd textbooks on composition and short-story writing, from which she lifted the most dogmatic sentences, or even whole paragraphs. When she did work, she worked extremely rapidly. It sounded like two or three typewriters instead of one, and the nervous typists kept running in from the big skylighted room and back again with the new material like relay racers. But she talked to me a great deal of the time, or stared gloomily out the window at the falling snow. Once she said, "Why don't you write a pretty poem about *that*?" Once or twice, smelling strongly of whiskey, she buried herself sulkily in a new proletarian novel for an entire afternoon.

We scarcely saw Mr. Black at all. He received a good many callers in his office, men who looked just like him, and he served them the George Washington instant coffee he made on a Sterno stove, which smelled unpleasantly through the partition into our room. Once in a while he would bring us both coffee, in ten-cent-store cups of milky green glass with very rough edges you could cut yourself on. He would ask, "And how's the Vassar girl?" and look over my shoulder at the letter I was slowly producing on the typewriter with three or four fingers, and say, "Fine! Fine! You're doing fine! They'll love it! They'll love it!" and give my shoulder an objectionable squeeze. Sometimes he would say to Rachel, "Take a look at this. Save it; put the carbon in your file. We'll use it again." Rachel would give a loud groan.

It was here, in this noisome place, in spite of all I had read and been taught and thought I knew about it before, that the mysterious, awful power of writing first dawned on me. Or, since "writing" means so many different things, the power of the printed word, or even that capitalized Word whose significance had previously escaped me but then made itself suddenly, if sporadically, plain.

Our advertisements specified that when an applicant wrote in inquiring about the course, he was to send a sample of his writing, a "story" of any sort, any length, for our "analysis," and a five-dollar money order. We sent him the "analysis" and told him whether or not he really did have the right stuff in him to make a successful writer. All applicants, unless analphabetic, did. Then he was supposed to complete the first lesson, I think it was either "Straight Reporting" or "Descriptive Writing," within a month and send it back to us with the remaining thirty-five dollars. We "analyzed" that and sent it back along with lesson number two, and he was launched on the course.

I forget all the lessons now, but "Advertising" was fitted in somewhere. The students were required to write advertisements for grapefruit, bread, and liquor. Why the emphasis on food and drink, I don't know, unless that too was a sign of the times. Also included were a short story and a "True Confession" lesson. Almost all the students had the two genres hopelessly confused. Their original "samples" were apt to fall into the True Confession form, too. This sample, expanded or cut, censored or livened up, and the first letter to Mr. Margolies that accompanied it constituted the most interesting assignment for all concerned. My job was to write an analysis of each lesson in five hundred words, if I could, and as many of them a day as I possibly could, using a collection of previous lessons and analyses as models. I also had to write a short personal reply to the inevitable letter that arrived with each lesson. I was to encourage the student if he was feeling hopeless, and discourage him firmly if he showed any signs of wanting his money back.

Henry James once said that he who would aspire to be a writer must inscribe on his banner the one word "Loneliness." In the case of my students, their need was not to ward off society, but to get into it. Their problem was that on their banners "Loneliness" had been inscribed despite them, and so they aspired to be writers. Without exception the letters I received were from people suffering from terrible loneliness in all its better-known forms, and in some I had never even dreamed of. Writing, especially writing to Mr. Margolies, was a way of being less alone. To be printed, and to be "famous," would be an instant shortcut to identity, and an escape from solitude, because then other people would know one as admirers, friends, lovers, suitors, etc.

In the forms they filled out, they gave their ages and occupations. There were a good many cowboys and ranch hands. One of them printed his lessons, not with the printing taught for a while in fashionable schools, although it resembled it, but with the printing of a child concentrating on being neat and careful. There was a sheepherder, a real shepherd, who even *said* he was lonely, "in my line of work." Writing cheered him up because "sheep aren't much company for a man (ha-ha)." There were the wives of ranchers as well. There were several sailors, a Negro cook, a petty officer on a submarine, and a real lighthouse keeper. There were a good many "domestics," some of whom said they were "colored," and several students writing from addresses in the Deep South told me, as if they had to, that they were Negroes.

Of all the letters and lessons I read during my stay at the U.S.A. School, only one set showed any slight sign of "promise" whatever. They were the work of a "lady cattle-rancher and poultry farmer," an "old maid," she wrote, living at an R.F.D. address somewhere in Kansas. The stories she sent in, regardless of the nature of the assignment, were real stories. The other students' heartbreaking attempts were always incoherent, abrupt, curtailed. Hers bounced along exuberantly, like a good talker, and were almost interesting, with a lot of local color and detail. They were filled with roosters, snakes, foxes, and hawks, and they had dramatic and possibly true plots woven around sick and dying cows, mortgages, stepmothers, babies, wicked blizzards, and tornadoes. They were also ten times longer than anyone else's stories. After I gave up my job, I used to look into farm magazines, like *The Country Gentleman*, on the news-stands, hoping that she might have made publication at last, but I never saw her name again.

Most of my pathetic applicants seemed never to have read anything in their lives, except perhaps a single, memorable story of the "True Confession" type. The discrepancy between the odd, colorless, disjointed little pages they sent me and what they saw in print just didn't occur to them. Or perhaps they thought Mr. Margolies would wave his magic wand and the little heaps of melancholy word-bones, like chicken bones or fish bones, would put on flesh and vitality and be transformed into gripping, compelling, thrilling, full-length stories and novels. There were doubtless other, deeper reasons for their taking the "course," sending in all their "lessons," and paying that out-rageous forty dollars. But I could never quite believe that most of my students really thought that they too could one day write, or even that they would really have to work to do so. It was more like applying for application blanks for a lottery. After all, they might win the prize just as well as the next person, and everyone knows those things aren't always run honestly.

There seemed to be one thing common to all their "primitive" writing, as I suppose it might be called, in contrast to primitive painting: its slipshodiness and haste. Where primitive painters will spend months or years, if necessary, putting in every blade of grass and building up brick walls in low relief, the primitive writer seems in a hurry to get it over with. Another thing was the almost complete lack of detail. The primitive painter loves detail and lingers over it and emphasizes it at the expense of the picture as a whole. But if the writers put them in, the details are often impossibly or wildly inappropriate, sometimes revealing a great deal about the writer without furthering the matter in hand at all. Perhaps it all demonstrates the professional writer's frequent complaint that painting is more fun than writing. Perhaps the ranchers' wives who sent in miserable little outlines for stories with no conversation and no descriptions of people or places wouldn't hesitate to spend long afternoons lovingly decorating birthday cakes in different-color icings. But the subject matter was similarly banal in both the paintings and the writing. There was also the same tendency in both primitive painting and writing to make it all right, or of real value to the world, by tacking on a grand, if ill-fitting, "moral," or allegorical interpretation. My students seemed to be saying: "Our experiences are real and true and from them we have drawn these unique, these noble conclusions. Since our sentiments are so noble, who could have the heart to deny us our right to Fame?"

What could I possibly find to say to them? From what they wrote me it was obvious they could hardly wait to receive my next analysis. Perhaps they hoped, each time, that Mr. Margolies would tell them he had found a magazine to publish their last lesson and was enclosing the check. All of them were eager, if not hardworking, or felt they had to pretend to be. One man wrote: "I slept on a hair all night, waiting to hear from you." They apologized for their slowness, for their spelling, for their pens or pencils (they were asked to use ink but quite a few didn't). One boy excused his poor handwriting by saying, "This is being written on the subway," and it may have been true. Some referred to the lessons as their "homework," and addressed Mr. Margolies as "Dear Teacher." One woman decorated her lessons with Christmas seals. To my surprise, there were two or three male students who wrote man-to-man obscenities, or retold well-worn dirty jokes.

I took to copying out parts of their letters and stories to take home with me. A Kansas City janitor wanted to learn to write in order to publish "a book about how to teach children to be good radicals, of the George Washington Type or the Jesus Christ Type." One woman revealed that her aged mother approved of her learning how to write to such an extent that she had given her the forty dollars and *"her own name* to write under." The daughter's name was Emma, the mother's was Katerina. Would I please address her as Katerina in the future?

Next to my "lady cattle-rancher and poultry farmer" I grew fondest of a Mr. Jimmy O'Shea of Fall River, aged seventy, occupation "retired." His was the nearest approach to a classical primitive style. His stories were fairly long, and like Gertrude Stein, he wrote in large handwriting on small pieces of paper. He had developed a style that enabled him to make exactly a page of every sentence. Each sentence—it usually began with *Also* or *Yes*—opened at the top left-hand and finished with an outsize dimple of a period in the lower right. Goodness shone through his blue-lined pages as if they had been little paper lanterns. He characterized everything that appeared in his simple tales with three, four, or even five adjectives and then repeated them, like Homer, every time the noun appeared. It was Mr. O'Shea who wrote me a letter which expressed the common feeling of time passing and wasted, of wonder and envy, and partly sincere ambition: "I wasn't feeling well over my teeth, and I had three large ones taken out, for they made me nervous and sick sometime, and this is the reason I couldn't send in my lesson. I am thinking of being able to write like all the Authors, for I believe that is more in my mind than any other kind of work. Mr. Margolies, I am thinking of how those Authors write such long stories of 60,000 or 100,000 words in those Magazines, and where do they get their imagination and the material to work upon? I know there is a big field in this art."

I stood the school for as long as I could, which wasn't very long, and the same week that I received this letter from Mr. O'Shea, I resigned. Mr. Black begged me to stay, I was just getting going, I was turning out more and more analyses every day, and he offered me two dollars and a half more a week. Rachel seemed sorry to see me go, too. We went out for a last lunch together, to a different cafeteria, one that had a bar, and, going Dutch, had a twenty-cent Manhattan each before lunch. When I was cleaning out my desk, she gave me a present, a strange paperbound book she had just finished reading, written by a Chinese, almost in the style of some of our students. It was all about his experiences as an agricultural slave in the United States and on the sugarcane plantations of Cuba. It may have been true, but it was not "realism" because he used odd, Oriental imagery.

About two years later I met Rachel in Times Square one night on my way to the theater. She looked just the same, perhaps a little heavier and perhaps a little less shabby. I asked her if she still worked for the U.S.A. School of Writing and how Mr. Black was. Mr. Black, she announced casually, was in jail, for a second or third offense, for misuse of the mails. The U.S.A. School of Writing had been raided by the police shortly after I left, and all our work, and all my poor students' accumulation of lessons and earnest, confiding letters, had been confiscated. She said, "I didn't tell you while you were there, but that's why we were doing that revising. The U.S.A. School was a new name; up until a month before you came, it was something else. Black paid a big fine that time, and we were starting all over again."

I asked her what she was doing now, but she didn't tell me. I was dressed to go to the theater, and she looked me up and down contemptuously, I felt, but tolerantly, as if she were thinking, Some anarchist! Then Mr. Hearn and Mr. Margolies shook hands and parted forever.

1966

Gregorio Valdes

§

The first painting I saw by Gregorio Valdes was in the window
of a barbershop on Duval Street, the main street of Key West.
The shop is in a block of cheap liquor stores, shoeshine parlors
and poolrooms, all under a long wooden awning shading the
sidewalk. The picture leaned against a cardboard advertisement
for Eagle Whiskey, among other window decorations of red-and-
green crepe-paper rosettes and streamers left over from Christ-
mas and the announcement of an operetta at the Cuban school
—all covered with dust and fly spots and littered with termites'
wings.

It was a view, a real View, of a straight road diminishing to a
point through green fields, and a row of straight Royal Palms on
either side, so carefully painted that one could count seven trees
in each row. In the middle of the road was the tiny figure of a
man on a donkey, and far away on the right the white speck of a
thatched Cuban cabin that seemed to have the same mysterious
properties of perspective as the little dog in Rousseau's *The
Cariole of M. Juniot*. The sky was blue at the top, then white,
then beautiful blush pink, the pink of a hot, mosquito-filled
tropical evening. As I went back and forth in front of the barber-
shop on my way to the restaurant, this picture charmed me, and

at last I went in and bought it for three dollars. My landlady had been trained to do "oils" at the Convent. —The house was filled with copies of *The Roman Girl at the Well, Horses in a Thunderstorm,* etc. —She was disgusted and said she would paint the same picture for me, "for fifteen cents."

The barber told me I could see more Valdes pictures in the window of a little cigar factory on Duval Street, one of the few left in Key West. There were six or seven pictures: an ugly *Last Supper* in blue and yellow, a *Guardian Angel* pushing two children along a path at the edge of a cliff, a study of flowers—all copies, and also copies of local postcards. I liked one picture of a homestead in Cuba in the same green fields, with two of the favorite Royal Palms and a banana tree, a chair on the porch, a woman, a donkey, a big white flower, and a Pan-American airplane in the blue sky. A friend bought this one, and then I decided to call on Gregorio.

He lived at 1221 Duval Street, as it said on all his pictures, but he had a "studio" around the corner in a decayed, unrentable little house. There was a palette nailed to one of the posts of the verandah with *G. Valdes, Sign Painter* on it. Inside there were three rooms with holes in the floors and weeds growing up through the holes. Gregorio had covered two sections of the walls with postcards and pictures from the newspapers. One section was animals: baby animals in zoos and wild animals in Africa. The other section was mostly reproductions of Madonnas and other religious subjects from the rotogravures. In one room there was a small plaster Virgin with some half-melted yellow wax roses in a tumbler in front of her. He also had an old cot there, and a row of plants in tin cans. One of these was Sweet Basil, which I was invited to smell every time I came to call.

Gregorio was very small, thin and sickly, with a childish face and tired brown eyes—in fact, he looked a little like the *Self-Portrait* of El Greco. He spoke very little English but was so polite that if I took someone with me who spoke Spanish he would almost ignore the Spanish and always answer in English, anyway, which made explanations and even compliments very difficult. He had been born in Key West, but his wife was from Cuba, and Spanish was the household language, as it is in most Key West Cuban families.

I commissioned him to paint a large picture of the house I was living in. When I came to take him to see it he was dressed in new clothes: a new straw hat, a new striped shirt, buttoned up but without a necktie, his old trousers, but a pair of new black-and-white Cuban shoes, elaborately Gothic in design, and with such pointed toes that they must have been very uncomfortable. I gave him an enlarged photograph of the house to paint from and also asked to have more flowers put in, a monkey that lived next door, a parrot, and a certain type of palm tree, called the Traveler's Palm. There is only one of these in Key West, so Gregorio went and made a careful drawing of it to go by. He showed me the drawing later, with the measurements and colors written in along the side, and apologized because the tree really had seven branches on one side and six on the other, but in the painting he had given both sides seven to make it more symmetrical. He put in flowers in profusion, and the parrot, on the perch on the verandah, and painted the monkey, larger than life-size, climbing the trunk of the palm tree.

When he delivered this picture there was no one at home, so he left it on the verandah leaning against the wall. As I came home that evening I saw it there from a long way off down the street—a fair-sized copy of the house, in green and white, leaning against its green-and-white prototype. In the gray twilight they seemed to blur together and I had the feeling that if I came closer I would be able to see another miniature copy of the house leaning on the porch of the painted house, and so on—like the Old Dutch Cleanser advertisements. A few days later when I had hung the picture I asked Gregorio to a vernissage party, and in spite of language difficulties we all had a very nice time. We drank sherry, and from time to time Gregorio would announce, "More wine."

He had never seemed very well, but this winter when I returned to Key West he seemed much more delicate than before. After Christmas I found him at work in his studio only once. He had several commissions for pictures and was very happy. He had changed the little palette that said *Sign Painter* for a much larger one saying *Artist Painter*. But the next time I went to see him he was at the house on Duval Street and one of his daughters told me he was "seek" and in bed. Gregorio came out as she said it, however, pulling on his trousers and apologizing for not having any new pictures to show, but he looked very ill.

His house was a real Cuban house, very bare, very clean, with a bicycle standing in the narrow front hall. The living room had a doorway draped with green chenille Christmas fringe, and six straight chairs around a little table in the middle bearing a bunch of artificial flowers. The bareness of a Cuban house, and the apparent remoteness of every object in it from every other object, gives one the same sensation as the bareness and remoteness of Gregorio's best pictures. The only decorations I remember seeing in the house were the crochet and embroidery work being done by one of the daughters, which was always on the table in the living room, and a few photographs—of Gregorio when he had played the trombone in a band as a young man, a wedding party, etc., and a marriage certificate, hanging on the walls. Also in the hall there was a wonderful clock. The case was a plaster statue, painted bronze, of President Roosevelt manipulating a ship's wheel. On the face there was a picture of a barkeeper shaking cocktails, and the little tin shaker actually shook up and down with the ticking of the clock. I think this must have been won at one of the bingo tents that are opened at Key West every winter.

Gregorio grew steadily worse during the spring. His own doctor happened to be in Cuba and he refused to have any other come to see him. His daughters said that when they begged him to have a doctor he told them that if one came he would "throw him away."

A friend and I went to see him about the first of May. It was the first time he had failed to get up to see us and we realized that he was dangerously sick. The family took us to a little room next to the kitchen, about six feet wide, where he lay on a low cot-bed. The room was only large enough to hold the bed, a wardrobe, a little stand, and a slop-jar, and the rented house was in such a bad state of repair that light came up through the big holes in the floor. Gregorio, terribly emaciated, lay in bed wearing a blue shirt; his head was on a flat pillow, and just above him a little holy picture was tacked to the wall. He looked like one of those Mexican retablo paintings of miraculous cures, only in his case we were afraid no miraculous cure was possible.

That day we bought one of the few pictures he had on hand— a still life of Key West fruits such as a coconut, a mango, sapodillos, a watermelon, and a sugar apple, all stiffly arranged against a blue background. In this picture the paint had cracked slightly, and examining it I discovered one eccentricity of Gregorio's painting. The blue background extended all the way to the tabletop and where the paint had cracked the blue showed through the fruit. Apparently he had felt that since the wall was back of the fruit he should paint it there, before he could go on and paint the fruit in front of it.

The next day we discovered in the Sunday *New York Times* that he had a group of fifteen paintings on exhibition at the Artists' Gallery in New York. We cut out the notice and took it to his house, but he was so sick he could only lie in bed holding out his thin arms and saying "Excuse, excuse." We were relieved, however, when the family told us that he had at last consented to have another doctor come to see him.

On the evening of the ninth of May we were extremely shocked when a Cuban friend we met on the street told us that "Gregorio died at five o'clock." We drove to the house right away. Several people were standing on the verandah in the dark, talking in low voices. One young man came up and said to us, "The old man die at five o'clock." He did not mean to be disrespectful but his English was poor and he said "old man" instead of "father."

The funeral took place the next afternoon. Only relatives and close friends attend the service of a Cuban funeral and only men go to the cemetery, so there were a great many cars drawn up in front of the house filled with the waiting men. Very quickly the coffin was carried out, covered with the pale, loose Rock Roses that the Valdeses grow for sale in their back yard. Afterwards we were invited in, "to see the children."

Gregorio was so small and had such a detached manner that it was always surprising to think of him as a patriarch. He had five daughters and two sons: Jennie, Gregorio, Florencio, Anna Louisa, Carmela, Adela, and Estella. Two of the daughters are married and he had three grandchildren, two boys and a girl.

I had been afraid that when I brought him the clipping from the *Times* he had been too sick to understand it, but the youngest daughter told me that he had looked at it a great deal and had kept telling them all that he was "going to get the first prize for painting in New York."

She told me several other anecdotes about her father—how when the battleships came into Key West harbor during the war he had made a large-scale model of one of them, exact in every detail, and had used it as an ice-cream cart, to peddle Cuban ices through the streets. It attracted the attention of a tourist from the North and he bought it, "for eighty dollars." She said that when the carnivals came to town he would sit up all night by the light of an oil lamp, making little pinwheels to sell. He used to spend many nights at his studio, too, when he wanted to finish a sign or a picture, getting a little sleep on the cot there.

He had learned to paint when he and his wife were "sweethearts," she said, from an old man they call a name that sounds like "Musi"—no one knows how to spell it or remembers his real name. This old man lived in a house belonging to the Valdeses, but he was too poor to pay rent and so he gave Gregorio painting lessons instead.

Gregorio had worked in the cigar factories, been a sign painter, an ice-cream peddler, and for a short time a photographer, in the effort to support his large family. He made several trips to Cuba and twenty years ago worked for a while in the cigar factories in Tampa, returning to Key West because his wife liked it better. While in Tampa he painted signs as well, and also the sides of delivery wagons. There are some of his signs in Key West—a large one for the Sociedad de Cuba and one for a grocery store, especially, have certain of the qualities of his pictures. Just down the street from his house, opposite the Sociedad de Cuba, there used to be a little café for the workers in a nearby cigar factory, the Forget-Me-Not Café, *Café no me Olvidades*. Ten years age or so Gregorio painted a picture of it on the wall of the café itself, with the blue sky, the telephone pole and wires, and the name, all very exact. Mr. Rafael Rodríguez, the former owner, who showed it to us, seemed to feel rather badly because since the cigar factory and the café have both disappeared, the color of the doors and window frames has been changed from blue to orange, making Gregorio's picture no longer as perfect as it was.

This story is told by Mr. Edwin Denby in his article on Valdes for the Artists' Gallery exhibition: "When he was a young man he lived with an uncle. One day when that uncle was at work, Valdes took down the towel rack that hung next to the washbasin and put up instead a painting of the rack with the towel on it. When the uncle came back at five, he went to the basin, bent over and washed his face hard; and still bent over he reached up for the towel. But he couldn't get hold. With the water streaming into his eyes, he squinted up at it, saw it and clawed at it, but the towel wouldn't come off the wall. 'Me laugh plenty, plenty,' Valdes said . . ."

This classical ideal of verisimilitude did not always succeed so well, fortunately. Gregorio was not a great painter at all, and although he certainly belongs to the class of painters we call "primitive," sometimes he was not even a good "primitive." His pictures are of uneven quality. They are almost all copies of photographs or of reproductions of other pictures. Usually when he copied from such reproductions he succeeded in nothing more than the worst sort of "calendar" painting, and again when he copied, particularly from a photograph, and particularly from a photograph of something he knew and liked, such as palm trees, he managed to make just the right changes in perspective and coloring to give it a peculiar and captivating freshness, flatness, and remoteness. But Gregorio himself did not see any difference between what we think of as his good pictures and his poor pictures, and his painting a good one or a bad one seems to have been entirely a matter of luck.

There are some people whom we envy not because they are rich or handsome or successful, although they may be any or all of these, but because everything they are and do seems to be all of a piece, so that even if they wanted to they could not be or do otherwise. A particular feature of their characters may stand out as more praiseworthy in itself than others—that is almost beside the point. Ancient heroes often have to do penance for and expiate crimes they have committed all unwittingly, and in the same way it seems that some people receive certain "gifts" merely by remaining unwittingly in an undemocratic state of grace. It is a supposition that leaves painting like Gregorio's a partial mystery. But surely anything that is impossible for others to achieve by effort, that is dangerous to imitate, and yet, like natural virtue, must be both admired and imitated, always remains mysterious.

Anyway, who could fail to enjoy and admire those secretive palm trees in their pink skies, the Traveler's Palm, like "the fan-filamented antenna of a certain gigantic moth . . ." or the picture of the church in Cuba copied from a liquor advertisement and labeled with so literal a translation from the Spanish, "Church of St. Mary Rosario 300 Years Constructed in Cuba."

1939

Mercedes Hospital

ༀ

One day in the summer of 1940 the following notice appears in the Key West *Citizen*:

JOSÉ CHACÓN DIED TODAY

José Chacón, 84, died three o'clock this afternoon in the Mercedes Hospital. Funeral services will be held 5:30 p.m. tomorrow from the chapel of the Pritchard Funeral Home, Rev. G. Perez of the Latin Methodist Church officiating.

The deceased leaves but one survivor, a nephew, José Chacón.

Directly underneath appears this poem:

FRIEND?

How often have you called
Someone a friend
And thought he would be
Everything it meant?

While you were on top of the world,
With money in your hands,
They flocked around everywhere,
Even at your command.

Now that you are old and gray,
Your friends look the other way
When you meet them on the street;
Never a "Hello" when you meet.

You go home to your little room
And sit silent in the gloom,
Thinking of the once bright day,
But now you are old and all alone.

But one comes to you every day
As on your bed you must lay.
He stops and takes you by the hand,
And the look on his face, you understand.

That smile on his face tells a lot
As he sits by your bed and watches the clock
Ticking the hours softly by.
With a tear in his eye, he says goodbye.

That was a Friend to the End.

I find this brief account of the death of an old man in what is really just the poorhouse, the Casa del Pobre, very touching. And of course the poem is touching too, but it naturally does not occur to me to connect them. Then I remember I am acquainted with a man named José Chacón who must be the nephew, but who certainly could never have written anything like it. He is a fat, talkative Cuban who runs a little open-air café, *La Estrella*. There are always several men sitting around the place, drinking coffee and playing dominoes, but the real money is made in the back room, where poker games and *bolito* drawings are held. José lives over the shop with his wife and several children; he is quite rich. Why he has let his uncle die in the Mercedes Hospital, I can't imagine.

I meet him on the street a few days later. José always speaks as though he were furiously angry, but it is just a rather common mannerism. I ask him what his uncle has died of, and he bursts out, as though the old man had been his bitterest enemy, that he died of drink, drink, drink. He demonstrates: he reels, emptying a bottle down his throat, and clutching at monsters in the air. He tells me a long story of how his uncle once hit a man with a bottle and had been taken to jail. I ask him why his uncle hasn't lived with him, and he says he couldn't live with anybody. He was a cigar maker for forty years; then he retired and pursued his real career of drinking. I ask if his uncle was a large or powerful man. "Yes, big and strong!" And again José expresses his opinion that it is drink that killed him.

It is a very hot day. The sky is thick bright blue, the same color as the painted lower halves of the windows of the Mercedes Hospital, as seen from the inside, where I am waiting for Miss Mamie Harris to appear. Miss Mamie has the local reputation of a saint. She is a nurse who has lived and worked at the Mercedes Hospital ever since it was opened. The parlor is hot and dark, as I examine the photographs of the hospital's founder.

The Mercedes Hospital was given to the town of Key West thirty years ago [in 1911] by Mr. Perro, the richest of the local cigar-factory owners. (Mr. Perro's favorite amusement was chess, and the high parapet of his former factory was adorned at intervals with knights cut from gray stones, as well as horse heads resting on little crenellated towers looking to all points of the compass. The inside covers of his cigar boxes had the same knights surrounded by gilt sunrays.) An enlarged photograph of Mr. Perro, yellow and indistinct, hangs in the parlor of the hospital, together with the original of his cigar-box decoration, done in watercolors.

On the walls there are also two or three mottoes, cross-stitched in wool on perforated cardboard; a crucifix; and a large lithograph, extremely yellow, of the life of the patriot Martí, with the major incidents of his life arranged in an oval; at the top, Martí in a toga is ascending into heaven. Besides the wall decorations, there are a few chairs, a Poor Box nailed to the wall for donations, and an old rolltop desk stuffed with forgotten papers. Mr. Perro left the hospital all these things, plus one hundred and thirty dollars a month forever and ever, and the name of his wife, Mercedes.

The hospital was originally his home. Being so rich, Mr. Perro had wanted to build his house in the Spanish style, like those of well-to-do businessmen in Cuba, but not wanting to go to the expense of importing stone, he had it built of wood. For that reason it looks a little strange—a high, square building with long Gothic windows, correctly built around a courtyard, but covered with clapboard and decorated here and there with quite American fretsaw work. The upstairs rooms rest on the thin wooden pillars around the patio, which is a dim, damp, battered square of cement with a drain in the middle. There is a well, but nothing at all picturesque—a square hole in the cement, with a galvanized bucket and a length of wet rope resting beside it. It is said that after Mr. Perro got his Spanish patio, he was uncertain as to what to do with it, so he stabled two horses there for several years.

The rooms, eight on each floor, are high and dark. The walls of horizontal boards were once painted in fearful shades of solid green, blue, or red, with moldings of contrasting fearful shades and gilt, but now they are as worn and faded as the painted walls of ancient tombs. Those of the parlor are different shades of blue, the dining room (at least I suppose it is a dining room, since there is a round table in the middle with four chairs pushed under it) different shades of brick and rose. One of the inmates' rooms suggests that it has been spinach-green, another ocher. But all these colors, once so rich and bright, are scarcely there at all. They look as if they had been soaked off by a long stay underwater. The whole hospital has the air of having been submerged: the damp cement, the bare floors worn away to the ridges of the grain, and the pillars and the patio so "sucked" by termites that they look like elongated sponges.

After a while I hear the staircase creaking and then Miss Mamie comes in. She is wearing a soiled white nurse's uniform, with a narrow white leather belt dangling around her waist, white cotton stockings, and soiled long white shoes. Her gray hair is cut very short, her face is full of indecipherable lines, and many of her teeth are missing. She always stands very close to me with one hand on her hip and the other usually on my shoulder, smiling, but watching my face closely like a doubtful child.

"My, how you keep plump," she says and gives me a leer and a pinch. "I wish I could."

We talk for a while about the weather, about how she would like to get out for a drive some evening soon but doesn't think she'll be able to, how she has been there for thirty years, and how the "Collector" is in Cuba on a little visit to her relatives, leaving her with more work to do than usual. The "Collector" is a very old lady, supposedly the superintendent of the hospital, who goes slowly around town from door to door, with a black imitation-leather market bag over her arm, begging money to add to the one hundred and thirty dollars a month.

After the "little talk," we take a tour around the ground floor to see the "patients." There are only four today, and three of them are permanent residents. First comes Mr. "Tommy" Cummers. Mr. Tommy has lived at the Mercedes Hospital for fourteen years, and his cousin Mr. "Sonny" Cummers has lived there for three. Miss Mamie always uses the Mister, and although they are both over seventy they are called "Sonny" and "Tommy." (It must be the idea of the helplessness it implies that makes the Southern use of childish names so sad. I hear old men speaking of "my daddy," and another man I know, aged sixty, was found dead drunk under the counter at the fish market, just two days after he had left his house, saying, "Mama, I'm going to be a good boy from now on.")

Mr. Tommy is singing hymns as we step across the patio to his room. His feet and ankles are paralyzed; he sits in an armchair beside the door with a sheet over his knees, and sings hymns, out of time and out of tune, in a loud rough voice all day long. He keeps a large Bible and two hymnbooks beside him and is rather inclined to boast that he reads nothing else. He sings the hymns partly to spite Mr. Sonny, who is sitting in the next room just behind the folding doors and who, before he came to Mercedes Hospital, was not able to lead as sheltered and virtuous a life as Mr. Tommy has for the last fourteen years.

While we are there, the housekeeper comes in. She is a plump little Cuban lady with little gold earrings shaking in her ears. She brings three cigars in a paper bag for Mr. Tommy, who takes a dime out of his breast pocket and pays her for them. As soon as we leave, he starts singing again, and while we call on Mr. Sonny, he is almost bellowing.

Mr. Sonny is dying of dropsy; we merely say good afternoon. He sits at the far end of one of the long side rooms, all alone, on a straight chair with his feet on a little footstool. His swollen body is wrapped in a gray blanket and his head is done up in a sort of turban of white. He bows to us indifferently; his thin pointed face is dark brown. He looks so exactly like an eighteenth-century poet that although Miss Mamie is chattering away to me about his desperate condition, I can't pay much attention to her. I'm expecting to hear him declaim from the shadows:

Cease, fond Nature, cease thy strife.

In another large room lies a tubercular Negro named Milton, here for the third time. Miss Mamie says, "We don't exactly take them, they have a place. But he is so sick and we have so few patients." She pulls me past the door, but I see a large black man with long thin legs stretched out on an iron cot under the mosquito bar. The walls of this room are ashes-of-roses. There are six beds but only Milton's is made up. It is on the sunny side of the building, it is hot, it smells strongly of disinfectant, and the long black legs look strange, seen through the ethereal cascade of mosquito netting.

Then we go into the sunlight, across a short gangplank, into a little square building.

"Our little crazy house," says Miss Mamie affectionately. "You haven't seen Antoñica, have you? Well, she isn't crazy any more. I'm going to take her back inside as soon as the doctor comes around again at the end of the week, but I have to keep her here awhile. She's only been here three weeks."

Sitting close to the window in an old-fashioned high-back

rocking chair is a tiny creature in a long ragged flannel night-gown with a ruffle around the neck. The sun falls directly on her face; the hot wind blows in on her straight from the embers of the huge red Poinciana tree outside the window.

"She can't hear nothing and she can't see nothing," says Miss Mamie, "she's just like a little baby. I do everything for her just like a little baby."

She unclasps a hand from the arm of the rocking chair and holds it. It holds hers tightly, and Antoñica raises her face to Miss Mamie's and begins in Spanish in a loud harsh voice. I try to make out what she is saying, but Miss Mamie says it doesn't make any sense.

"She's terrible fond of me," she says. The old woman's hair has been cut so that it is about an inch long. Miss Mamie keeps rubbing her hand over the small skull, rather roughly, I think. But yes, it is true—Antoñica does appear to be fond of her. She snatches Miss Mamie's hand to her cheek, and jabbers louder than ever.

"She outlived all her folks, she ain't got anyone left, she's way over ninety," says Miss Mamie in a sort of coarse singsong, rubbing the old woman's white head and rocking her back and forth. "Terrible fond of me. I feed her just like a baby, just like a baby."

Antoñica's wool-white hair glistens in the sun. The ruff, the unnatural motion, her feet curled up off the floor, and her clutching hands make her look like a rare and delicate specimen of Chinese monkey. But her eyes, which are bright milky blue, like the flames of a gas burner when they have just been turned off and are about to sink back into the black pipes, give her an apocryphal appearance.

Perhaps she is an angel, speaking with "tongues."

Miss Mamie and I go back to the parlor and stand and talk some more. I know that some people consider her a saint.

Probably they are right. She is capable of arousing the same feelings that the saints do: profoundest admiration and suspicion. Thirty dollars a month wages, thirty years of unselfish labor, "managing" on one hundred and thirty dollars a month for "everything" are all incredible feats—unless one does believe she is a saint.

There are other proofs of Miss Mamie's unusual character. There is her indifference to personal cleanliness (although she keeps her patients very clean). There is her solitariness: she rarely, if ever, leaves the hospital. There is her appearance: her face, her hands, and those long ascetic feet are all in her favor. Above all, there is her inquisitiveness and talkativeness and that childlike expression in her eyes when she takes hold of my shoulders and peers into my face and asks question after question—just as St. Anthony might have rushed out of his cell, and seized a traveler by the elbow and naïvely but determinedly asked him for news of the world. In fact, all the saints must have been insistent buttonholers, like Miss Mamie.

I suddenly remember José Chacón. Seeing Miss Mamie now, as sitting patiently at the mouth of her cavern on the edge of an endless desert, I wonder if the old man had been the wild "lion of the desert," coming to her roaring, with thorns in his paws? I ask about him.

"Oh, José. He was here lots of times, seven or eight times."

"He was a very big man, wasn't he?"

"José? Oh no, he wasn't big at all. I could lift him myself. He'd come here for a while, then he'd get better and go home again. He had a bad heart." If she knew about his alcoholism, she says nothing about it.

"How did he die?"

"He died so quick. The day he died, he seemed pretty good. I thought he was going to go home the next day, he seemed so good. I had his bed out in the front room by the window to get the air. Then I went to push it back into his room; he didn't weigh much. He was talking to me and, all of a sudden just as we got there, going through his door"—Miss Mamie cracked her finger—"it was his heart. Just stopped like that." Bump, the bed went over the threshold and José Chacón died.

Of course Miss Mamie could not have been the "Friend to the End" in the poem. If she read it in the paper, she wouldn't understand its sentiments, of which she certainly would have disapproved wholeheartedly, especially its self-praise. I could not conceive of such a poem being written or read there in Mercedes Hospital. Among Miss Mamie's saintly qualities, tenderness is lacking. In fact, it is the absence of tenderness that is the consoling thing about her.

It is time for me to leave, and after a little conversation about the "Collector" and about finances, I put ten dollars into Miss Mamie's hands, "for the Poor Box," and say goodbye. As I leave, I begin to think, Why didn't I put the money in the Poor Box myself? I know perfectly well that she won't do it.

It is a foolish as well as an unkind thought, because naturally Miss Mamie would have the key to the Poor Box; probably she wears it around her neck on a string. I realize my doubt is another proof of Miss Mamie's saintliness, and therefore of her ability to arouse suspicion. I've always thought the reason we suspect saints is the ambiguous nature of all good deeds, the impossibility of ever knowing why they are being performed. But that reasoning fails to explain Miss Mamie. She does away with the feeling that possibly she may be a saint for the wrong reason, by convincing one that she is being a saint for no ulterior reason at all.

There is no reason for or against her robbing the Poor Box, no more than there are reasons for or against her staying at the Mercedes Hospital, or being kind or cruel to the patients. St. Simeon Stylites probably thought he knew exactly what he was doing at the top of his pillar and rejoiced in it. Miss Mamie hasn't any idea that what she is doing where she is needs explaining. She has managed to transfer the same feeling to her patients—giving them security from hopelessness. Simplicity of heart, never the vulgarity of putting two and two together.

I go out, and the palm branches move slowly like prehistoric caryatids. The Mercedes Hospital seems so remote and far away now, like the bed of a dried-up lake. Out of the corner of my eye I catch a glimpse of the salty glitter at its bottom, a slight mica-like residuum, the faintest trace of joyousness.

1941

To the Botequim & Back

༇

I go out to the botequim to buy some cigarettes and a Merenda, a soft drink similar to Orange Crooshy, and in the twenty minutes or so the expedition takes me I see "the following," as they say here.* (The slight pretentiousness in speech of semi-literacy. Workmen love to say, "I want to say *the following*," colon, then say it. Or, "Now I shall say *the following*," after which they do.)

It is a beautiful bright morning, big soft clouds moving rather rapidly high up, making large patches of opaque blue on the green hills and rocky peaks. The third of February; summer has come. Everything has grown amazingly in a week or so. Two kinds of morning glory adorn the standing walls of a ruined house—a pale lavender kind and a bright purple, pink-centered kind, hundreds of gaudy flowers stretching open to the sun as wide as they possibly can. All along the way the stone walls are flourishing after the January rains with mosses, maidenhair ferns, and a tiny yellow flower. I look down at a garden inside another ruin, an attempt at beauty and formality about ten feet square: there are a square border and two

* That is, in the town of Ouro Prêto ("Black Gold"), over 300 miles northwest of Rio de Janeiro, where EB lived.

diagonals, with a rosebush in the middle covered with small red roses. Everything straggly and untidy, unpruned, long shoots on the bushes swaying in the breeze. Two Monarch butterflies are flickering, with hundreds of bees getting at the blossoms. Two hummingbirds sucking at the morning glories— one the little brilliant iridescent kind, the other the big long-bodied hummingbird, gray, with white edges to its tail. A tree (almost) of orange-yellow dahlias; white roses; a common variety, yellow-white, untidy; lavender flowers in profusion, onions mixed up with them all along the border, and a little kale. Where a cascade passes under the street, and comes out below, there is a rank growth of "lily of the valley," a wild water plant with lush long leaves and big tired white blossoms that drag in the water. Every once in a while I catch their scent, overstrong and oversweet.

Palmyra had asked to leave work early this morning to go to have her throat blessed. Father Antonio was holding a Throat Blessing at the church at 6 a.m. (It's the feast of St. Blasius, the patron saint of throats.) Aurea had had a sore throat; Palmyra didn't, so apparently she was taking precautions. I asked her how the blessing had gone. There had been "many folks"; the priest had blessed them all in general, then at the railing he had come up close to each one, with his arms crossed and candles burning on either side of him, murmuring a blessing.

The botequim is a little shop or "grocery store," where I buy a liter of milk every morning—that is, if it hasn't already turned sour. The bottles are usually left standing on the sidewalk, in a frame, all morning or all day, until they are sold. This store is owned by João Pica Pau, John Woodpecker. But, on the way, there is something new today. A "poolroom" has just opened, and there are five or six men and boys blocking the narrow sidewalk in front of the two open doors. It is a snooker table, I suppose, but so small it looks like a toy one, brand-new, with bright green felt. Two boys are playing, almost on the sidewalk.

Just before I get to João Pica Pau's, which is next to the barbershop, I meet three boys of twelve or so, brothers by their looks, all about the same size, mulattoes, with dark gray eyes. The two outside boys are helping the middle one, who is very thin, wasted, pale, wearing boots on his bare feet. He is languid and limp; his ragged shirt and blue trousers are very clean. He drags his feet and bends and sways like a broken stalk. His head turns toward me and he seems to have only one eye, a sunken hole for the other one—or is it an eye? I can't bear to look. His brother suddenly puts an arm under his knees and picks him up and takes him into the barber's. The barbershop is barely big enough for the chair, the barber, a fly-specked mirror, and an enormous atomizer. (At other times I've gone by, a child has been playing with the atomizer, spraying a rich synthetic scent out the door at his friends.) I glance in now and there are *two* people in the barber chair, the one-eyed boy sitting on his brother's lap, while the barber cuts his long frizzy hair. Everyone is silent as the brother holds him in a tight embrace. The boy cocks his one eye helplessly at the mirror.

Constant coming and going on the sidewalk, hot in the sun. A large black lady holds an apricot-colored umbrella, sheer and shiny, high over her head to give as much shade as possible to herself, the baby in her arms, and two little ones trailing behind. One of the local "characters" comes toward me, a miserable and shuffling old woman. She is broad and sagging; everything sags—breasts and stomach. She carries a black umbrella as a sunshade. Her shoes don't match; one is an old tennis shoe, almost falling off, the other an old black slipper. Her hair is wild and white; her crazy little eyes glitter at me. Two little girls follow, giggling. I give them a look.

I reach the botequim, but I find it closed. João Pica Pau has set up shop in the small cloth store next door. He has moved shop to the extent of pushing his milk bottles along the sidewalk a few feet, and setting up his glass case, which is filled with a wild variety of cheap cigarettes. I also see his pair of red scales, a huge knife, and a mess of small salamis in a basket, sitting on top of bolts of yard goods. He seems to be handling the sale of cloth as well. Ropes of garlic and a box of half-ripe tomatoes are all he has to offer fresh this morning. I drink a Pepsi-Cola, small size, while he wraps up the others for me. I also buy a pack of razor blades and some cheap candies. He spills the candies out all over the dirty counter for me to make my selection.

He tells me and anyone else interested—there are several men and boys in the shop, as usual, one already quite drunk at the far end drinking straight *cachaça* and another eating a small loaf of bread, all just staring and listening—about the awful fight last night. One man had a machete, another had a pocket knife, the third had a stick, and they were all drunk. He got them separated and closed his doors. "I hate fights, don't you?" he asks me. I say I do. "Someone might get killed," he says. He wanted three policemen to come and hit them with their rubber truncheons—he demonstrates—and that would have put a stop to the fighting, but he had no telephone, as the men well knew. But he wasn't afraid of them, or only of the one with the machete. Yes, too much killing goes on, it is easy to kill someone. He ends his little sermon by saying, "It is stupid, it is great nonsense to kill a man. Imagine, the police would catch him, he'd spend a year in jail, and lose his job, and confound his life completely." Everyone nods in agreement.

The *cachaça* drinker, in a thick voice, asks for another. I take my purchases and leave the botequim.

Home again. No, the dishonest antique dealer hails me from his pale blue house hung with fake-antique lanterns and with a front yard full of old tables and cupboards. "Do you want an antique cupboard? I have three or four nice ones." He comes running across the road, wagging his fat hands like a baby. He's obviously making money. Three years ago he was just a day laborer and knew nothing of antiques. Now he has customers all over the state [of Minas Gerais] and sends things to dealers in Rio and Saõ Paulo. "I want to show you a house. I want the senhora to see it because she has such *good taste*." I stopped speaking to him for two years because of a dirty trick he played on me over the most beautiful statue of St. Sebastian I have ever seen. I've started speaking again; it's useless to try to make him understand ethics. His fat wife smiles and waves her hands at me like a baby too.

At home I find a flyer, thrown in the yard—an invitation from the Ouro Prêto Department of Tourism inviting the people of the town and visitors

> to witness the monumental parade of the Carnival Clubs in Tooth-puller Square on the 7th, 8th, 9th and 10th of the month of February. The following clubs will parade: Zé Pereira of the Lacaios [footmen], Conjunto Brito Filho, Clube Recreative XV de Novembere, Escola de Samba Morro de Sant'ana, Bloco Estrela Dalva, Zé Pereira Infantil, and Escola do Bairro do Padre Faria.
>
> On the 10th there will be a great competition for the prize for the best of the Carnival of 1970, and the great parade of Allegorical Cars [floats].

About a mile above the city, up a winding steep dirt road, you reach a high plateau. On the way you pass two small chapels in the distance, Our Lady of the Safe Delivery and Santa Ana. Up through Burnt Hill, past steep fields full of ruins. After two hundred years, a few ruins have turned back into houses again: one very small one, just four standing walls with openings for a door and window, now has a roof of tarpaulin, weighted with stones. It is hard to see how anyone lives in it, but a few hens scratch around the door and there's some washing spread out over the tops of the nearest weeds.

The tiniest house of all, mud brick, wattles showing through, stands against a magnificent view, overlooking a drop of a thousand feet or so, one end of the house merging into a small and very old bus body. The windows and door of the bus are all faded green, with a black rounded roof. Whether the house is an extension of the bus, or the bus the "new wing" of the house, is a hideous little riddle against a majestic backdrop. But someone lives there! It is a magnificent sight to the east, seemingly all the way to the coast, miles and miles and miles of blue hills, the nearer ones topped by crazy spars of gray stone, and one tall cross slanting slightly to the north.

On the left you can see where a small mill stood and fell down. There used to be a strange old iron mill wheel there, but some time ago the boys who came to make a very arty movie of the town stole it. (The boys then lived below me; I smelled their pot every evening and one, the youngest, stayed home alone and sniffed ether, almost etherizing me, in the bedroom above his, every night.)

The fields are filled with wild flowers. At first you see only tall ones, all nameless, yellow and purple, fuzzy seed-heads, red pods, and white ones too. Then you realize the ground is carpeted with flowers, short, shorter ones, moss-height ones. I pick dozens of wild flowers, little bright orange-and-yellow ones on a dry fine little bush, brilliant like orchids; lovely tall single white-yellow ones, each on its own thin green stock; hanging magenta bells. Before you can get these home, they have shut up tight forever.

This is the field of the Waterfall of the Little Swallows, and this is where the stream disappears, like the sacred river Alph in Coleridge's dream. It fans out over the red stone, narrows and rises in cold gray ridges, disappears underground, and then shows up again farther off, dashing downwards now through more beautiful rocks. It then takes off downwards for the Underworld. You can hang over the rocks and see it far below. It keeps descending, disappears into a cavern, and is never seen again. It talks as it goes, but the words are lost . . .

1970

The Diary of "Helena Morley":
The Book & Its Author

ℰ

When I first came to Brazil, in 1952, I asked my Brazilian friends which Brazilian books I should begin reading. After naming some of Machado de Assis's novels or short stories, or Euclides da Cunha's *Os Sertões,* they frequently recommended this little book, *Minha Vida de Menina.* Two or three even said it was the best thing that had appeared in Brazilian letters since Machado de Assis, and then they were apt to launch into animated exchanges of their favorite stories from it.

In English the title means "My Life as a Little Girl," or "Young Girl," and that is exactly what the book is about, but it is not reminiscences; it is a diary, the diary actually kept by a girl between the ages of twelve and fifteen, in the far-off town of Diamantina, in 1893–1895. It was first published in 1942 in an edition of two thousand copies, chiefly with the idea of amusing the author's family and friends, and it was never advertised. But its reputation spread in literary circles in Rio de Janeiro and there was a demand for it, so in 1944 a second edition was brought out, then two more, in 1948 and 1952, making ten thousand copies in all. Georges Bernanos, who was living in the country as an exile when it first appeared, discovered it and gave away a good many copies to friends, a fact to which the author and her husband modestly attribute much of its success. He wrote the author a letter which has been used, in part, on the jackets of later editions. Copies of *Minha Vida de Menina* are now presented every year as prize books to students of the Convent of the Sacred Heart in Rio.

The more I read the book the better I liked it. The scenes and events it described were odd, remote, and long ago, and yet fresh, sad, funny, and eternally true. The longer I stayed on in Brazil the more Brazilian the book seemed, yet much of it could have happened in any small provincial town or village, and at almost any period of history—at least before the arrival of the automobile and the moving-picture theater. Certain pages reminded me of more famous and "literary" ones: Nausicaa doing her laundry on the beach, possibly with the help of *her* freed slaves; bits from Chaucer; Wordsworth's poetical children and country people, or Dorothy Wordsworth's wandering beggars. Occasionally entries referring to slavery seemed like notes for an unwritten, Brazilian, feminine version of Tom Sawyer and Nigger Jim. But this was a real, day-by-day diary, kept by a real girl, and anything resembling it that I could think of had been observed or made up, and written down, by adults. (An exception is Anne Frank's diary; but its forced maturity and closed atmosphere are tragically different from the authentic childlikeness, the classical sunlight and simplicity of this one.) I am not sure now whether someone suggested my translating it or I thought of it myself, but when I was about halfway through the book I decided to try.

I learned that "Helena Morley" was still very much alive; that the name was the pseudonym of Senhora Augusto Mario Caldeira Brant and that she was living in Rio, well known and much loved in Rio society. Her husband was then, although almost eighty years old, acting as president of the Bank of Brazil for the second time. The poet Manuel Bandeira, an old friend of the family, kindly gave me an introduction. Armed with a friend, Lota de Macedo Soares, to serve as interpreter because my spoken Portuguese was very limited, I went to call.

Senhora Brant, or Dona Alice as I shall call her in the Brazilian way ("Helena" and "Morley" are both names from her English father's family), now lives in a large, stuccoed, tile-roofed house, on the street that borders the "Lagoa," or lagoon. It is a fashionable place to live. The house is set in a yard with flower beds, coconut palms, eight fruit trees, and a servants' house and vegetable garden at the back. A stuccoed fence and wooden gates protect it from the street. A large Cadillac is sometimes parked in the driveway, and its mulatto chauffeur wears a white yachting cap: Cadillac, chauffeur, and white cap are all contemporary Rio fashion. Nearby rise the extravagant Rio mountains and across the lagoon towers the one called the "Gavea," or crow's nest, because its shape reminded the six-teenth-century Portuguese explorers of the lookout platforms on their little vessels.

On our first visit we were ushered into a large living room, parlor, rather, with its silk-and-lace curtains closely drawn, luxuriously furnished: vases, bronzes, and clocks on small tables, rugs, a chandelier, chairs and sofas covered in gold-colored satin. This room is divided from the hall and another living room opposite by a fence and gateway of wrought iron, painted white. One of Dona Alice's daughters, Dona Sarita, appeared and started talking to my friend. Although they had not met before, very shortly they were identifying and placing each other's relatives, something that seems to happen in Brazil as quickly as it does in the South of the United States, when Dona Alice herself came in.

She is a large woman, very tall for a Brazilian, looking younger than seventy-six, her hair not yet entirely white, with a handsome, lively, high-cheekboned face lit up by two small but exceedingly bright and gay reddish-brown eyes. Her half-English blood shows, perhaps, in the unusual fairness of her skin, the fairness that made her liable to the freckles she used to complain of in her diary. She began talking, laughing and talking, immediately, and in no time at all we were telling each other stories and Dona Alice was leaning forward to pat our knees with the greatest ease and intimacy. (This warmth and ease in meeting strangers is a Brazilian characteristic especially charming to Nordic visitors.) At the first interview a great deal of the conversation was lost to me. However, I did gather that Dona Alice was proud of the book she had unwittingly written more than sixty years before, pleased at the thought of its being put into English, and still somewhat puzzled by its success in Brazil and the fact that Georges Bernanos, French people, and more recently, Americans, had seemed to like it, too. I could also recognize her retelling of some of the anecdotes in the very words of the diary, or in more detail, and with a great deal of hilarity.

Presently Dr. Brant came home from the Bank of Brazil, a small, modest-appearing man of brilliant intelligence, who also looks much younger than his age. He is proud of his wife and it was he who had undertaken to put together all the old scraps and notebooks and prepare them for publication. He has been a lawyer, a journalist, and was five times elected to the National Congress; under the Vargas dictatorship he was exiled, and spent five years in France and England. He reads English; that day, I remember, he told me he was reading Boswell's *Journals*. In answer to my question he said no, that Dona Alice had never written anything since her early diaries, nothing, that was, but "letters, letters, letters!"

I don't believe we accepted the invitation to stay to dinner on this first call, but we did on our second, even though we had

taken along two friends, admirers of the book, to meet Dona
Alice. Dona Sarita, another daughter, a son-in-law, a grandson
of sixteen or so, a nephew—the number of people at the long
table seemed to be constantly expanding and contracting. Dona
Alice, very much a matriarch, sat at the head, Dr. Augusto Mario
beside her at her left. She told stories, ladled soup, told stories,
carved, told stories, and served the multiple Brazilian desserts,
occasionally interrupting herself to scold the maid, or the
nephew, who used up a whole cake of soap, or so she said, every
time he took a bath, in a sort of head-tone of mock-rage that
disturbed no one in the slightest.

On one of our visits we were taken upstairs in Dona Alice's
own elevator, to a paneled library, and shown various copies of
the book, the original of the letter from Bernanos, and some old
photographs. By then it had been settled that I was to do the
translation and I had hoped they might have some photographs
of Diamantina and the people in the diary. They did have a
few, but in poor condition. One was of Dona Alice's old home
in the Old Cavalhada: plastered stone, two-storied, severe, with
a double door opening onto a wide stoop. I said that I would
like to get a copy of it for the book, but Dona Alice and Dona
Sarita said, Oh no, not *that* house, suggesting that I use a picture
of Dona Alice's present house on the Lagoa in Rio. I'm not sure
that my arguments for using the old photographs of Diamantina
ever quite convinced them.

Diamantina is in the state of Minas Gerais (General Mines)
and *mineiros,* miners, as the people who come from there are
called, have the reputation of being shrewd and thrifty. There
is a saying that the *mineiro* eats out of an open drawer, ready to
close it quickly if unexpected company shows up. Dona Alice's
hospitality belied this legend, but once when Lota de Macedo
Soares went to see her she found Dona Alice seated in the up-

stairs hall darning linen, and was rather taken aback to be asked severely if she didn't employ her time on such chores when she was at home.

The diaries, I found, had been cut short where they now end by Dr. Brant because the next year marks his own appearance in them, and his acceptance as a suitor. I feel it is a pity he so firmly omits every incident of their courtship. By the time she was seventeen, "Helena" had already received five proposals of marriage from "foreign" miners living in Diamantina. Her girl cousins and friends had been reduced to hinting to her that if she didn't want any of her suitors, perhaps she would let *them* have them. She had indeed become what she admits to yearning to be in her diary: "the leading girl of Diamantina." In true Brazilian fashion she chose a Brazilian and a cousin and at eighteen married Dr. Augusto Mario, whose family had been prominent in Diamantina since the eighteenth century. I am sure she has never for a moment regretted turning down those other offers, and that this is one of those rare stories that combine worldly success and a happy ending.

One story she told us, not in the book, was about the first time she received a serious compliment from one of the rejected suitors and at last became convinced that she was pretty, really pretty. She said that she had sat up in bed studying her face, or what she could see of it by the light of a candle, in a broken piece of looking glass, all night long.

Dr. Brant has provided the following information about "Helena Morley's" English background:

"The family name is really Dayrell. Dona Alice's grandfather, Dr. John Dayrell, studied medicine in London. He married a Miss Alice Mortimer, the daughter of an Irish Protestant, Henry Mortimer, who was, or had been, a government official in Barbados, where he also had a sugarcane plantation producing sugar and rum. His children were educated in London, and it was there that Alice Mortimer met and married Dr. John Dayrell.

"Dr. Dayrell left England between 1840 and 1850 to serve as physician to a gold mining concern at Morro Velho [Old Hill] belonging to the famous English São João del Rey Mining Company. A short while later there was a flood in the mine and work came to a halt. The other officials went back to England, but Dr. Dayrell, who had a 'weak chest,' remained in Brazil and went to live in Diamantina, a town five thousand feet high and famous for its fine climate.

"In Diamantina he established himself as a doctor, acquired a *fazenda* [farm or country seat] near town, and practiced medicine for about forty years. He and his wife were the only Protestants in the town. He had eight children, two born in England and the rest in Diamantina."

Richard Burton, in *Explorations of the Highlands of the Brazil* (Tinsley Brothers, London, 1869), speaks of meeting Dr. Dayrell in 1867, and also Felisberto Dayrell, the real name of "Helena Morley's" father, who was even then at work mining diamonds, as he is later, throughout the pages of his daughter's diary.

Diamantina

Like most children, Helena Morley seems to have taken her surroundings and the scenery of the region where she lived very much for granted. There are few direct references to them in *Minha Vida de Menina*. She does speak of the streams where she and her sister and brothers take baths, or catch the most fish, of places where there are wild flowers and fruits, or where she can set her bird traps. And she says a good many times that she likes "the country better than the city," the "city" being, of course, the tiny provincial town of Diamantina. But whatever love of nature she has seems part utilitarian and part, the greater part, sheer joy at not being in school.

However, what impresses the occasional traveler who visits Diamantina these days first of all is its wild and extraordinary setting. Diamantina, the highest town in Brazil, is about two hundred miles northeast of Belo Horizonte, the modern capital of Minas Gerais, a state bigger than Texas. At the time of the diary the railway had not yet been put through; now, sixty years later, trains still run but are already outmoded for passengers, and a once-a-day plane makes the trip from the capital in a little less than an hour.

I went there in May, when the worst of the rains are over but roads are supposedly not yet too dusty. After leaving Belo Horizonte the plane flies higher and higher, the land below grows rockier and rockier, wilder and more desolate; not a sign of life is to be seen. A high sea of waves and crests of steely-gray rock, eroded and fragmented, appears; the rolling land between is covered with greenish grass, but barely covered. There are unexpected streams among the rocks; slender waterfalls fall into small black pools or the streams fan out glittering over beds of white sand. Never a village nor a house; only hundreds of the pockmarks, or large pits, of old gold and diamond mines, showing red and white.

The plane comes down on a bare, slightly swelling field. There is nothing to be seen but a long red dust cloud settling behind it, an open shed with names and comic heads splashed on it in black paint, and a wretched little house with a baby and a few hens against a ragged washing strung on a barbed-wire fence. But the air is crisp and delicious and the horizon is rimmed all around with clear-etched peaks of rock. The three or four passengers descend, immediately feeling that they are *up* and exclaiming about the change in temperature. There is no sign of Diamantina. The highest peak of rock, to the northeast, is the mountain of Itambé, sharp and looking deceptively near.

A lone taxi drives to town. A church tower suddenly appears between the brown-green waves of grass and the wilder, broken waves of gigantic rocks; then other church towers, and then almost the whole of the red-tiled cluster of roofs comes into sight at once. The town climbs one steep hill, extends sidewise over a lower one and down the other side. The highway enters from above along the line of the railway, passing under the striped arm of a police "barrier."

There are sixteen churches, most of them diminutive, no more than chapels; the Cathedral is new and very ugly. The famous churches of the gold-mining town of Ouro Prêto are small, too, but with their baroque façades trimmed with green soapstone, their heavy curves and swirls and twin mustard-pot towers, they are opulent and sophisticated, while the little churches of Diamantina are shabby, silent, and wistful. For one thing, although they are built of stone, plastered and painted white, the window and door frames are of wood, in dark blues, reds, or greens, or combinations of all three colors. Ornamentation is skimpy or nonexistent, and belfries on clock towers are square. The comparative poverty of the town is shown in the way, once the walls were up, the rest of the façade and the tower were simply constructed of boards and painted white to match the stone. Because of the steepness of the streets there is often a flight of stone steps at an angle across the front and off one side, and some churches are still fenced in by high old blue or red picket fences, giving them a diffident, countrified appearance.

The Church of the Rosario that figures prominently in Helena's diary, standing next door to her grandmother's house as it does, is still the most impressive. It is the Negroes' church, built by slaves in the middle of the eighteenth century; inside are three black saints: St. Benedict, St. Iphigenia, and St. Somebody; his name was unidentifiable. There are three crystal chandeliers, a great deal of red dust and faded blue paint, and a slightly rickety blue gallery for the black choir. The church has settled and everything is now askew. As in many old Brazilian churches, the ceilings are made of narrow boards, so that the scenes from the Life of the Virgin painted on them, copied from heaven knows what hand-me-down sources, are scored through by black lines. These ceilings have a sad appeal, like letters written in old copybook handwriting on lined paper.

In front of this church there is a big tree of the ficus family. Looking up into its branches, one is surprised to see a large black beam stuck in them, crosswise, then a rusty lantern and other indistinguishable rusty odds and ends that have no business being thirty feet up off the ground, in a tree. This is one of the town's modest "sights," and proves to be what is left of an enormous crucifix that once stood where the tree now stands. The airborne seed started growing out from the side of the cross, grew upwards and downwards and took root, and now has taken over, broken up, and lifted the whole cross in the air: ladder, lantern, pliers, hammer, and all.

These crosses are a common feature of the countryside around Diamantina, sometimes with all their accoutrements, sometimes bare or simply with stiff wooden streamers arranged over the arms and a flat tin rooster on top. The bird called João de Barro, John of the Mud, or Clay, builds his beehive-shaped adobe nests on the arms, and the hammock bird slings his woven ones underneath. One cross, on the high ridge of rock opposite the town, now burns brightly at night with hundreds of electric light bulbs. At Sopa (soup), where Helena's father went "to open a mine," there is a fine one, with a white skull and crossbones on the black wood, silvered Roman centurions' helmets, and a flat rose-red "seamless garment" like a pattern for a child's dress. It stands near a small church known as the "Chinese church" because the eaves of the roof and tower are turned upwards in Oriental style, a common feature of Brazilian colonial architecture, traced directly to the Portuguese colony of Macão. One becomes accustomed to it in Rio de Janeiro, but here far off in a desolate countryside it is strange to come across this church like a baby pagoda, and a crucifix almost as tall, loaded with its grim set of Christian iconography-toys.

The interiors of Helena's various churches are disappointing, cramped and musty, the Portuguese-style wedding-cake altars crowded with old artificial flowers and incongruously dressed, bewigged saints. The confessionals, however, are sometimes quaint and pretty: upright boards about five feet high; the priest sits on one side on a chair, the penitent kneels on the other; but the boards are gilded and painted in pastel blues and pinks, the upper part pierced with holes like a colander, or with long slits that make them vaguely resemble Biblical musical instruments, possibly some sort of organ. And the "masts" Helena speaks of as being set up on certain holy days lie in the sacristies or along the side aisles of their churches the rest of the year, big as telephone poles, painted in winding blue-and-white stripes.

I came upon the Church of the Amparo, which figures in the diary, unexpectedly, as it was getting dark. Its trim is dark peacock blue; on top a rusty rooster perches on a rusty globe; there is a minute balcony on either side of a large, faded coat of arms cut out of tin above the door, and over it a three-dimensional Dove of the Holy Spirit, dimly illuminated, nesting behind a quatrefoil window. Seen suddenly blocking the end of an alleyway, this church is stricken but dignified, like a person coming toward one whom one expects to beg, who doesn't beg after all.

Some of the church clocks by which Helena told the time have been removed. At about seven o'clock the light leaves the town rapidly and the surrounding sea of rocks, and the peak of Itambé, turn red. A few church bells ring and then a great noise comes from the loudspeaker over the Cathedral door and reverberates all over town. *Ave Maria, gratia plena*; the town vibrates with it and the light bulbs on the high cross opposite snap into activity. It is the hour of the rosary, Helena's *terço*, which caused her so much "suffering" at family prayers and which is now broadcast every evening during the month of May. On Sundays the same loudspeaker is used to draw people to Mass; at five o'clock it was blaring out *The Stars and Stripes Forever*.

In spite of these innovations and the Betty Grable film showing at the one cinema, the town has changed very little since the youthful Helena lived there and raced up and down its steep streets. Most of the streets have no sidewalks, some have narrow ones, two feet or so wide, long slabs of greenish stone raised a little above the cobblestones, the *pé de muleque,* or "ragamuffin's foot"—that is, the confection we call peanut brittle, which it is supposed to resemble. Down the middle of the street runs another strip of long stones, set flush, much easier to walk on than the sidewalks, which every so often stop altogether, or break up into steps. These footpaths are called *capistranas,* after a mayor of Ouro Prêto, who introduced them there.

The houses are thick-walled and solid, in the middle of the town of two or even three stories, but as one gets away from the Cathedral they become smaller and lower and the tile roofs turn to thatched ones. The taller houses have balconies, formerly often completely covered in by the latticework cages, called *muxarabis* (from the Arabian *muxara,* a shelter), showing the influence of the Moors on the architecture and way of life of Portugal. From them the women could watch what went on in the streets, in an Oriental seclusion. On either side of the windows giving onto these balconies are little lanterns, globes of colored or milk glass, *luminarias*. (The word has been extended to mean a kind of small cream-filled tart, highly thought of by our diarist.) The same kind of globe, without lights, decorates the railings, and sometimes Tecoma vines or grapevines are trained along the ironwork.

The window frames are curved at the top, with double sashes of a dozen small panes each. Here the trimming becomes confusing, since some of the wooden frames are marbleized or painted to imitate stone, and some of the stone ones are painted to imitate grained wood. A good many of the windows still have stencils on the lower panes, a form of folk art that also served to protect the privacy of rooms right on the street. A paper stencil in a formalized leaf-and-flower or other design is held against the glass and patted with a rag dipped in white paint. The effect is very decorative, like frost on the window-panes in northern climates, only geometrical. The wide over-hang of the eaves contributes to the town's surprisingly Oriental air, and this overhang is filled in solid with molding and is a favorite place for colored stripes and other ornamentation. The houses are in admirably bold or pretty colors. I particularly liked a crushed-strawberry pink one, with a double staircase of blue, and window frames and under-eaves marbleized in the same blue. There are mustard-colored houses with bright yellow and dark green shutters, white with dark blue and peach, mauve with dark blue and yellow. So that passers-by will not be drenched in the rainy season, the mouths of the rain pipes are carried out two feet or more, across the sidewalks, and the funnels flare like trumpets. It is as if a band had suddenly stopped playing. Sometimes they have tin petals or feathers down them and around the mouth, and this decoration is re-

peated in tiles set edgewise up the ridges of the roofs, dragon-
like and very "Chinese."

The grandmother's house still stands, to the right of the
Rosario Church, but the Teatro Isabel, formerly on the other
side, has been torn down and in its place is a large baby-pink
jail from whose barred windows a drunken prisoner yelled at
me incomprehensibly. The house is low, its stoop just a few
inches off the ground, a deceptively small-looking house with
a sweeping, concave old tile roof. The woman who lives there
now knew *Minha Vida de Menina* and its author and kindly
showed me through. The old rooms for slaves, extending along
the street by the church, are let out. Inside there is room after
room, high, square, sadly neglected, almost devoid of furniture.
The walls are a yard thick, wooden shutters can be closed and
barred on the inside; the ceilings are of boards or woven rushes
painted white, the two common Brazilian types. After a good
many of these high dark rooms we reached the kitchen, where
a girl was cooking over an open fire. Stoves here consist of a
long iron plate with four potholes in it, laid on the edges of a
stone trough full of embers. A wood called *candeia* is com-
monly used. It has a peculiar sweetish smell, sickening until
one gets used to it; at the dinner hour this sweetish stench
hovers bluely over Brazilian towns and villages.

Behind the house the grandmother's former garden covers
about five acres, sloping down to a brook and a jungle of banana
trees. There are huge *jaboticaba* trees, the same ones that
Helena used to climb into for refuge. There are a few beds
of lettuce and cabbages, and a grove of coffee trees, but every-
thing is overgrown and gone to seed and it is hard to imagine
how it must have looked in the old days, tended by the grand-
mother's ex-slaves. A big sociable pig stood up on his hind
legs in his pen, to watch us.

One of the handsomest buildings is Helena's "Normal

School," now the Grupo Escolar, and located in the middle of the town; big, white, rectangular, with bright blue doors and window frames. Juscelino Kubitschek, the present President of Brazil and a former governor of Minas, was born in Diamantina. He had visited recently and a great canvas banner bearing his smiling face almost concealed the front of the building. There are also a Kubitschek Street and a Kubitschek Place with his head in bronze in it, less than life-size, as if done by the Amazonian head shrinkers.

The market is a large wooden shed, with blue and red arches, and a sparse forest of thin, gnawed hitching posts around it. The drovers are still there, with loads of hides and corn, but because of trains, better roads, and trucks, trade has dwindled to next to nothing since Helena's day. Near the Cathedral one is warned from the street or alley where the "bad girls" live. They are extremely juvenile mulattoes, sitting on their door-steps with their feet stuck out on the cobblestones, gossiping and sucking sugarcane in the sunshine. The live-forevers that Helena used to pick are still very much in evidence; in fact, they are one of the town's few industries besides diamond mining. They are a tiny yellow-white straw flower, less than half an inch in diameter, on a long fine shiny brown stalk. Tied up in bunches, the bundle of stems bigger than two hands can hold, they lie drying in rows on the streets all around the Cathedral, and freight cars full of flowers are sent off every year, on their way to Japan. They are used, I was told, for "fireworks," or "ammunition," but I suspect that, dyed and glued, they merely reappear in the backgrounds of Japanese trays, plaques, etc. Brazilian-made fireworks play an important role in Diamantina, as they do in all provincial Brazilian towns, and are used in staggering quantities for religious holidays. I was shown a warehouse packed to the ceiling with fire-crackers, Catherine wheels, and Roman candles; the supply looked much larger than that of foodstuffs on hand at the same wholesaler's.

Diamonds and gold, but chiefly diamonds, still obsess the economy. The hotel manager (a new hotel, designed by Oscar Niemeyer, was finished in 1956), using almost the very words that Helena used in 1893, complained that he had to fly in vegetables from Belo Horizonte. "Here no one's interested in anything but gold and diamonds," he said. "They say they can't grow vegetables in this soil, but it isn't true. They think of nothing but diamonds, diamonds, diamonds." It is strange to see, on the side of a miserable little house, a blue-and-white enameled sign announcing that here is a diamond dealer. I looked inside one of these houses and could see nothing but overhead a lurid plaster statue of St. George killing the dragon, with a small red electric light bulb glowing in front of it, and under it, on the table, a bunch of live-forevers and a fine pair of scales in a glass case. The scales are covered up at night, like the innumerable caged birds hanging everywhere. Curiously shaped stones, lumps of ores, clusters and chunks of rock crystal and quartz are everywhere, too, used as doorstops and sideboard decorations. In the cold clear air, the town itself, with its neatness, rockiness, and fine glitter, seems almost on the point of precipitation and crystallization.

In the recently opened museum there are the usual polychrome saints and angels, sedan chairs and marriage beds, and then suddenly and horribly an alcove hung with the souvenirs of slavery: rusty chains, handcuffs, and leg and neck irons draped on the wall; pointed iron prods originally fastened to poles; and worse things. As one drives about the region, the sites of the old slave encampments are pointed out. Trees, and a very fine short grass, supposedly from Africa, distinguish them, and they are usually beside a stream and near the pits of old mines. But now there is only the small Negro and mulatto population to show for all the million or more slaves who came here in the eighteenth and early nineteenth centuries.

I made an excursion to Boa Vista, where Helena's father mined. The mines are abandoned now, although they were worked on a large scale by foreign companies up until a few years ago. There is nothing to be seen but an immense excavation exposing soils of different colors (each with a different name; Burton's book gives an excellent account of them and the different methods of mining), and endless iron pipes. Boa Vista is slightly higher than Diamantina; although it is six or seven miles away, one can see a church tower. The road there is dirt, narrow, winding, and eventually the taxi scrapes over outcroppings of naked rock and splashes through streams. Battalions of grotesque rocks charge across the fields, or stand like architecture, pierced by Gothic-ruin windows. Large slabs balance on top of moldering turrets, with vines, bushes, and even stunted palm trees on their tops. Helena Morley was not a fanciful child but I wondered at her riding on her borrowed horse, before sunup, along this nightmare road, hurrying to get back to Diamantina in time for school.

I took with me a lifelong friend of Helena's future husband, Dr. Brant, Senhor Antonio Cicero de Menezes, former local director of the post-office service, now eighty years old, a very distinguished-looking man with a white Vandyke beard and mustache, like an older, frailer Joseph Conrad. We came back through the hamlet of twenty or so houses that is Palha (straw) today and Seu Antonio Cicero said, in Helena's very phrase, "Now let us descend and suck fruit." So we sat in the tiny general store, surrounded by household and mining necessities: iron kettles and frying pans, salt beef and soap, and sucked a good many slightly sour oranges. A little boy brought them in a gold-panning bowl and Seu Antonio Cicero prepared them for me with his pocket knife faster than I could suck. The storekeeper showed me a storeroom full of these wooden bowls, cowhides and tarry lumps of brown sugar and sieves for panning diamonds, piled on the floor, and boxes and boxes of dusty rock crystals, bound, he said, for the United States, for industrial purposes.

Near there we stopped again to watch a group of men looking for diamonds in a stream beside the road. The head of the group had four men, black and white, working for him; he gave me his name and asked me to print it; here it is: Manoel Benicio de Loyola, "diamond-hunter of Curralinho." They were shoveling in the shallow, sparkling water, damming it up, releasing it, and arranging piles of gravel on the bank. One of them took up a small quantity of gravel in the wide round sieve and held it just beneath the surface of the water, swirling it skillfully around and around. In a few minutes he lifted it out; the gravel was distributed evenly over the sieve in one thin layer. With the gesture of a quick-fingered housewife turning out a cake, he turned the whole thing upside down on the ground, intact. Senhor Benicio de Loyola then put on his horn-rimmed glasses, lowered himself to his knees in the wet mud, and stared, passing a long wooden knife over the gravel from side to side. In a second he waved his hand, got up, and put his glasses back in his pocket, and his assistant got ready to turn out another big gravel pancake, while he and Seu Antonio Cicero talked about a large blue diamond someone had found somewhere a day or two before.

This is the simplest of all forms of diamond "mining." It goes on all around Diamantina constantly, and enough diamonds are found in this way to provide a meager living for some thousands of people. One sees them, sometimes all alone, sometimes in groups of three or four, standing in every stream. Sometimes they are holding a sieve just under the water, looking for diamonds, sometimes they are sloshing their wooden bowls from side to side in the air, looking for gold. The bent heads and concentration of these figures, in that vast, rock-studded, crucifix-stuck space, give a touch of dementia to the landscape.

I also made an excursion to Biribiri (accented on the second and last *i*'s), an enchanting spot, where Helena used to dance, and leap through St. John's Day bonfires. The factory, for weaving cotton, is still there, but nothing could look less like industrialization. One descends to a fair-sized river and the landscape is green and lush; there are many trees, and fruit trees around the blue- or whitewashed stone houses along the one unpaved street. In the middle is the church, better kept up than any of the others I saw, trim, almost dainty. Indeed, it looks like an old-fashioned chocolate box. A blue picket fence encloses the flourishing flower garden and over the door, below the twin towers, is a large rounded pink Sacred Heart with a crown of realistic ten-inch thorns, green wooden palm branches, and blue wooden ribbons. Close around the church stand a dozen real palms, royal palms, enormously tall and slender, their shining heads waving in the late afternoon sun.

"Helena Morley"

In one of his letters to Robert Bridges, Hopkins says that he has bought some books, among them Dana's *Two Years Before the Mast,* "a thoroughly good one and all true, but bristling with technicality—seamanship—which I most carefully go over and even enjoy but cannot understand; there are other things, though, as a flogging, which is terrible and instructive *and it happened*—ah, that is the charm and the main point." And that, I think, is "the charm and the main point" of *Minha Vida de Menina.* Its "technicalities," diamond digging, say, scarcely "bristle," and its three years in Diamantina are relatively tame and unfocused, although there are incidents of comparable but casual, small-town cruelty. But—*it really happened*; everything did take place, day by day, minute by minute, once and only once, just the way Helena says it did. There really was a grandmother, Dona Teodora, a stout, charitable old lady who walked with a cane and managed her family and her freed slaves with an iron will. There really was a Siá Ritinha who stole her neighbors' chickens, but not Helena's mother's chickens; a Father Neves; a spinster English Aunt Madge, bravely keeping up her standards and eking out a living by teaching small obstreperous Negroes, in a town financially ruined by the emancipation of the slaves and the opening of the Kimberly diamond mines.

Some of the people in the diary are still alive, and the successors of those who are dead and gone seem to be cut very much from the same cloth. Little uniformed girls, with perhaps shorter skirts, carrying satchels of books, press their noses against the dining-room windows of the new hotel and are overcome by fits of giggling at seeing the foreigner eat her lunch—on their way to the school run by the Sisters of Charity, the same school that Helena ran away from. The boys still give them the same nicknames. (They call a freckled child of my acquaintance *Flocos*, "Flakes," but that is a new product in Brazil and Helena was spared it.) Mota's store, where she bought her boots, is now Mota's Son's store. There is still a garrison of soldiers, now outside the town; there is a seminary, and young priests walk in the streets and people talk to them through the latticed windows.

When the diary happened, Helena was tall and thin and freckled and always, always hungry. She worries about her height, her thinness, her freckles, and her appetite. She is not a very good scholar and fails in her first year at Normal School. Her studies can always be interrupted by her brother, her many cousins, or even the lack of a candle. (The diary was mostly written by candlelight.) She is greedy; sometimes she is unfair to her long-suffering sister, Luizinha, but feels properly guilty afterwards, rationalize as she may. She is obviously something of a show-off and saucy to her teachers; but she is outspoken and good-natured and gay, and wherever she is, her friends may be getting into mischief but they are having a good time; and she has many friends, old and young, black and white. She is willing to tell stories on herself, although sometimes she tries to ease her conscience, which has "a nail in it." She thinks about clothes a great deal, but, under the circumstances—she has only two or three dresses and two pairs of boots—who wouldn't?

She may grow tedious on the subject of stealing fruit, but it is, after all, the original sin, and remember St. Augustine on the subject of the pear tree. On the other hand, she seems to take the Anglo-Saxon sin of sins, "cheating," rather lightly. If she is not always quite admirable, she is always completely herself; hypocrisy appears for a moment and then vanishes like the dew. Her method of composition seems influenced by the La Fontaine she hates to study; she winds up her stories with a neat moral that doesn't apply too exactly; sometimes, for variety's sake, she starts off with the moral instead. She has a sense of the right quotation, or detail, the gag line, and where to stop. The characters are skillfully differentiated: the quiet, humorous father; the devout, doting, slightly foolish mother; the rigid Uncle Conrado. Occasionally she has "runs" on one subject; perhaps "Papa" had admired a particular page and so she wrote a sequel to it or remembered a similar story.

In matters of religion, Helena seems to have been somewhat of an eighteenth-century rationalist. She steps easily in and out of superstition, reason, belief, and disbelief, without much adolescent worrying. She would never for a moment doubt, one feels, that the church is "a good thing." With all its holidays, processions, mast-raisings, and fireworks, its christenings, first communions, and funerals, it is the fountainhead of the town's social life. Her father remains in the background, smiling but tolerant, while her mother pleads with him to go to church and constantly prays for all the family. Like him, Helena is at first skeptical of a schoolmate who dies and acquires a reputation for working miracles; then she veers toward her mother's party. Her religion, like her feeling for nature, is on the practical side.

She lives in a world of bitter poverty and isolation. A trip to the capital, Rio de Janeiro, where a few boys go to study, takes ten days: eight on muleback to Sabara, and from there two days by very slow train to Rio. Supplies are brought to town by the drovers, on long lines of mules or horses. One of the greatest problems is what to do with the freed slaves who have stayed on. Reading this diary, one sometimes gets the impression that the greater part of the town, black and white, "rich" and poor, when it hasn't found a diamond lately, gets along by making sweets and pastries, brooms and cigarettes, and selling them to each other. Or the freed slaves are kept busy manufacturing them in the kitchen and peddling them in the streets, and the lady of the house collects the profits—or buys, in her parlor, the products of her kitchen.

Now that I can join in my friends' exchanges of anecdotes from the book, and have seen Diamantina, I think that one of my own favorite entries is Helena's soliloquy on November 5, 1893, on the meaning of Time (her style improves in the later years):

"The rooster's crow never gives the right time and nobody believes it. When a rooster crows at nine o'clock they say that a girl is running away from home to get married. I'm always hearing the rooster crow at nine o'clock, but it's very rarely that a girl runs away from home.

"Once upon a time I used to believe that roosters told the time, because in Boa Vista when you ask a miner the time he looks at the sun and tells you. If you go and look at the clock, he's right. So I used to think that the sun kept time during the day and the rooster at night. Now I realize that this was a mistake . . .

"In Cavalhada only the men have watches. Those who live in the middle of the town don't feel the lack of them because almost all the churches have clocks in their towers. But when Papa isn't home the mistakes we make about the hours are really funny . . . The rooster is Mama's watch, which doesn't run very well. It's already fooled us several times." She goes on to tell about "Mama's" waking her and Luizinha up to go to four o'clock Mass, because the rooster has already crowed twice. They drink their coffee and start out. "I kept looking at the moon and the stars and saying to Mama, 'This time the Senhora's going to see whether the rooster can tell time or not.' The street was deserted. The two of us walked holding on to Mama's arms. When we passed by the barracks the soldier on duty looked at Mama and asked, 'What's the Senhora doing in the street with these little girls at this hour?' Mama said, 'We're going to Mass at the Cathedral.' The soldier said, 'Mass at midnight? It isn't Christmas Eve. What's this all about?'

"I was afraid of the soldier. Mama said, 'Midnight? I thought it was four o'clock. Thank you very much for the information.'

"We went home and lay down in our clothes. But even so we missed Mass. When we got to church later Father Neves was already in the Hail Marys."

I like to think of the two tall, thin little girls hanging on to their mother's arms, the three figures stumbling up the steep streets of the rocky, lightless little town beneath the cold bright moon and stars; and I can hear the surprised young soldier's voice, Mama's polite reply, and then three pairs of footsteps scuttling home again over the cobblestones.

Food

The staple diet of Brazil consists of dried black beans and rice, with whatever meat, beef or pork, salted or fresh, can be afforded or obtained. And black beans, instead of the "bread" of other countries, seem to be equated with life itself. An example of this: when the Brazilian football team went to play in the Olympic Games recently, thirty-three pounds of black beans were taken along for each man. And recently in Rio the court ordered a taxi driver to pay alimony to his wife and children in the form of twenty-two pounds of rice and twenty-two pounds of black beans monthly.

They are boiled separately and seasoned with salt and pepper, garlic, and lard. The common vegetables, such as pumpkin, okra, *couve* (a kind of cabbage), are usually made into stews with small quantities of meat or chicken. As in other Catholic countries, salt codfish is a common dish. But black beans and rice form the basis of the main meal, the heavy lunch, usually served early, between eleven and half past twelve. At the time of the diary, lunch was even earlier, at half past ten or eleven, and dinner was eaten at three or four o'clock. This explains why everyone is always ready to eat again in the evenings.

A dish of roasted manioc flour is always served with the beans and rice, indeed it is what the unqualified word "flour" signifies. It is sprinkled over the food, to thicken the sauce, and perhaps to add a little textural interest to the monotonous diet, since its nutritional value is almost nothing. It is also used in making various cakes and pastries. There is an impressive variety of these in Brazil, using manioc and cornmeal as well as wheat flours, coconut, brown sugar, etc., each with its own name, frequently religious in origin and varying from region to region. Helena mentions a dozen or more and there are whole books on the subject. Desserts are often *pudims,* usually, or unusually, heavy, and a great variety of fruit pastes, guava, quince, banana, etc., served with a small piece of hard white cheese. On a good Brazilian table, desserts appear, or always used to, several at a time. Cinnamon is the universal spice. Most Brazilians have very sweet tooths.

Breakfast is simply coffee, black or with boiled milk, and a piece of bread, although Helena varies hers strangely with cucumbers. Coffee is served after the other meals, at intervals in the day, and inevitably to callers at any time, in the form of *cafezinhos,* "little coffees," black, boiling hot, and with the tiny cup half-filled with sugar. (The sugar is only partially refined, so it takes quite a lot to sweeten a cup.) It is made by stirring the very finely ground coffee into boiling water, then pouring it through a coffee bag. These brown-stained bags and their high wooden stands are a symbol of Brazil, like black beans, and they are seen everywhere, even in miniature, as toys. There are laws to ensure that the coffee served in the innumerable cafés is unadulterated and of the required strength. (In an American movie being shown in Rio a character was told that he'd feel better after he had "a good breakfast, porridge and bacon and eggs and coffee," and this speech was rendered by the Portuguese subtitle, "Come and take coffee.")

A glance at the photographs will perhaps explain what may seem like Helena's overemphasis on fruit, or unnatural craving for it. Through June, July, and August, the long dry winters in that stony region, when everything is covered with red dust, with a constant shortage of fresh vegetables and the only drinking water running in open gutters as it was at that time, "sucking oranges" must have been the best way to quench one's thirst, and stealing fruit an almost irresistible impulse.

Money

Dr. Brant has given me the following information about the value of money at the time the diary was kept.

The *mil reis* (a thousand *reis*, the plural of *real*, or "royal") was worth twenty cents of U.S. money. (As a banker, Dr. Brant points out that the dollar has since been devalued, so that a *mil reis* would be worth ten cents of today's money. But as Helena says, we are speaking of "bygone days" and it seems simpler to keep it at the earlier evaluation.) Five *mil reis* would therefore be a dollar, 100 *reis* two pennies, and so on. Dr. Brant gives a list of approximate prices of goods and labor at the time:

> A pound of meat: 10¢
>
> A pound of sugar: 3¢
>
> A dozen eggs: 4¢
>
> A quart of milk: 4¢
>
> A pound of butter: 12¢
>
> A pair of shoes: $3.00
>
> A good horse: $20.00
>
> Average rent for a good house: $8.00 a month
>
> A cook: $2.00 a month
>
> Wages of Negroes employed in mining: 40¢ a day
> (paid to the whites who rented them out. In
> the town, or in agriculture, Negro wages were
> less)

Arinda receives about $100 for the diamond she finds; Helena makes $6 by selling her mother's gold brooch without a diamond in it; and the grandmother sends home a present of $10 to her daughter.

Acknowledgments

I am indebted to many friends and acquaintances for the help they have given me, both as sources of information about Diamantina and its life and vocabulary, and with the actual work of translation. Thanks are due:

In Diamantina, to Antonio Cicero de Menezes and his granddaughter; to Armando Assis, manager of the Hotel de Tourismo; and to many other inhabitants who showed me the way or went with me, invited me into their houses, and patiently repeated and spelled out the names of things.

To Vera Pacheco Jordão, who went with me to Diamantina and came to my assistance when my Portuguese failed me; to Manuel Bandeira; to Dora Romariz; to Otto Schwartz; and to Mary Stearns Morse, who typed the difficult manuscript.

To Rodrigo Melo Franco de Andrade, head of the Patrimonio Artistico of the Brazilian Department of Education, who took an interest in the book and who got out the Department's collection of photographs of Diamantina for me to choose from.

To my friend Pearl Kazin, who, in New York, received the manuscript and gave me invaluable help with it.

To my friend Lota de Macedo Soares, who reluctantly but conscientiously went over every word of the translation with me, not once, but several times.

To Dr. Augusto Mario Caldeira Brant, who also went over every word of the translation, and without whose remarkable memory for the customs and idioms of Diamantina in the nineties a great deal of detail might have been lost. I am grateful to him for many suggestions, and many of the footnotes are his.

But most thanks of all are, of course, due to Dona Alice herself for her wonderful gift: the book that has kept her childhood for us, as fresh as paint. Long may she live to retell the stories of "Helena Morley" to her grandchildren and great-grandchildren.

Sítio da Alcobacinha
Petrópolis
September 1956

The above note was written over twenty years ago and its possibly excessive length and detail are probably due to the pleasure and excitement I felt in translating the book and then actually seeing all the places, and even some of the people, mentioned in it. Since its first appearance in English translation, in 1957, both Dona Alice and Dr. Augusto Mario Brant, her husband, have died, and several of the friends mentioned in the Acknowledgments are also dead. But the diary itself lives on and on, continuing to be reissued in Brazil. It has also appeared in French and, I think, in Japanese. (Dr. and Mrs. Brant refused, characteristically, to let it be translated into Russian.)

From what later visitors to Diamantina have told me, I think that my impressions, observations, and the information I was able to gather during my week's stay there in 1955 still hold fairly true: the fantastic landscape, the minute churches and houses, the narrow economy, and the characteristics of the people have changed very little. Diamantina today seems to strike other visitors very much as it struck me then. However, it is more accessible: there is now a paved road from Belo Horizonte, or at least a *better* road than the old, almost impassable one, and I believe the plane goes and returns every day instead of—rather unpredictably—once or twice a week. I know quite a few people who have driven, or flown, there, as "tourists"—and in some cases the real attraction was to see the little town where the famous "Helena" grew up.

The small-scale Oscar Niemeyer hotel (for most of my stay I was its only guest) was closed for some years, but now, with the new "highway" and more regular plane service, it has opened up again. (Or had when I last heard of it; one shouldn't speak too confidently of such things in the interior of Brazil.) I have not been back to Diamantina, nor have I ever really wanted to go back. Remote, sad, and impoverished as it was, I liked the little town very much, perhaps because it seemed so close to the Diamantina of Helena's childhood, the writing coming off the pages of her diary, and turning to life again, as it had happened. I am superstitious about going "back" to places, anyway: they have changed; you have changed; even the weather may have changed. I am glad to see Helena's youthful book appear again; both it and my memories of Diamantina remain, as I'm afraid I said once before, in the earlier Introduction, still "as fresh as paint."

Boston, Massachusetts
June 1977

A Trip to Vigia

The shy poet, so soiled, so poor, so polite, insisted on taking us
in his own car. A friend would go along as *mechanista*. The car
was on its last legs; it had broken down twice just getting us
around Belem the day before. But what could we do? I couldn't
very well flaunt my dollars in his face and hire a better one.

He arrived at our hotel at nine (he had said eight) with José
Augusto, one of his little boys, aged eleven, fair, and also very
shy. Ruy, the poet, was dark, quiet, and softly heavy, his waxy
face spattered with fine black moles like shot. His other children,
four or five of them, were at home with "fever." They were
sick all the time we were in Belem. This José Augusto scarcely
spoke, but in the course of the long day his expression became
by degrees more animated, more childlike. By mid-afternoon he
grew restless, even active; he slept all the way back from the
expedition in his father's arms.

Ruy was nervous. He kept telling us we probably wouldn't
like the famous church at Vigia; it would be too "baroque" for
us. Each time he said this, our imaginations added more bel-
fries and a slightly wilder wave of carved stone. M. and I got
into the back seat that slanted downwards so that our bottoms

felt as if they were gently grazing the road. The *mechanista,* José Augusto, and Ruy were in front. Most of the time they kept their heads bent as if in prayer. Perhaps they were praying to the tired heart of the car to keep on beating just a little longer, until the expedition was safely over.

We had met Ruy just two days before. That morning I asked M. to let me know when the mystic moment arrived and she'd shift gears from addressing him as "Dr. Ruy" to "you." This use of the *você* or second person is always a delicate problem and I wanted to see how M., who has the nicest Brazilian manners, would solve it. Since Ruy was a poet and therefore could be considered sensitive, and since we found him very sympathetic, I felt it would be happening very soon.

Outside Belem we crossed a dead-looking railroad yard with old red freight cars scattered about in it, the end of the line. We passed under a fretwork arch, decorated with a long and faded banner and with cut bamboos turned sere brown. It had been set up to celebrate the opening of the new highway to Brasilia. Just beyond it, the paved road stopped for good. However, the very thought of this new road to the capital had cheered up all of Belem considerably. Even the resigned Ruy spoke about the future optimistically.

Vigia was about a hundred kilometers away. We went off toward it on another narrower road to the left that went up and down, up and down, in low wavy hills, mostly through bushes. Because of the two daily rains (it was the rainy season), there was little dust. Slowly, slowly we rose and fell over the gravel. The silent *mechanista* was like a mother teaching the car to walk. But after a while it stopped.

He got out and lifted the hood. M. talked gaily of this and that. After fifteen minutes or so, the car started again: up a slight grade; down faster; up. The day was getting hot. The car was getting hot. But still it seemed as if we had just left Belem. We passed fields of pepper, big leafy pillars. It is grown on poles, like string beans, and is called Pimenta da Rainha, Queen's Pepper, because it originally belonged to the crown. They say that the whole history of Portugal since the fourteenth century is the history of pepper. It had recently become a big crop in the north. Ruy complained about it, saying it was already overplanted, the way any successful crop always is in Brazil, and the price was dropping. On the left, where an unseen stream ran, were occasional plantations of jute, a bright and tender green.

More pepper. A mud-and-wattle house or two. An oxcart: mild, lovely *zebus* with high humps and long hanging ears, blue-gray, a well-matched team. Skinny horses scrambled off into the bushes, or stood pat while we edged around them. A dismal mud-and-wattle church, half-painted bright blue: IGREJA BATISTA. Then a little bridge with half the planks missing. The *mechanista* got out and squatted to study it from the far side, before taking us over.

Fine and blue, the morning rain arrived. The gravel darkened and spurted away slowly on either side. We plowed dreamily along. Ruy was talking about T. S. Eliot. He read English, some, but spoke not a word. I tried a story about Ezra Pound. It was very well received but, I felt, not understood. I undertook some more literary anecdotes. Smiling politely, Ruy waited for every joke until the faithful M. had helped me put them into Portuguese. Often they proved to be untranslatable. The car stopped.

This time the *mechanista* took much longer. M. talked ever more gaily. Suddenly the rain came down hard, great white lashings. The bushes crouched and the gravel danced. M. nudged me, whispered "*Now*," and in her next sentence to Ruy used a noticeable *você*; the mystic moment was past. The *mechanista* got back in, his clothes several shades darker with wet, and said we would stop at the next village for repairs.

The rains stopped and the sun came out. Certain varieties of glazed tropical leaves reflected the light like nickel, or white enamel, but as the car passed they returned to their actual gray-green. It was confusing, and trying to the eyes. Palm trees, more pepper and jute, more bushes. Here and there a great jungle tree had been left standing, and black specks were busy high around the tops; each tree held a whole community of birds. At least two hundred feet high, a Brazil nut tree blossomed; one could tell only by a smell like that of a thousand lilacs.

Three teams of *zebus*, loaded with jute. A small shower, like an afterthought right through the sunshine. We were driving north-northeast, skirting the great bay of Marajó, but we might as well have been in the middle of Africa or the Yucatan. (It *looked* a bit like the Yucatan.) More wretched little houses, with pigs, and naked children shining from the rain. The "village" was a crossroads, with a combined drink-shop and grocery store, a botequim, beside a spreading flamboyant tree. It took a moment to realize the car had really stopped; we stopped talking, and got out.

The store had been raided, sacked. Oh, that was its normal state. It was quite large, no color inside or cloud-color perhaps, with holes in the floor, holes in the walls, holes in the roof. A barrel of kerosene stood in a dark stain. There were a coil of blue cotton rope, a few mattock heads, and a bundle of yellow-white handles, fresh cut from hard *ipé* wood. Lined up on the shelves were many, many bottles of *cachaça*, all alike: Esperança, Hope, Hope, Hope. There was a counter where you could drink, if you wanted. A bunch of red-striped lamp wicks hung beside a bunch of rusty frying pans. A glass case offered brown toffees leaking through their papers, and old, old, old sweet buns. Some very large ants were making hay there while the sun shone. Our eyes negotiated the advertisements for Orange Crush and Guaraná on the cloud-colored walls, and we had seen everything. That was all.

The shopkeeper had gone off with our *mechanista,* so Ruy helped us to warm Orange Crush and over our protests put the money for it on the counter. "No cheese?" he inquired, poking about in back, as if he were in the habit of eating quantities of cheese with an Orange Crush every morning. He asked if we'd like a toffee, and urged us to take another *crooshy.* Then he said, "Let's go see the manioc factory."

This was right behind the botequim. It was an open-air affair of three thatched roofs on posts, one a round toadstool. A dozen women and girls sat on the ground, ripping the black skins off the long roots with knives. We were the funniest things they had seen in years. They tried not to laugh in our faces, but we "slayed" them. M. talked to them, but this did not increase their self-control. *Zebus* stood looking on, chewing their cuds. A motor, with belts slanting up under the thatch, chugged away, grinding up the raw manioc. The place smelled of *zebu,* gasoline, and people. Everyone talked, but it was murky and peaceful.

The greatest attraction was the revolving metal floor, a big disk, for drying out the flour. It was heated underneath by a charcoal fire and the area was partly railed off, like a small rink, so one could lean over and watch. The coarse white flour went slowly round and round, pushed back and forth in drifts by two men with long wooden hoes. The flour got whiter and whiter, but they were careful not to let it brown. In the north, people usually eat it white; in the south, they prefer it roasted to a pale tan.

We almost forgot we were on our way to Vigia. Then the *mechanista* collected us; in we got, out again, in again, and finally off. The motor now sounded languid and half sick but uncomplaining, like the poet himself.

Another ten kilometers and we came to a small house on the left, set among fruit and banana trees growing directly from the bare, swept earth. A wash was strung on the barbed-wire fence. Several skinny dogs appeared and a very fat young woman came out, carrying a baby, with two little boys tagging along behind. We all shook hands, even the baby boys. Her husband, a friend of Ruy's, was away but she invited us in—"for lunch," said the poor woman. We quickly explained we had brought our lunch with us. Ruy did the honors. "Ah! the water here is a *delicia*, isn't it, Dona Sebastiana? It's the best water, the only water, from here to Vigia. People come for miles to get water here. Wait till you try it."

Pegged to the side of the house was a fresh snake skin, a monster over ten feet long the husband had shot two days before. Dona Sebastiana brought out three glass jars, and a large tin can full of fat she'd rendered from the snake. She said it was the best remedy in the world for a great variety of ailments, including tuberculosis and "sore legs." Then she hurried in to make the coffee.

There were several small rooms in her house, and they were almost bare. There was no glass in the windows, and only the front room had a floor. It also had the *oratorio*, a yellowed print of Our Lady of Nazareth, with red paper roses in front of it, and that other light of the world, the sewing machine, a hand-run *Sin-ger*.

In the kitchen Dona Sebastiana was fanning hard, with a

plaited palm leaf held in both hands, a charcoal fire in a clay trough. We admired a hanging lamp of tin, homemade, cleverly constructed to stay upright. It was the only thing to admire. "Oh," she said, "my girl friend left that to me when she died. We went to school together." There was almost nothing in her kitchen except a black pot or two. The only signs of food were some overripe cucumbers on the windowsill. How had she managed to be so fat? The upside-down *cafezinho* cups were modestly hidden under a fringed napkin, with a little boy pushing a wheelbarrow embroidered in red outline. Dona Sebastiana had no white sugar, and she apologized for the cake of brown she scraped for us herself. We drank it down, the hot, bad, sad coffee, and went out back to see her river.

It really was a beautiful river. It was four yards across, dark, clear, running rapidly, with white cascades and deep pools edged with backed-up foam, and its banks were a dream of the tropics. It splashed, it sang, it glittered over white pebbles. Little did it reck that it had almost reached the vast muddy bay, the mouth of the Amazon. It made up for a lot, and Dona Sebastiana was proud of it. José Augusto and the little boys went wading. The thin dogs stood in the water, and gulped at it, then looked back at us over their shoulders from *their* river.

It was one o'clock by now and we were starving. The hotel had given us a lunch, a good-sized roast hen, fresh rolls, butter, oranges, a hunk of desirable white cheese. But no one would eat a bite. They *never* ate lunch—what an idea! I made a chicken sandwich and offered it to José Augusto. He looked shocked and frightened, and moved closer to his father's knee. Finally M. and I miserably gobbled up some lunch by ourselves. The *mechanista* soaked his feet, and rolled and smoked corn-husk cigarettes. Ruy let José Augusto accept one orange; Dona Sebastiana let her little boys accept two oranges. Then we shook hands all around, and back in our car we crawled away.

After a while, we got there. But first, from far off, we could see the pinnacled tops of two square towers, dazzling white against the dark rainclouds. The church looked like a sacred bull, a great white zebu. The road was level now, the landscape low and flat; we were near the coast. The church towers could be seen a long way off, rising very high above the tops of the tall green-black mango trees around them.

The plaza was dark red, laid out with cement benches and lampposts stuck with round globes, like artificial pearls. Smack in the middle was a blue-and-white bandstand. It was hideous, but because it was so small it didn't spoil the effect at all— rather as if these absurd offerings had been laid out on the ground in front of the great, indifferent, sacred white zebu. The dark green mango trees were dwarfed by the church. On either side the little old houses were tile-covered, with Gothic blue-and-white, or yellow-and-white, tile-covered *azulejos*.

Ruy watched us. But we liked the church very much and said so. He looked greatly relieved. The church danced in the light. I climbed on a stone wall, the remains of another abandoned house, to get a photograph of the whole thing, if possible, but there was nothing high enough to take it all in. It started to rain. I got a picture, jumped down—a dozen people had gathered to watch me, all looking scandalized—tripped, and tore my petticoat, which fell down below my skirt. The rain poured.

The others were all inside the church. It was mostly blue and white—bare, cold, huge, echoing. Little children followed us and ran shouting up and down; Ruy's little boy joined in. We went out on the second-story galleries, beneath the row of huge whitewashed pillars. You could see a pattern of tile roofs and mango trees through the rain tapestry, red-brown, down to the river, where the masts of ships and boats showed. A battered blue truck ground along below, and the driver came in, too— another friend of Ruy's.

The sacristan, an old fisherman, appeared. There was little enough to be seen in the sacristy. He went to a cupboard, with the little children pressing close around him and me, crying, "Show her Father! Show her Father!" and he handed me—a bone. A skull. The children reached up for it. He patted the skull and said yes, that was Father So-and-So, a saint if ever there was one, a really holy man. Never went anywhere, thought of nothing but prayer, meditated and prayed seven hours a day. I thought he was speaking of some forgotten saint of the seventeenth century who had never been properly recognized. No, Father had died two years before. I kept trying to hand the skull back. He was too busy telling me about the final illness, his *agonia,* his death. It was the most wonderful thing in Vigia. The sacristan put the skull back in the corner of the bare cupboard. It was so dark in the sacristy we could scarcely see.

We went out. Huge thunderclouds rolled back and forth, the river was higher, the tide had turned. All the lights went on in the forsaken plaza, although it was not dark. The pearly, silent, huge church of Vigia had made us all feel somehow guilty at abandoning it once again. The town's little white houses were turning mauve. In the high, high skies, shafts of long golden beams fell through the thunderclouds. Nature was providing all the baroque grandeur the place lacked. We started back to Belem, and it soon began to get really dark.

The car didn't stop all the way home, except once on purpose for gasoline. The trip seemed to take forever and we all fell silent. The little boy fell sound asleep. There wasn't even a light for miles, and never a car; we met two trucks and over-took two. Our eyes fastened on the slightest light or movement —an oil lamp, like an ancient Greek lamp, on a bicycle; a few people on foot carrying umbrellas.

Then lights. We were coming to Belem. Lights on the mud walls and their political posters and endless slogans, with all the *N*'s and *S*'s written backwards. Tall narrow doorways, the murky light of an oil lamp, warm, yellow and black. A man carrying a lantern—oh, he's leading a cow and a calf. Goats. Look out, a zebu! We almost hit him, a high bony gray wall across the road. He lowered his horns sharply and snorted softly.

Suddenly we are in Belem. Huge black mango trees. Cars bumping over the cobblestones, bumpety-bump. How very, very bright this dim city can look! We ache in the dark. The church at Vigia, huge, white, alone on our consciences, has become a ghost story.

The hotel at last. It is almost nine o'clock. We invite Ruy in for a drink, at least. He comes, but will take only another *cafezinho*. The dingy café looks brilliant. The young literary men are there, with their rolled umbrellas, moving hands and black neckties, their hair slicked back. They all greet Ruy. Half asleep, we swallow the coffee and, behind our backs, Ruy pays for it.

1967

Efforts of Affection:

A Memoir of Marianne Moore

In the first edition of Marianne Moore's *Collected Poems* of 1951 there is a poem originally called "Efforts and Affection." In my copy of this book, Marianne crossed out the "and" and wrote "of" above it. I liked this change very much, and so I am giving the title "Efforts of Affection" to the whole piece.

I first met Marianne Moore in the spring of 1934 when I was a senior at Vassar College, through Miss Fanny Borden, the college librarian. A school friend and the friend's mother, both better read and more sophisticated in their literary tastes than I was, had told me about Marianne Moore's poetry several years earlier. I had already read every poem of Miss Moore's I could find, in back copies of *The Dial*, "little magazines," and anthologies in the college library. I hadn't known poetry could be like that; I took to it immediately, but although I knew there was a volume of hers called *Observations*, it was not in the library and I had never seen it.

Because Miss Borden seems like such an appropriate person to have introduced me to Marianne Moore, I want to say a little about her. She was the niece of the Fall River Lizzie Borden, and at college the rumor was that Lizzie Borden's lurid career had had a permanently subduing effect on Miss Fanny Borden's personality. She was extremely shy and reserved and spoke in such a soft voice it was hard to hear her at all. She was tall and thin; she always dressed in browns and grays, old-fashioned, muted, and distinguished-looking. She also rode a chainless bicycle. I remember watching her ride slowly up to the library, seated very high and straight on this curiosity, which somehow seemed more lady-like than a bicycle with a chain, and park it in the rack. (We didn't padlock bicycles then.) Once, after she had gone inside, I examined the bicycle, which was indeed chainless, to see if I could figure out how it worked. I couldn't. Contact with the librarian was rare; once in a long while, in search of a book, one would be sent into Miss Borden's office, shadowy and cave-like, with books piled everywhere. She weighed down the papers on her desk with smooth, round stones, quite big stones, brought from the seashore, and once when my roommate admired one of these, Miss Borden said in her almost inaudible voice, "Do you like it? You may *have* it," and handed it over, gray, round, and very heavy.

One day I was sent in to Miss Borden's office about a book, I no longer remember what. We continued talking a little, and I finally got up my courage to ask her why there was no copy of *Observations* by that wonderful poet Marianne Moore in the Vassar library. She looked ever so gently taken aback and inquired, "Do you *like* Marianne Moore's poems?" I said I certainly did, the few I'd been able to find. Miss Borden then said calmly, "I've known her since she was a little girl," and followed that with the question that was possibly to influence the whole course of my life: "Would you like to meet her?" I was painfully—no, excruciatingly—shy and I had run away many times rather than face being introduced to adults of much less distinction that Marianne Moore, but I immediately said, "Yes." Miss Borden said that she would write to Miss Moore, who lived in Brooklyn, and also that she would be glad to lend me *her* copy of *Observations*.

Miss Borden's copy of *Observations* was an eye-opener in more ways than one. Poems like "An Octopus," about a glacier, or "Peter," about a cat, or "Marriage," about marriage, struck me, as they still do, as miracles of language and construction. Why had no one ever written about things in this clear and dazzling way before? But at the same time I was astonished to discover that Miss Borden (whom I now knew to be an old family friend of the Moores) obviously didn't share my liking for these poems. Tucked in the back of the book were quite a few reviews that had appeared when *Observations* was published, in 1924, and most of these were highly unfavorable, some simply obtuse. There was even a parody Moore poem by Franklin P. Adams. Even more revealing, Miss Borden hadn't seen fit to place a copy of her friend's book in the college library. (Later that year I found a copy for myself, on a secondhand-book table at Macy's.)

The day came when Miss Borden told me that she had heard from Miss Moore and that Miss Moore was willing to meet me in New York, on a Saturday afternoon. Years later I discovered that Marianne had agreed to do this with reluctance; in the past, it seems, dear Miss Borden had sent several Vassar girls to meet Miss Moore and sometimes her mother as well, and every one had somehow failed to please. This probably accounted for the conditions laid down for our first rendezvous: I was to find Miss Moore seated on the bench at the right of the door leading to the reading room of the New York Public Library. They might have been even more strict. I learned later that if Miss Moore really expected *not* to like would-be acquaintances, she arranged to meet them at the Information Booth in Grand Central Station—no place to sit down, and, if necessary, an instant getaway was possible. In the meantime, I had been told a little more about her by Miss Borden, who described her as a child, a strange and appealing little creature with bright red hair—playful, and, as might have been expected, fond of calling her family and friends by the names of animals.

I was very frightened, but I put on my new spring suit and took the train to New York. I had never seen a picture of Miss Moore; all I knew was that she had red hair and usually wore a wide-brimmed hat. I expected the hair to be bright red and for her to be tall and intimidating. I was right on time, even a bit early, but she was there before me (no matter how early one arrived, Marianne was always there first) and, I saw at once, not very tall and not in the least intimidating. She was forty-seven, an age that seemed old to me then, and her hair was mixed with white to a faint rust pink, and her rust-pink eyebrows were frosted with white. The large flat black hat was as I'd expected it to be. She wore a blue tweed suit that day and, as she usually did then, a man's "polo shirt," as they were called, with a black bow at the neck. The effect was quaint, vaguely Bryn Mawr 1909, but stylish at the same time. I sat down and she began to talk.

It seems to me that Marianne talked to me steadily for the next thirty-five years, but of course that is nonsensical. I was living far from New York many of those years and saw her at long intervals. She must have been one of the world's greatest talkers: entertaining, enlightening, fascinating, and memorable; her talk, like her poetry, was quite different from anyone else's in the world. I don't know what she talked about at that first meeting; I wish I had kept a diary. Happily ignorant of the poor Vassar girls before me who hadn't passed muster, I began to feel less nervous and even spoke some myself. I had what may have been an inspiration, I don't know—at any rate, I attribute my great good fortune in having known Marianne as a friend in part to it. Ringling Bros. and Barnum & Bailey Circus was making its spring visit to New York and I asked Miss Moore (we called each other "Miss" for over two years) if she would care to go to the circus with me the Saturday after next. I didn't know that she *always* went to the circus, wouldn't have missed it for anything, and when she accepted, I went back to Poughkeepsie in the grimy day coach extremely happy.

The Circus

I got to Madison Square Garden very early—we had settled on the hour because we wanted to see the animals before the show began—but Marianne was there ahead of me. She was loaded down: two blue cloth bags, one on each arm, and two huge brown paper bags, full of something. I was given one of these. They contained, she told me, stale brown bread for the elephants, because stale brown bread was one of the things they liked best to eat. (I later suspected that they might like stale white bread just as much but that Marianne had been thinking of their health.) As we went in and down to the lower level, where we could hear (and smell) the animals, she told me her preliminary plan for the circus. Her brother, Warner, had given her an elephant-hair bracelet, of which she was very fond, two or three strands of black hairs held together with gold clasps. One of the elephant hairs had fallen out and been lost. As I probably knew, elephant hairs grow only on the tops of the heads of very young elephants. In her bag, Marianne had a pair of strong nail scissors. I was to divert the adult elephants with the bread, and, if we were lucky, the guards wouldn't observe her at the end of the line where the babies were, and she could take out her scissors and snip a few hairs from a baby's head, to repair her bracelet.

She was quite right; the elephants adored stale brown bread

and started trumpeting and pushing up against each other to get it. I stayed at one end of the line, putting slices of bread into the trunks of the older elephants, and Miss Moore went rapidly down to the other end, where the babies were. The large elephants were making such a to-do that a keeper did come up my way, and out of the corner of my eye I saw Miss Moore leaning forward over the rope on tiptoe, scissors in hand. Elephant hairs are tough; I thought she would never finish her hair-cutting. But she did, and triumphantly we handed out the rest of the bread and set off to see the other animals. She opened her bag and showed me three or four coarse, grayish hairs in a piece of Kleenex.

I hate seeing animals in cages, especially small cages, and especially circus animals, but I think that Marianne, while probably feeling the same way, was so passionately interested in them, and knew so much about them, that she could put aside any pain or outrage for the time being. That day I remember that one handsomely patterned snake, writhing about in a glass-walled cage, seemed to raise his head on purpose to look at us. "See, he knows me!" said Miss Moore. "He remembers me from last year." This was a joke, I decided, but perhaps not altogether a joke. Then we went upstairs and the six-ring affair began. The blue bags held our refreshments: thermos jugs of orange juice, hard-boiled eggs (the yolks only), and more brown bread, but fresh this time, and buttered. I also remember of this first visit to the circus (there were to be others) that in front of us sat a father with three young children, two boys and a girl. A big circus goes on for a long time and the children began to grow restless. Marianne leaned over with the abruptness that characterized all her movements and said to the father that if the little girl wanted to go to the bathroom, she'd be glad to take her.

260 Cumberland Street

After graduating from Vassar I lived for a year in New York City; I returned to live there from time to time for thirty years or so, but it was during this first year that I got to know Miss Moore and her mother and became familiar with their small apartment in Brooklyn. It was in the fourth floor front of an ugly yellow brick building with a light granite stoop and a big white glass globe on a pillar at either side of the door. (Marianne told taxi drivers to stop at the apartment with the "two mothballs" in front.) The elevator was small and slow. After I had buzzed, I used to try to get up in it to the fourth floor before Marianne could get down in it to take me up personally, but I rarely managed to. A very narrow hall, made narrower by waist-high bookcases along one side, and with doors to two tiny bedrooms opening off it, led back to the living room. On the end of the bookcase nearest the front door sat the famous bowl of nickels for subway fare (nickels for years, then dimes, then nickels *and* dimes, and finally quarters). Every visitor was made to accept one of these upon leaving; it was absolutely *de rigueur*. After one or two attempts at refusing, I always simply helped myself to a nickel as I left, and eventually I was rewarded for this by Marianne's saying to a friend who was protesting, "Elizabeth is an *aristocrat;* she *takes* the money." (I should like to mention here the peculiar way Marianne had of pronouncing my Christian name. She came down very hard on the second syllable, Eli*z*abeth. I liked this, especially as an exclamation, when she was pretending to be shocked by something I had said.)

The small living room and dining room were crowded with furniture that had obviously come from an older, larger home, and there were many pictures on the walls, a mixture of the old and the new, family possessions and presents from friends (these generally depicted birds or animals). One painting of trees and a stream had suffered an accident to its rather blurry tree passage, and Marianne herself had restored this—I felt, unkindly, not too successfully—with what she said was "Prussian blue." She was modestly vain of her manual skills. A set of carpenter's tools hung by the kitchen door, and Marianne had put up some of the bookshelves herself. In one doorway a trapeze on chains was looped up to the lintel. I never saw this in use, but it was Marianne's, and she said that when she exercised on it and her brother was there, he always said, "The ape is rattling her chains again." A chest stood in the bay window of the living room with a bronze head of Marianne on it by Lachaise. The chest was also always piled high with new books. When I first knew Marianne she did quite a bit of reviewing and later sold the review copies on West Fourth Street.

I was always seated in the same armchair, and an ashtray was placed on a little table beside me, but I tried to smoke no more than one or two cigarettes a visit, or none at all. I felt that Mrs. Moore disapproved. Once, as I was leaving and waiting for the slow elevator, I noticed a deep burn in the railing of the staircase and commented on it. Mrs. Moore gave a melancholy sigh and said, "*Ezra* did that. He came to call on Marianne and left his cigar burning out here because he knew I *don't like cigars* . . ." Many years later, in St. Elizabeths Hospital, I repeated this to Ezra Pound. He laughed loudly and said, "I haven't smoked a cigar since I was eighteen!" Beside the ashtray and even a new package of Lucky Strikes, I was sometimes given a glass of Dubonnet. I had a suspicion that I was possibly the only guest who drank this Dubonnet, because it looked very much like the same bottle, at the level it had been on my last visit, for many months. But usually we had tea and occasionally I was invited for dinner. Mrs. Moore was a very good cook.

Mrs. Moore was in her seventies when I first knew her, very serious—solemn, rather—although capable of irony, and very devout. Her face was pale and somewhat heavy, her eyes large and a pale gray, and her dark hair had almost no white in it. Her manner toward Marianne was that of a kindly, self-controlled parent who felt that she had to take a firm line, that her daughter might be given to flightiness or—an equal sin, in her eyes—mistakes in grammar. She had taught English at a girls' school and her sentences were Johnsonian in weight and balance. She spoke more slowly than I have ever heard anyone speak in my life. One example of her conversational style has stayed with me for over forty years. Marianne was in the kitchen making tea and I was alone with Mrs. Moore. I said that I had just seen a new poem of Marianne's, "Nine Nectarines & Other Porcelain," and admired it very much. Mrs. Moore replied, "Yes. I am so *glad* that Marianne has *decided* to give the inhabitants of the *zoo* . . . a *rest*." Waiting for the conclusion of her longer statements, I grew rather nervous; nevertheless, I found her extreme precision enviable and thought I could detect echoes of Marianne's own style in it: the use of double or triple negatives, the lighter and wittier ironies—Mrs. Moore had provided a sort of ground bass for them.

She wrote me one or two beautifully composed little notes on the subject of religion, and I know my failure to respond made her sad. At each of my leave-takings she followed me to the hall, where, beside "Ezra's" imagined cigar burn, she held my hands and said a short prayer. She said grace before dinner, and once, a little maliciously, I think, Marianne asked *me* to say grace. Mercifully, a childhood grace popped into my mind. After dinner Marianne wrote it down.

Of course Mrs. Moore and her daughter were what some people might call "prudish"; it would be kinder to say "over-fastidious." This applied to Mrs. Moore more than to Marianne; Marianne, increasingly so with age, was capable of calling a spade a spade, or at least calling it by its archaic name. I remember her worrying about the fate of a mutual friend whose sexual tastes had always seemed quite obvious to me: "What are we going to do about X . . . ? Why, sometimes I think he may even be in the clutches of a *sodomite* . . . !" One could almost smell the brimstone. But several novels of the thirties and forties, including Mary McCarthy's *The Company She Keeps*, were taken down to the cellar and burned in the furnace. I published a very bad short story a year or two after I first knew the Moores and I was reprimanded by both of them for having used the word "spit." (Two or three years later I was scolded for having used "water closet" in a poem, but by then I had turned obstinate.) Marianne once gave me her practical rules for the use of indecent language. She said, "Ordinarily, I would never use the word *rump*. But I can perfectly well say to Mother, 'Mother, there's a thread on your *rump*, because *she* knows that I'm referring to Cowper's pet hare, 'Old Tiney,' who liked to play on the carpet and 'swing his rump around!' "

I was shown many old photographs and snapshots and, once, a set of postcards of their trip to England and Paris—at that time the only European traveling Marianne had done. The post-cards were mostly of Oxford, and there was a handwritten menu, including the wines, of the luncheon George Saintsbury had given for her. I was also privileged to look into the note-books, illustrated with Marianne's delicate sketches.

Besides exercising on the trapeze, Marianne was very fond of tennis. I never saw her play, but from the way she talked about it, it seemed as if she enjoyed the rules and conventions of the

game as much as the sport. She engaged a young black boy to
play with her, sometimes in Prospect Park and sometimes on
the roof of the apartment house. He was finally dismissed be-
cause of his lack of tennis manners; his worst offense seemed
to be that instead of "Serve!" he *would* say "Okay!"

The bathroom in the apartment was small, long, and narrow,
and as if I were still a child, I was advised to go there when
Marianne thought it would be a good idea. (Also in subway
stations: "I'll hold your bag and gloves, Elizabeth.") In their
bathroom was an object I liked, an old-fashioned shoeshine box
with an iron footrest. On one visit this had just been repainted
by Marianne, with black enamel, and so had a cast-iron horse,
laid out on a piece of newspaper on its side, running, with
a streaming mane. It looked as if it might have originally been
attached to a toy fire engine. I asked about this little horse, and
Mrs. Moore told me that when Marianne was two and a half
years old she had taken her to visit an aunt; the horse had had
to go along too. Mrs. Moore had gone into the guest room and
discovered that Marianne had taken a length of lace, perhaps a
lace collar, from the bureau and dressed the horse up in it.
"Marianne!" she had said—one could imagine the awful
solemnity of the moment—"You wouldn't take Auntie Bee's
lace to put on your horse, would you?" But the infant Marianne,
the intrepid artist, replied, "Pretty looks, Ma! Pretty looks!"

Mrs. Moore's sense of honesty, or honor, like her respect for
the proprieties, was staggering. Marianne occasionally teased
her mother about it, even in front of me. One story was about
the time Mrs. Moore had decided that five empty milk bottles
must be returned to the grocery store, and thence to the dairy.
They were not STORE BOTTLES, as bottles then said right in the
glass, nor the kind that were to be put out on the doorstep, but
they all came from the same dairy. The grocer looked at them
and pushed them back on the counter toward Mrs. Moore, say-

ing, "You don't have to return these bottles, ma'am; just throw them away." Mrs. Moore pushed the bottles back again and told him quietly, "It *says* BORDEN on the bottles; they belong to the dairy." The grocer: "I know it does, ma'am, but it doesn't say STORE BOTTLES or RETURN. Just throw them away." Mrs. Moore spoke more slowly and more quietly, "But they don't belong to me. They are *their bottles*." "I know, ma'am, but they really don't want them back." The poor man had underestimated Mrs. Moore. She stood firm, clarifying for him yet again the only honorable line of action to be pursued in regard to the five bottles. Finally the grocer took them all in his arms and, saying weakly, "My *God*, ma'am!" carried them into the back of the store.

Clothes were of course an endless source of interest to Marianne, increasingly especially so as she grew older. As she has written herself (in a piece for *The Christian Science Monitor*), her clothes were almost always hand-me-downs, sometimes very elegant ones from richer friends. These would be let out or, most frequently, let down (Marianne preferred clothes on the loose side, like the four-sizes-too-large "polo shirts"). The hats would be stripped of decorations, and ribbons changed so all was black or navy blue, and somehow perhaps *flattened*. There was the Holbein/Erasmus-type hat, and later the rather famous tricorne, but in the first years I knew her, only the large, flat, low-crowned hats of felt or summer straw.

Once when I arrived at the Brooklyn apartment, Marianne and her mother were occupied with the old-fashioned bit of sewing called "making over." They were making a pair of drawers that Marianne had worn at Bryn Mawr in 1908 into a petticoat or slip. The drawers were a beautiful garment, fine white batiste, with very full legs that must have come to below the knee, edged with lace and set with rows of "insertion."

These I didn't see again in their metamorphosed state, but I did see and was sometimes consulted about other such projects. Several times over the years Marianne asked me abruptly, "Elizabeth, what do you have on under your dress? How much underwear do *you* wear?" I would enumerate my two or perhaps three undergarments, and Marianne would say, "Well, I know that I [or, Mother and I] wear many too many." And sometimes when I arrived on a cold winter evening dressed in a conventional way, I would be greeted by "Elizabeth, silk stockings!" as if I were reckless or prone to suicide. My own clothes were subject to her careful consideration. The first time I ever met a publisher, I reported the next day by telephone and Marianne's first question was "What did you *wear*, Elizabeth?"

Marianne's hair was always done up in a braid around the crown of her head, a style dating from around 1900, I think, and never changed. Her skin was fair, translucent, although faded when I knew her. Her face paled and flushed so quickly she reminded me of Rima in W. H. Hudson's *Green Mansions*. Her eyes were bright, not "bright" as we often say about eyes when we really mean alert; they were that too, but also shiny bright and, like those of a small animal, often looked at one sidewise—quickly, at the conclusion of a sentence that had turned out unusually well, just to see if it had taken effect. Her face was small and pointed, but not really triangular because it was a little lopsided, with a delicately pugnacious-looking jaw. When one day I told her she looked like Mickey Rooney, then a very young actor (and she did), she seemed quite pleased.

She said her poem "Spenser's Ireland" was not about *loving* Ireland, as people seemed to think, but about *disapproving* of it. Yet she liked being of Irish descent; her great-great-grandfather had run away from a house in Merrion Square, Dublin (once, I went to look at it from the outside), and I remember her delight when the book in which the poem appeared was bound in Irish green.

She had a way of laughing at what she or someone else had just said if she meant to show outrage or mock disapproval—an *oh-ho* kind of sound, rough, that went with a backwards and sidewise toss of the head toward the left shoulder. She accepted compliments with this laugh too, without words; it disparaged and made light of them, and implied that she and her audience were both far above such absurdities. I believe she was the only person I have ever known who "bridled" at praise, while turning pink with pleasure. These gestures of her head were more pronounced in the presence of gentlemen because Marianne was innately flirtatious.

The Moore *chinoiserie* of manners made giving presents complicated. All of her friends seemed to share the desire of giving her presents, and it must sometimes have been, as she would have said, a "burden." One never knew what would succeed, but one learned that if a gift did not succeed it would be given back, unobtrusively, but somehow or other, a year or two later. My most successful gift was a pair of gloves. I don't know why they made such a hit, but they did; they weren't actually worn for a long time, but they appear in a few of her photographs, held in one hand. Marianne brought them to the photographer wrapped in the original tissue paper. Another very successful gift was a paper nautilus, which became the subject of her poem "The Paper Nautilus":

> . . . *its wasp-nest flaws*
> *of white on white, and close-*
>
> *laid Ionic chiton-folds*
> *like the lines in the mane of*
> *a Parthenon horse . . .*

Fruit or flowers were acclaimed and examined but never, I felt, really welcomed. But a very unbeautiful bracelet from Morocco, alternate round beads of amber and black ambergris on a soiled string, was very well received. I was flattered to see this worn at a poetry reading, and afterwards learned that, as it was too loose for Marianne's wrist, Mother had carefully sewn it onto the edge of her sleeve. But another friend's attempt to give her a good gramophone was a disaster, a drama that went on for months. Eventually (it was portable but very heavy) it was carried back by Marianne to the shop in New York.

She liked to show her collection of jewelry, which had a few beautiful and valuable pieces. I once gave her a modest brooch of the semi-precious stones of Brazil, red and green tourmalines and amethysts; this she seemed to like so much that I gave her a matching bracelet. A few years later I wrote her from Brazil asking what I could bring her on my return to New York, and she wrote back, "I like *jewels*."

Knowing her fondness for snakes, I got for her when I was in Florida a beautiful specimen of the deadly coral snake with inch-wide rose-red and black stripes separated by narrow white stripes, a bright new snake coiled in liquid in a squat glass bottle. This bottle sat on her hall bookcase, at the other end from the bowl of nickels, for many years. The colors gradually faded, and the formaldehyde grew cloudy, and finally I said I thought she could dispense with the coral snake. A mutual friend told me that Marianne was relieved; she had always hated it. Perhaps it had only been brought out for my visits.

Marianne once told me a story on herself about her aversion to reds. Her physician in Brooklyn for some years was a Turkish woman, Dr. Laf Loofy, whom she often quoted as a great authority on health. Dr. Loofy had prescribed for Marianne a large bottle of red pills, but before taking one, Marianne would wash it thoroughly until all the shiny red coating had disappeared. Something, perhaps digestive symptoms, made her confess this to Dr. Loofy, who was incredulous, then appalled. She explained that medical genius and years of research, expressly for Marianne's benefit, had gone into developing the red enamel-like coating that she had deliberately washed away. Marianne was completely stoical about herself; once, at a New York doctor's office, she proved to have a temperature of 104 degrees. The doctor wanted to call a cab for her for the long trip back to Brooklyn, but Marianne would have none of it. She insisted on returning by subway, and did.

Despite what I assumed to be her aversion to reds, she once showed me a round, light tan, rather pig-like piece of luggage, bought especially for her first trip to give readings on the West Coast, saying, "You will think this too *showy*, Elizabeth." The long zipper on the top could be locked with a bright red padlock. I said no, I thought it a very nice bag. "Of course," Marianne said, "the red padlock is the very best thing about it."

One winter Mrs. Moore was sick for a long time with a severe case of shingles. She was just recovering from this long illness when she also had to go to the dentist, whose office was in Manhattan. A friend who had a car and I went to Brooklyn to take Marianne and her mother to the city. Mrs. Moore was still feeling poorly. She was wearing a round flat fur cap, a very 1890-ish hat, mink, I think, or possibly sable, and since she couldn't bear to put her hair up yet, the remarkably un-gray hair hung down in a heavy pigtail. The dentist's office was high up in a tall office building. There were a good many passengers in the elevator and an elevator boy; we shot upwards. What I remember most is that at the proper floor, as the passengers stared, Marianne and her mother both bowed to the elevator boy pleasantly and thanked him, Mrs. Moore the more profusely, for the ride. He was unaccustomed to such civility, but he was very pleased and tried hard not to push his handle or close the doors as quickly as on the other floors. Elevator men, subway changemakers, ticket takers, taxi drivers—all were treated to these formalities, and, as a rule, they were pleasantly surprised and seemed to respond in kind.

A very well known and polished writer, who had known Marianne since he was a young man and felt great admiration for her, was never invited to Cumberland Street although his friends were. Once, I asked innocently why I never saw him there and Marianne gave me her serious, severe look and said, "He *contradicted* Mother."

The atmosphere of 260 Cumberland Street was of course "old-fashioned," but even more, otherworldly—as if one were living in a diving bell from a different world, let down through the crass atmosphere of the twentieth century. Leaving the diving bell with one's nickel, during the walk to the subway and the forty-five-minute ride back to Manhattan, one was apt to have a slight case of mental or moral bends—so many things to be remembered; stories, phrases, the unaccustomed deference, the exquisitely prolonged etiquette—these were hard to reconcile with the New Lots Avenue express and the awful, jolting ride facing a row of indifferent faces. Yet I never left Cumberland Street without feeling happier: uplifted, even inspired, determined to be good, to work harder, not to worry about what other people thought, never to try to publish anything until I thought I'd done my best with it, no matter how many years it took—or never to publish at all.

To change the image from air to water: somehow, under all the subaqueous pressure at 260 Cumberland Street—admonitions, reserves, principles, simple stoicism—Marianne rose triumphant, or rather her voice did, in a lively, unceasing jet of shining bubbles. I had "taken" chemistry at preparatory school; I also could imagine that in this water, or heavy water glass, I saw forming the elaborate, logical structures that became her poems.

Writing and a Few Writers

On the floor of the kitchen at 260 Cumberland Street I once saw a bushel basket, the kind used for apples or tomatoes, filled to overflowing with crumpled papers, some typed, some covered with Marianne's handwriting. This basketful of papers held the discarded drafts of one review, not a long review, of a new book of poems by Wallace Stevens. When it was published I found the review very beautiful, as I still do. Nevertheless, Marianne chose to omit it from her collected essays; it didn't come up to her standards.

If she was willing to put in so much hard work on a review running to two or two and a half pages, one can imagine the work that went into a poem such as "The Jerboa," or "He 'Digesteth Harde Yron' " (about the ostrich), with their elaborate rhyme schemes and syllable-counting meters. When not at the desk, she used a clipboard with the poem under construction on it, carrying it about the apartment, "even when I'm dusting or washing the dishes, Elizabeth."

Her use of "light" rhymes has been written about by critics. On principle, she said, she disapproved of rhyme. Nevertheless, when she read poems to me, or recited them, she obviously enjoyed rhymes very much, and would glance up over her reading glasses and exclaim that *that* was "gusto"—her favorite word of praise. With great gusto of her own, she read:

> *Strong is the lion—like a coal*
> *His eye-ball—like a bastion's mole*
> *His chest against the foes:*

Strong, the gier-eagle on his sail,
Strong against tide, th'enormous whale
Emerges as he goes.

She admired Ogden Nash and liked to quote his poem about the baby panda for the sake of its rhyme:

I love the Baby Giant Panda;
I'd welcome one to my veranda.

Once, I found her consulting a large rhyming dictionary and she said, yes, it was "indispensable"; and I myself was congratulated on having rhymed "antennae" with "many."

Besides "gusto" she admired the "courageous attack," and for this reason she said she thought it a good idea to start off a poem with a spondee.

In *Observations* she seems undecided between free verse and her own strict stanza forms with their variations on "light" rhyme. Although she still professed to despise it, rhyme then seemed to win out for some years. However, by the time *Collected Poems* was published, in 1951, she had already begun a ruthless cutting of some of her most beautiful poems, and what suffered chiefly from this ruthlessness were those very rhymes and stanza forms she had so painstakingly elaborated in the years just before.

A conflict between traditional rhymes and meters came during the seven years (1946–53) Marianne worked on translating La Fontaine's *Fables*. For my own amusement, I had already made up a completely unscientific theory that Marianne was possessed of a unique, involuntary sense of rhythm, therefore of meter, quite unlike anyone else's. She looked like no one else; she talked like no one else; her poems showed a mind not much like anyone else's; and her notions of meter and rhyme were unlike all the conventional notions—so why not believe that the old English meters that still seem natural to most of us (or *seemed* to, at any rate) were not natural to her at all? That Marianne from birth, physically, had been set going to a different rhythm? Or was the explanation simply that she had a more sensitive ear than most of us, and since she had started writing at a time when poetry was undergoing drastic changes, she had been free to make the most of it and experiment as she saw fit?

When I happened to be in New York during those seven years, I was usually shown the fable she was working on (or she'd read it on the phone) and would be asked to provide a rhyme, or to tell her if I thought the meter was right. Many other people must have had the same experience. These were strange requests, coming from someone who had made contemporary poets self-conscious about their crudities, afraid to rhyme "bone" with "stone," or to go *umpty-umpty-um*. Marianne was doing her best, one saw, to go *umpty-umpty-um* when she sensed that La Fontaine had gone that way, but it seemed to be almost —I use the word again—physically impossible for her to do so. If I'd suggest, say, that "flatter" rhymed with "matter," this to my embarrassment was hailed as a stroke of genius; or if I'd say, "If you leave out 'and' or 'the' [or put it in], it will go *umpty-umpty-um*," Marianne would exclaim, "Elizabeth, thank you, you have saved my life!" Although I too am mentioned in the introduction, I contributed next to nothing to the La Fontaine —a few rhymes and metrically smoothed-out or slicked-up lines. But they made me realize more than I ever had the rarity of true originality, and also the sort of alienation it might involve.

Her scrupulous and strict honesty could be carried to extremes of Protestant, Presbyterian, Scotch-Irish literalness that amazed me. We went together to see an exceptionally beautiful film, a documentary in color about Africa, with herds of gazelles and giraffes moving across the plains, and we loved it. Then a herd of elephants appeared, close up and clear, and the narrator commented on their feet and tread. I whispered to Marianne that they looked as if their feet were being lifted up off the ground by invisible threads. The next day she phoned and quoted my remark about the elephants' walk, and suddenly came out with, "Elizabeth, I'll give you ten dollars for that." There was often no telling how serious she was. I said something like "For heaven's sake, Marianne, please take it," but I don't believe it ever made an appearance in a poem. I confess to one very slight grudge: she *did* use a phrase of mine once without a note. This may be childish of me, but I want to reclaim it. I had been asked by a friend to bring her three glass buoy-balls in nets, sometimes called "witch balls," from Cape Cod. When I arrived at the old hotel where I lived, a very old porter took them with my bag, and as I watched him precede me down the corridor, I said to myself, "The bellboy with the buoy-balls." I liked the sound of this so much that in my vanity I repeated the phrase to Marianne a day or so later. You will find "The sea- / side burden should not embarrass / the bell-boy with the buoy-ball / endeavoring to pass / hotel patronesses" in the fifth stanza of "Four Quartz Crystal Clocks." It was so thoroughly out of character for her to do this that I have never understood it. I am sometimes appalled to think how much I may have unconsciously stolen from her. Perhaps we are all magpies.

> *The deepest feeling always shows*
> *itself in silence;*
> *not in silence, but restraint.*

These lines from her early poem "Silence" are simply another one of Marianne's convictions. Like Auden, whom she admired, she believed that graceful behavior—and writing, as well—

demands a certain reticence. She told me, "Ezra says all dedications are *dowdy*," but it was surely more than to avoid dowdiness that caused her to write this postscript in *Selected Poems* (1935): "Dedications imply giving, and we do not care to make a gift of what is insufficient; but in my immediate family there is one 'who thinks in a particular way' and I should like to add that where there is an effect of thought or pith in these pages, the thinking and often the actual phrases are hers." This postscript was obviously meant for Mrs. Moore, and after her mother's death in 1947, Marianne became more outspoken about dedications; however, when she wrote an acrostic on the name of one of her oldest and closest friends, it too was semiconcealed, by being written upside down.

The first time I heard Marianne read poetry in public was at a joint reading with William Carlos Williams in Brooklyn. I am afraid I was a little late. There was a very small audience, mostly in the front rows, and I made my way as self-effacingly as I could down the steep red-carpeted steps of the aisle. As I approached the lower rows, she spotted me out of the corner of her eye and interrupted herself in the middle of a poem to bow and say, "Good evening!" She and Dr. Williams shared the rather small high stage and took turns reading. There were two high-backed chairs, far apart, and each poet sat down between readings. The decor seemed to be late-Victorian Gothic; I remember a good deal of red plush, dark wood, and Gothic points, knobs, and incised lines. Marianne, wearing a hat and a blue dress, looked quite small and seemed nervous. I had the impression that Williams, who was not nervous in the slightest, was generously trying to put her at her ease. As they changed places at the lectern, he would whisper to her and smile. I have no recollection of anything that was read, except for a sea-monster poem of Williams's, during which he gave some loud and realistic roars.

She seldom expressed opinions of other writers, and the few I remember were, to say the least, ambiguous or ambivalent. She developed the strategy of damning with faint praise to an almost supersonic degree. One writer whom I rather disliked, and I suspect she did too, was praised several times for her "beautifully laundered shirtwaist." One day when I was meeting her in New York, she said she had just run into Djuna Barnes again, after many years, on the steps of the Public Library. I was curious and asked her what Djuna Barnes was "like." There was rather a long pause before Marianne said, thoughtfully, "Well . . . she looked very smart, and her shoes were *beautifully* polished."

I do not remember her ever referring to Emily Dickinson, but on one occasion, when we were walking in Brooklyn on our way to a favored tea shop, I noticed we were on a street associated with the *Brooklyn Eagle*, and I said fatuously, "Marianne, isn't it odd to think of you and Walt Whitman walking this same street over and over?" She exclaimed in her mock-ferocious tone, "Elizabeth, don't speak to me about that man!" So I never did again. Another time, when she had been talking about her days on *The Dial*, I asked how she had liked Hart Crane when he had come into her office there. Her response was equally unexpected. "Oh, I *liked* Hart! I always liked him very much—he was so *erudite*." And although she admired Edmund Wilson very much and could speak with even more conviction of *his* erudition, she once asked me if I had read his early novel *I Thought of Daisy*, and when I said no, she almost extracted a promise from me that I would *never* read it. She was devoted to W. H. Auden, and the very cat he had patted in the Brooklyn tearoom was produced for me to admire and pat too.

Lately I have seen several references critical of her poetry by feminist writers, one of whom described her as a "poet who controlled panic by presenting it as whimsy." Whimsy is sometimes there, of course, and so is humor (a gift these critics sadly seem to lack). Surely there is an element of mortal panic and fear underlying all works of art? Even so, one wonders how much of Marianne's poetry the feminist critics have read. Have they really read "Marriage," a poem that says everything they are saying and everything Virginia Woolf has said? It is a poem which transforms a justified sense of injury into a work of art:

> *This institution . . .*
> *I wonder what Adam and Eve*
> *think of it by this time . . .*
>
> *Unhelpful Hymen!*
> *a kind of overgrown cupid*
> *reduced to insignificance*
> *by the mechanical advertising*
> *parading as involuntary comment,*
> *by that experiment of Adam's*
> *with ways out but no way in—*
> *the ritual of marriage . . .*

Do they know that Marianne Moore was a feminist in her day? Or that she paraded with the suffragettes, led by Inez Milholland on her white horse, down Fifth Avenue? Once, Marianne told me, she "climbed a lamppost" in a demonstration for votes for women. What she did up there, what speech she delivered, if any, I don't know, but climb she did in long skirt and petticoats and a large hat. Perhaps it was pride or vanity that kept her from complaints, and that put her sense of injustice through the prisms dissected by "those various scalpels" into poetry. She was not too proud for occasional complaints; she was humorously angry, but nevertheless angry, when her publisher twice postponed her book in order to bring out two young male poets, both now almost unheard of. Now that everything can be said, and done, have we anyone who can compare with Marianne Moore, who was at her best when she made up her own rules and when they were strictest—the reverse of "freedom"?

Soon after I met Marianne in 1934—although I concealed it for what seemed to me quite a long time—somehow or other it came out that I was trying to write poetry. For five or six years I occasionally sent her my poems. She would rarely say or write very much about them except that she liked such and such a phrase or, oddly, the alliteration, which I thought I tended to overdo. When I asked her what the poems she had written at Bryn Mawr were like, she said, "*Just* like Swinburne, Elizabeth." Sometimes she suggested that I change a word or line, and sometimes I accepted her suggestions, but never did she even hint that such and such a line might have been influenced by or even unconsciously stolen from a poem of her own, as later on I could sometimes see that they were. Her notes to me were often signed "Your Dorothy Dix."

It was because of Marianne that in 1935 my poems first appeared in a book, an anthology called *Trial Balances*. Each of the poets in this anthology had an older mentor, who wrote a short preface or introduction to the poems, and Marianne, hearing of this project, had offered to be mine. I was much too shy to dream of asking her. I had two or three feeble pastiches of late seventeenth-century poetry called "Valentines," in one of which I had rhymed "even the English sparrows in the dust" with "lust." She did not like those English sparrows very much, and said so ("Miss Bishop's sparrows are not revolting, merely disaffecting"), but her sponsorship brought about this first appearance in a book.

One long poem, the most ambitious I had up to then attempted, apparently stirred both her and her mother to an immediate flurry of criticism. She telephoned the day after I had mailed it to her, and said that she and her mother had sat up late rewriting it for me. (This is the poem in which the expression "water closet" was censored.) Their version of it arrived in the next mail. I had had an English teacher at Vassar whom I liked very much, named Miss Rose Peebles, and for some reason this name fascinated Marianne. The revised poem had been typed out on very thin paper and folded into a small square, sealed with a gold star sticker and signed on the outside "Lovingly, Rose Peebles." My version had rhymed throughout, in rather strict stanzas, but Marianne and her mother's version broke up the stanzas irregularly. Some lines rhymed and some didn't; a few other colloquialisms besides "water closet" had been removed and a Bible reference or two corrected. I obstinately held on to my stanzas and rhymes, but I did make use of a few of the proffered new words. I am sorry to say I can't now remember which they were, and won't know unless this fascinating communication should turn up again.

Marianne in 1940 gave me a copy of the newly published *Last Poems and Two Plays*, by William Butler Yeats, and though I dislike some of the emphasis on lechery in the poems, and so did she, I wrote her that I admired "The Circus Animals' Desertion" and the now famous lines "I must lie down where all the ladders start, / In the foul rag-and-bone shop of the heart." She replied:

> I would be "much disappointed in you" if you
> *could* feel about Yeats as some of his acolytes
> seem to feel. An "effect," an exhaustively great
> sensibility (with insensibility?) and genius for
> word-sounds and sentences. But after all, what is
> this enviable apparatus for? if not to change our
> mortal psycho-structure. It makes me think of

the Malay princes—the *horde* of eunuchs and entertainers and "bearers" of this and that; then suddenly the umbrella over the prince lowered, because a greater prince was passing. As you will suspect from my treachery to W. B. Yeats, I've been to a lecture on Java by Burton Holmes, and one on Malay . . .

One day she abruptly asked me, "Do you like the *nude*, Elizabeth?" I said yes I did on the whole. Marianne: "Well, so do I, Elizabeth, but *in moderation*," and she immediately pressed on me a copy of Sir Kenneth Clark's new book, *The Nude*, which had just been sent to her.

Some Expeditions

This was a story told me by Mrs. Moore, of an outing that had taken place the summer before I met them. There had been a dreadful heat wave, and Marianne had been feeling "over-burdened" (the word *burden* was an important one in the Brooklyn vocabulary) and "overtaxed." Her mother decided that Marianne "should take a course in the larger mammals" and said, "Marianne, I am going to take you to Coney Island to see Sheba," an unusually large and docile elephant then on view at a boardwalk sideshow. Coney Island is a long subway ride even from Brooklyn, but in spite of the heat and the crowds, the two ladies went. Sheba performed her acts majestically, and slowly played catch with her keeper with a shiny white ball. I asked about the elephant's appearance, and Marianne said, "She was very simply dressed. She was lightly powdered a matte rose all over, and wore ankle bracelets, large copper hollow balls, on her front legs. Her headdress consisted of three white ostrich plumes." Marianne was fond of roller coasters; a fearless rider, she preferred to sit in the front seat. Her mother told me how she waited below while the cars clicked agonizingly to the heights, and plunged horribly down. Marianne's long red braid had come undone and blew backwards, and with it went all her cherished amber-colored "real tortoiseshell" hairpins, which fortunately landed in the laps of two sailors in the car behind her. At the end of the ride, they handed them to her "very politely."

Two friends of Marianne's, two elderly Boston ladies, shared an exquisitely neat white clapboard house in northern Maine. I once spent a day there, and they teased Marianne about her habit of secreting food. She laughed, blushed, and tossed her head, and did not seem to mind when one of them told of going into Marianne's room for a book only to discover two boiled potatoes lying on the dresser. Some years later the older lady phoned Marianne from Boston and told her she was dying of cancer. She was perfectly stoical about it, and said she was in a hospital and knew she could not last very long. She asked Marianne to come and stay near her until she died, and Marianne went. At the hospital, she told Marianne that while she would be grateful to her if she came to see her every day, she knew that Marianne couldn't possibly spend all her time with her, so she had arranged for her to take driving lessons. Marianne, who must have been nearly seventy at the time, agreed that this was a good idea; she had always wanted to learn to drive, and she did, with a lesson at the driving school every day and a visit to the hospital. A day or so after her friend died, Marianne passed her driving test. She said she had a little trouble with the lights in Copley Square and confessed she thought the "policeman" giving her the test had been a little overlenient. I said I hoped she hadn't driven too fast, and she replied, "A steady forty-five, Elizabeth!" On her return she proudly showed her driving license to her brother, Warner, and he, sounding no doubt very much as her mother used to sound, said, "There must be some mistake. This must be sent back *immediately*."

Marianne was intensely interested in the techniques of things —how camellias are grown; how the quartz prisms work in crystal clocks; how the pangolin can close up his ear, nose, and eye apertures and walk on the outside edges of his hands "and save the claws / for digging"; how to drive a car; how the best pitchers throw a baseball; how to make a figurehead for her nephew's sailboat. The exact way in which anything was done, or made, or functioned, was poetry to her.

She even learned to tango. Before she acquired a television set of her own, she was in the habit of going down to the basement apartment at 260 Cumberland Street to watch the baseball games with the janitor and his wife, who had a set. During one of the games there was a commercial that advertised a Brooklyn dancing school. Any viewer who telephoned in was guaranteed a private tango lesson at a Brooklyn academy. Marianne announced that she had always liked the tango, and hurried to the fourth floor to put in her call, and got an appointment. The young dancers, male and female, may have been a little surprised, but soon they were competing with each other to dance with her. She was given a whole short course of lessons. I asked about the tango itself, and she allowed that they had felt perhaps it was a little too strenuous and had taught her a "modified" version of it. She had also learned several other steps and dances in more current use, and insisted everyone had enjoyed himself and herself thoroughly.

In the late winter or early spring of 1963, when I was in New York, one evening around eight I emerged from a Lexington Avenue subway station on my way to a poetry reading at the YMHA. Suddenly I realized that Marianne was walking ahead of me over half a block away, alone, hurrying along with a bag of books and papers. She reached the YMHA before I did, but she was not present at the function I was attending; I wondered what she could be up to. Later she informed me that she was attending the YMHA Poetry Workshop, conducted that term by Louise Bogan. She said she was learning a great deal, things she had never known before; Miss Bogan was another of the people she considered "erudite." Shortly afterwards I met Miss Bogan at a party and asked her about the workshop and her famous student. Poor Miss Bogan! I am sure Marianne never dreamed what suffering she was causing her. It seemed that Marianne took notes constantly, asked many questions, and entered into discussions with enthusiasm. But the other students were timid and often nonplused, and so was Miss Bogan, besides feeling that she was sailing under false colors and never knowing what technical question she might be expected to answer next.

I attended very few literary events at which Marianne was present, but I did go with her to the party for Edith and Osbert Sitwell given at the Gotham Book Mart. I hadn't intended to go to this at all; in fact, I really didn't want to, but Marianne, who was something of an Anglophile, was firm. "We must be *polite* to the Sitwells," she said.

The party was given by *Life* magazine and was rather awful. The photographers behaved as photographers do: strewing wires under our feet, calling to each other over our heads, and generally pushing us around. It took some time to separate the poets, who were the subjects of the picture, from the non-poets, and this was done in a way that made me think of livestock being herded into cattle cars. Non-poets and some real poets felt insulted; then the photographer announced that Miss Moore's hat was "too big." She refused to remove it. Auden was one of the few who seemed to be enjoying himself. He got into the picture by climbing on a ladder, where he sat making loud, cheerful comments over our heads. Finally the picture was taken with a sort of semicircular swoop of the camera. Marianne consented to let a friend and me take her to dinner and afterwards back to Brooklyn in a cab. I had on a small velvet cap and Marianne said, "I wish I had worn a *minimal* hat, like yours." The taxi fare to Brooklyn at that time was something over five dollars, not counting the tip. That evening my friend was paying for dinner and the cab. Between comments on the Sitwell party, Marianne exclaimed at intervals, "Mr. W——, this is *highway robbery!*"

She told me about another, more elegant literary party she had been to in a "penthouse," to celebrate the publication of a deluxe edition of a book, I think by Wallace Stevens. The chairs were upholstered in "lemon-colored velvet," there was a Matisse drawing she didn't altogether like, and she had taken a glass of champagne and regretted it all evening; it had made her face burn. I asked for further details. She became scornful: "Well, we signed our names several times, and after *that* thrill was over, I came home."

Sometimes we went to movies together, to *Kon-Tiki* twice, I recall. I never attempted to lure her to any dramatic or "artistic" films. Since Dr. and Mrs. Sibley Watson were her dearest friends, she must have seen his early experimental films, such as *Lot in Sodom*. I heard the sad story of two young men, however, who when they discovered that she had never seen Eisenstein's *Potemkin* insisted on taking her. There was a short before *Potemkin*, a Walt Disney film; this was when the Disney films still had charm and humor. After the movies they went to tea and Marianne talked at length and in detail about the ingenuity of the Disney film, and nothing more. Finally they asked her what she had thought of *Potemkin*. Her opinion was brief but conclusive: "Life," she said, "is not like that."

Twice we went together to the Saturday-morning lectures for

children at the Museum of Natural History—once, to see Meshie, the three-year-old chimpanzee, who came onstage pedaling her tricycle and offered us bites of her banana. And once to see a young couple I had known in Mexico show their collection of pets, including Aguilla, the bald-headed American eagle they had trained to hunt like a falcon, who had ridden all the way to Mexico and back perched on a broomstick in their car. There were more lovable pets as well: Marianne held the kinkajou in her arms, an affectionate animal that clutched on to one tightly with his tail. In a homemade movie the couple also showed us, the young man himself was shown in his library taking a book from the shelf. As he did so, he unselfconsciously blew the dust off the top of its pages. Marianne gave one of her laughs. She loved that; it was an example of the "spontaneity" that she admired as much as she admired "gusto."

The next-to-last outing I went on with Marianne was in the summer of 1968. This was long after her mother's death, when she had moved from Brooklyn and was living at 35 West Ninth Street in Manhattan. I was staying nearby in the Village, and one day she telephoned and asked me if I would come over and walk with her to the election polls; she wanted to vote. It was the first time, I think, she had ever actually asked me for assistance. It was a very hot day. She was ready and waiting, with her hat on. It was the usual shape, of navy-blue straw, and she wore a blue-and-white-checked seersucker suit and blue sneakers. She had become a bit unsteady and was supposed to use a cane, which was leaning against the door frame. She hated it, and I don't think I ever saw her use it. The voting booths were quite near, in the basement of a public school off Sixth Avenue; there were a good many people there, sitting around, mostly women, talking. Marianne made quite a stir; they seemed to know who she was and came up to talk to her and to ask me about her while she voted. They were Greenwich Village mothers, with intellectual or bluestocking types among them. I thought to myself that Marianne's was probably the only Republican vote cast there that day.

It was the originality and freshness of Marianne's diction, in the most casual conversation, as well as her polysyllabic virtuosity, that impressed many people. She once said of a well-known poet, "That man is freckled like a trout with impropriety." A friend has told me of attending a party for writers and artists at which she introduced a painter to Marianne by saying, "Miss Moore has the most interesting vocabulary of anyone I know." Marianne showed signs of pleasure at this, and within a minute offhandedly but accurately used in a sentence a word I no longer remember that means an addiction, in animals, to licking the luminous numbers off the dials of clocks and watches. At the same party this friend introduced the then comparatively young art critic Clement Greenberg; to her surprise and no doubt to Mr. Greenberg's, Marianne seemed to be familiar with his writing and said, on shaking hands, "Oh, the *fearless* Mr. Greenberg."

There was something about her good friend T. S. Eliot that seemed to amuse Marianne. On Eliot's first visit to Brooklyn after his marriage to Valerie, his young wife asked them to pose together for her for a snapshot. Valerie said, "Tom, put your arm around Marianne." I asked if he had. Marianne gave that short deprecatory laugh and said, "Yes, he did, but very *gingerly*." Toward the last, Marianne entrusted her Eliot letters for safekeeping with Robert Giroux, who told me that with each letter of the poet's she had preserved the envelope in which it had come. One envelope bore Marianne's Brooklyn address in Eliot's handwriting, but no return address or other identification. Within, there was a sheet of yellow pad paper on which was drawn a large heart pierced by an arrow, with the words "from an anonymous and grateful admirer."

Last Years

The dictionary defines a memoir as "a record of events based on the writer's personal experience or knowledge." Almost everything I have recorded was observed or heard firsthand, mostly before 1951–1952, the year—as Randall Jarrell put it—when "she won the Triple Crown" (National Book Award, Bollingen and Pulitzer Prizes) and became really famous. She was now Marianne Moore, the beloved "character" of Brooklyn and Manhattan; the baseball fan; the friend of many showier celebrities; the faithful admirer of Presidents Hoover and Eisenhower and Mayor Lindsay; the recipient of sixteen honorary degrees (she once modeled her favorite academic hoods for me); the reader of poetry all over the country, in settings very unlike the Brooklyn auditorium where in the thirties I heard her read with William Carlos Williams. She enjoyed every bit of the attention she received, although it too could be a "burden." After those long years of modest living and incredibly hard work, she had—until the helplessness at the very last—thank heavens, an unusually fortunate old age.

She once remarked, after a visit to her brother and his family, that the state of being married and having children had one enormous advantage: "One never has to worry about whether one is doing the right thing or not. There isn't time. One is always having to go to market or drive the children somewhere. There isn't time to wonder, 'Is this *right* or isn't it?' "

Of course she did wonder, and constantly. But, as in the notes to her poems, Marianne never gave away the whole show. The volubility, the wit, the self-deprecating laugh, never really clarified those quick decisions of hers—or decisive intuitions, rather

—as to good and bad, right and wrong; and her meticulous system of ethics could be baffling. One of the very few occasions on which we came close to having a falling out was when, in the forties, I told her I had been seeing a psychoanalyst. She disapproved quite violently and said that psychoanalysts taught that "Evil is not *evil*. But we know it *is*." I hadn't noticed that my analyst, a doctor of almost saintly character, did this, but I didn't attempt to refute it, and we didn't speak of it again. We never talked about Presbyterianism, or religion in general, nor did I ever dare more than tease her a little when she occasionally said she believed there was something *in* astrology.

Ninety years or so ago, Gerard Manley Hopkins wrote a letter to Robert Bridges about the ideal of the "gentleman," or the "artist" versus the "gentleman." Today his ideas may sound impossibly Victorian, but I find this letter still applicable and very moving: "As a fact poets and men of art are, I am sorry to say, by no means necessarily or commonly gentlemen. For gentlemen do not pander to lust or other basenesses nor . . . give themselves airs and affectations, nor do other things to be found in modern works . . . If an artist or thinker feels that were he to become in those ways ever so great, he would still be essentially lower than a gentleman that was no artist and no thinker. And yet to be a gentleman is but on the brim of morals and rather a thing of manners than morals properly. Then how much more must art and philosophy and manners and breeding and everything else in the world be below the least degree of true virtue. This is that chastity of mind which seems to lie at the very heart and be the parent of all good, the seeing at once what is best, and holding to that, and not allowing anything else whatever to be even heard pleading to the contrary . . . I agree then, and vehemently, that a gentleman . . . is in the position to despise the poet, were he Dante or Shakespeare, and the painter, were he Angelo or Apelles, for anything that showed him *not* to be a gentleman. He is in a position to do it, but if he is a gentleman perhaps this is what he will not do." The word "gentleman" makes us uncomfortable now, and its feminine counterparts, whether "lady" or "gentlewoman," embarrass us even more. But I am sure that Marianne would have "vehemently agreed" with Hopkins's strictures: to be a poet was not the be-all, end-all of existence.

I find it impossible to draw conclusions or even to summarize. When I try to, I become foolishly bemused: I have a sort of subliminal glimpse of the capital letter *M* multiplying. I am turning the pages of an illuminated manuscript and seeing that initial letter again and again: Marianne's monogram; mother; manners; morals; and I catch myself murmuring, "Manners and morals; manners *as* morals? Or it is morals *as* manners?" Since like Alice, "in a dreamy sort of way," I can't answer either question, it doesn't much matter which way I put it; it *seems* to be making sense.

c. 1969

STORIES

The Baptism

It was November. They bent in the twilight like sea plants, around their little dark center table hung with a cloth like a seaweed-covered rock. It seemed as if a draft might sway them all, perceptibly. Lucy, the youngest, who still did things for her sisters, rose to get the shawls and light the lamp. She sighed. How would they get through the winter?

"We have our friends!"

Yes, that was true and a consolation. They had several friends. They had old Mrs. Peppard and young Mrs. Gillespie and old Mrs. Captain Green and little Mrs. Kent. One of them was bound to drop in almost every afternoon.

When the weather was fine they themselves could make a call, although they preferred to stay at home. They were more in command of conversation when they sat close together around their own table. Antiphonally, they spoke to their friends of the snowstorm, of health, of church activities. They had the church, of course.

When the snow grew too deep—it grew all winter, as the grain grew all summer, and finally wilted away unharvested in April—old Mr. Johnson, who had the post office now, would bring the newspaper on his way home.

They would manage, but winter was longer every year. Lucy thought of carrying wood in from the woodshed and scratching her forearms on the bark. Emma thought of hanging out the washing, which was frozen before you got it onto the line. The sheets particularly—it was like fighting with monster icy seagulls. Flora thought only of the difficulties of getting up and dressing at six o'clock every morning.

They would keep two stoves going: the kitchen range and an airtight in the sitting room. The circulatory system of their small house was this: in the ceiling over the kitchen stove there was an opening set with a metal grill. It yielded up some heat to the room where Lucy and Emma slept. The pipe from the sitting-room stove went up through Flora's room, but it wasn't so warm, of course.

They baked bread once a week. In the other bedroom there were ropes and ropes of dried apples. They ate applesauce and apple pie and apple dumpling, and a kind of cake paved with slices of apple. At every meal they drank a great deal of tea and ate many slices of bread. Sometimes they bought half a pound of store cheese, sometimes a piece of pork.

Emma knitted shawls, washcloths, bed socks, an affectionate spiderweb around Flora and Lucy. Flora did fancy work and made enough Christmas presents for them to give all around: to each other and to friends. Lucy was of no use at all with her fingers. She was supposed to read aloud while the others worked.

They had gone through a lot of old travel books that had belonged to their father. One was called *Wonders of the World*; one was a book about Palestine and Jerusalem. Although they could all sit calmly while Lucy read about the tree that gave milk like a cow, the Eskimos who lived in the dark, the automaton chess player, etc., Lucy grew excited over accounts of the Sea of Galilee, and the engraving of the Garden of Gethsemane

as it looks today brought tears to her eyes. She exclaimed "Oh
dear!" over pictures of "An Olive Grove," with Arabs squatting
about in it; and "Heavens!" at the real, rock-vaulted Stable,
the engraved rocks like big black thumbprints.

They had also read: (1) *David Copperfield*, twice; (2) *The
Deer-Slayer*; (3) *Samantha at the World's Fair*; (4) *The Auto-
crat of the Breakfast Table.*

Also two or three books from the Sunday School library,
which none of them liked. Because of the source, however, they
listened as politely as to the minister's sermons. Lucy's voice
even took on a little of his intonation, so that it seemed to take
forever to get through them.

They were Presbyterians. The village was divided into two
camps, armed with Bibles: Baptists and Presbyterians. The
sisters had friends on both sides.

Prayer meeting was Friday night. There was Sunday School
and church on Sunday, and Ladies' Aid every other week at
different friends' houses. Emma taught the smallest children in
Sunday School. Lucy and Flora preferred not to teach, but to
attend the class for adults held by the minister himself.

Now each was arranging the shawl over her shoulders, and
just as Lucy lit the lamp, old Mrs. Peppard came to call. She
opened the back door without knocking, and said, "Anybody
home?" This was the thing to do. She wore a very old mud-
brown coat with large black frogs down the front and a black,
cloth-covered hat with a velvet flower on it.

Her news was that her sister's baby had died the day before,
although they had done everything. She and Emma, Flora, and
Lucy discussed infant damnation at some length.

Then they discussed the care of begonias, and Mrs. Peppard
took home a slip of theirs. Flora had always had great luck with
house plants.

Lucy grew quite agitated after Mrs. Peppard had gone, and could not eat her bread and butter, only drank three cups of tea.

Of course, as Emma had expected because of the tea, Lucy couldn't sleep that night. Once she nudged Emma and woke her.

"Emma, I'm thinking of that poor child."

"Stop thinking. Go to sleep."

"Don't you think we ought to pray for it?"

It was the middle of the night or she couldn't have said that. Emma pretended to be asleep. In fact, she was asleep, but not so much that she couldn't feel Lucy getting out of bed. The next day she mentioned this to Flora, who only said "Tsch—Tsch." Later on they both referred to this as the "beginning," and Emma was sorry she'd gone back to sleep.

In prayer meeting one Friday the minister called for new members, and asked some of those who had joined the church lately to speak. Art Tinkham stood up. He talked for a long time of God's goodness to him, and said that now he felt happy all the time. He had felt so happy when he was doing his fall plowing that he had kept singing, and at the end of every furrow he'd said a Bible verse.

After a while the minister called on Lucy to give a prayer. She did it, quite a long one, but at last her voice began to tremble. She could scarcely say the Amen, and sat down very quickly. Afterwards her sisters said it had been a very pretty prayer, but she couldn't remember a word of it.

Emma and Lucy liked the dreamy hymns best, with vague references in them to gardens, glassy seas, high hills, etc. Flora liked militant hymns; almost her favorite was "A Mighty Fortress."

Lucy's was: "Sometimes a light surprises the Christian while he sings." Emma's: "There is a green hill far away without a city wall."

Lucy was not yet a church member. Emma and Flora were, but Lucy had been too young to join when they had. She sometimes asked her sisters if she were good enough.

"You are too good for us, Lucy."

"That's not what I mean," Lucy said.

At night she felt that Emma's prayers were over all too quickly. Her own sometimes lasted almost an hour, and even then did not seem quite long enough. She felt very guilty about something. She worried about this so much that one day she almost convinced Flora that she must have been guilty of the gravest misdemeanor as a young girl. But it was not so.

It got to be Christmastime. The snow was up to the window-sills, practically over, as if they inhabited a sinking ship. Lucy's feeling of guilt grew heavier and heavier. She talked constantly about whether she should join the church or not.

At Christmas an elderly missionary, Miss Gillespie, young Mr. Gillespie's aunt, came home from India on furlough. The Ladies' Aid had special meetings for her. At them this tall, dark brown, mustached woman of sixty-four talked, almost shouted, for hours about her lifework. Photographs were handed around. They represented gentle-faced boys and young men, dressed in pure-white loincloths and earrings. Next, the same boys and young men were shown, in soiled striped trousers and shirts worn with the tails outside. There were a few photographs of women, blurred as they raised a hand to hide their faces, or backed away from the camera's Christian eye.

Emma and Flora disliked Miss Gillespie. Flora even said she was "bossy." But Lucy liked her very much and went to see her several times. Then for three weeks she talked about nothing but going as a missionary. She went through all the travel books again.

Flora and Emma did not really think she would ever go, but the thought of living without her sometimes horrified one or the other of them. At the end of the third week she stopped speaking of it and, in fact, became very untalkative.

Lucy was growing thinner. The skin of her forehead seemed stretched too tightly, and although she had never had a temper in her life, Flora and Emma could see that it was sometimes an effort for her not to speak crossly to them.

She moved very slowly. At supper she would eat half a slice of bread and put the other half back in the bread dish.

Flora, who was bolder to say things than Emma, said: "She makes me feel that I'm not as good as she is."

Once when Lucy went out to get wood from the woodshed she didn't come back for fifteen minutes. Emma, suddenly realizing how long it had been, ran outside. Lucy, with no coat or shawl, stood holding on to the side of the house. She was staring at the blinding dazzle the sun made on the ice glaze over the next field. She seemed to be humming a little, and the glaring strip made her half shut her eyes. Emma had to take hold of her hand before she would pay any attention. Speaking wasn't enough.

It was the night of the day after this that the strange things began to happen.

Lucy kept a diary. It was written in pencil in a book that said "Jumbo Scribbler" in red letters on a tan cover. It was really a record of spiritual progress.

"*January 3rd.* This morning was clear again so Flora did some of the wash and we hung it in the garden, although it was hard to with the wind. For dinner we had a nice stew with the rest of the lamb and the carrots Mr. Jonson brought in. I say a nice stew, but I could not touch a bite. The Lord seems very far away. I kept asking the girls about my joining but they did not help me at all."

Here Lucy copied out three Bible verses. Sometimes for several days the diary was made up of nothing but such quotations.

"*January 16th.* It was 18 below zero last night. We had to get Father's old buffalo robe from the spare room. I didn't like the smell, but Emma didn't mind it. When the lamp was out I prayed for a long time, and a little while after I got into bed I felt that face moving toward me again. I can't make it out, but it is very large and close to mine. It seemed to be moving its lips. Is it reproachful?"

Four days after this Lucy began crying in the afternoon and cried almost all evening. Emma finally cried a little, too. Flora shook her by the shoulder, but left Lucy alone.

Emma wished that she and Flora slept together instead of she and Lucy, so that they could talk about Lucy together privately.

Flora said: "What has she ever done wrong, Emma? Why should she weep about her soul?"

Emma said: "She's always been as good as gold."

"*January 20th.* At last, at last, I know my own mind," she began, "or rather I have given it up completely. Now I am going to join the church as soon as I can. But I am going to join the *Baptist* church, and I must not tell Flora and Emma beforehand. I cannot eat, I am so happy. Last night at four o'clock a terrible wind began to blow. I thought all the trees were breaking, I could hear the branches crashing against the house. I thought the chimney would come down. The house shook, and I thought about the House founded on the Rock. I was terribly frightened. Emma did not wake up. It went on for hours in the dark and I prayed that we would all be safely delivered. Then there was a lull. It was very black and my heart pounded so I thought I was dying. I couldn't think of a prayer. Then suddenly a low voice began to talk right over the head of the bed. I couldn't make out the words, they weren't exactly words I knew, but I seemed to understand them. What a load dropped from my mind! Then I was so happy I woke Emma and said: 'Emma,

Emma, Christ is here. He was here just now, in this room. Get up and pray with me.' Emma got out of bed and knelt, then she said the floor was cold and wanted to pull the rug over under our knees. I said: 'No, Emma. Why do we need rugs when we have all Christ's love to warm our hearts?' She did not demur after that, and I prayed a long time, for Flora, too. When we got back in bed I told Emma about the voice I had heard."

The next day Lucy called on the Baptist minister and told him she had decided to join his church. He was very severe, older than the Presbyterian minister, and Lucy felt at once that he was a much better man.

But a problem came up that she had not considered. She now believed ardently in the use of total immersion as practiced by the Baptists, according to their conception of the methods of John the Baptist. She could not join without that, and the river, of course, was frozen over. She would have to wait until the ice went out.

She could scarcely bear it. In her eagerness to be baptized and her disappointment she forgot she had intended not to tell her sisters of her change of faith. They did not seem to mind so much, but when she asked them, they would not consider changing with her.

She was so overexcited they made her go to bed at five o'clock. Emma wrapped up a hot stove lid to put at her feet.

"*January 25th.* I felt very badly last night and cried a great deal. I thought how Mother always used to give me the best of everything because I was the smallest and I took it not thinking of my sisters. Emma said, 'For mercy's sake, Lucy, stop crying.' I explained to her and she became much softened. She got up and lit the lamp. The lamplight on her face made me cry afresh. She went and woke Flora, who put on her gray wrapper and sat in the rocking chair. She wanted to make me something, but I said No. The lamp began to smoke. The smoke went right up to the ceiling and smelled very strong and sweet, like rose geranium. I began to laugh and cry at the same time. Flora and Emma were talking together, but other people seemed to be talking too, and the voice at the head of the bed."

A few days later Lucy became very sad. She could neither pray nor do anything around the house. She sat by the window all day long.

In the afternoon she pointed at the road which went off toward the mountains between rows of trees, and said: "Flora, what does it matter where the road goes?"

Emma and Flora were taking apart Emma's blue silk dress and making a blouse. A moth crawled on the windowpane. Emma said, "Get the swatter, Lucy."

Lucy got up, then sat down and said again: "What does it matter?"

She got out the scribbler and wrote in it from memory all the stanzas of "Return, O heavenly Dove, return."

After supper, she seemed more cheerful. They were sitting in the kitchen evenings now, because it was warmer. There was no light but one lamp, so the room was quite dark, making the red circle around the stove lids show.

Lucy suddenly stood up.

"Emma, Emma, Flora. I see God."

She motioned toward the stove.

God, God sat on the kitchen stove and glowed, burned, filling all the kitchen with a delicious heat and a scent of grease and sweetness.

Lucy was more conscious of his body than his face. His beautiful glowing bulk was rayed like a sunflower. It lit up Flora's and Emma's faces on either side of the stove. The stove could not burn him.

"His feet are in hell," she remarked to her sisters.

After that, Lucy was happy for a long time and everything

seemed almost the way it had been the winter before, except for Lucy going to the Baptist church and prayer meeting by herself.

She spoke often of joining. It had happened once or twice that when people had wanted to join the church in the winter a hole had been broken in the ice to make a font. Lucy begged the minister that this might be done for her, but he felt that it was unnecessary in her case.

One had been a farmer, converted from drinking and abusing his wife. He had chopped the ice open himself. Another had been a young man, also a reformed drunkard, since dead.

Flora said: "Oh, Lucy, wait till the ice goes out."

"Yes," Lucy said in bitterness, "and until my soul is eternally lost."

She prayed for an early spring.

On the nineteenth of March, Flora woke up and heard the annually familiar sound, a dim roaring edged with noises of breaking glass.

"Thank goodness," she thought. "Now, maybe, Lucy won't even want to be baptized."

Everyone had heard the cracking start, off in the hills, and was at the bridge. Lucy, Emma, and Flora went too. The ice buckled up in shining walls fifteen or twenty feet high, fit for heavenly palaces, then moved slowly downstream.

Once in a while a space of dark brown water appeared. This upset Lucy, who had thought of the water she would be baptized in as crystal-clear, or pale blue.

The baptism took place on the twenty-fourth. It was like all the others, and the village was even used to such early ones, although they were usually those of fervent young men.

A few buggies were on the bank, those of the choir, who stood around in coats and hats, holding one hymnbook among three or four people. Most of the witnesses stood on the bridge, staring

[handwritten marginalia:] Morgesons. alcoholism anorexia- addiction to abstinence

down. One boy or young man, of course, always dared to spit over the railing.

The water was muddy, very high, with spots of yellow foam. The sky was solid gray cloud, finely folded, over and over. Flora saw the icy roots of a tree reaching into the river, and the snowbanks yellow like the foam.

The minister's robe, which he wore only on such occasions, billowed until the water pulled it all down. He held a clean, folded handkerchief to put over Lucy's mouth at the right minute. She wore a robe, too, that made her look taller and thinner.

The choir sang "I am coming, Lord, coming now to Thee," which they always dragged, and "Shall we gather at the river where bright angel feet have trod?" After the baptism they were to sing something joyful and faster, but the sisters did not remain to hear it.

Lucy went under without a movement, and Flora and Emma thought she'd never come up.

Flora held Emma's heavy coat all ready to put around her. Rather unconventionally, Emma sat in the buggy, borrowed from Mrs. Captain Green, so as to drive off home as soon as Lucy reached the bank. She held the reins and had to keep herself from taking up the whip in her other hand.

Finally it was over. They put the dripping Lucy in the middle. Her hair had fallen down. Thank goodness they didn't live far from the river!

The next day she had a bad head cold. Emma and Flora nursed her for a week and then the cold settled in her chest. She wouldn't take to bed. The most they could get her to do was to lie on the couch in the kitchen.

One afternoon they thought she had a high fever. Late in the day, God came again, into the kitchen. Lucy went toward the stove, screaming.

Emma and Flora pulled her back, but not before she had burned her right hand badly.

That night they got the doctor, but the next night Lucy died, calling their names as she did so.

The day she was buried was the first pleasant day in April, and the village turned out very well, in spite of the fact that the roads were deep with mud. Jed Leighton gave a beautiful plant he had had sent from the city, a mass of white blooms. Everyone else had cut all their geraniums, red, white, and pink.

1937

The Sea & Its Shore

⁂

Once, on one of our large public beaches, a man was appointed to keep the sand free from papers. For this purpose he was given a stick, or staff, with a long, polished wire nail set in the end.

Since he worked only at night, when the beach was deserted, he was also given a lantern to carry.

The rest of his equipment consisted of a big wire basket to burn the papers in, a box of matches for setting fire to them, and a house.

This house was very interesting. It was of wood, with a pitched roof, about four by four by six feet, set on pegs stuck in the sand. There was no window, no door set in the door frame, and nothing at all inside. There was not even a broom, so that occasionally our friend would get down on his knees and with his hands brush out the sand he had tracked in.

When the wind along the beach became too strong or too cold, or when he was tired, or when he wanted to read, he sat in the house. He either let his legs hang over the doorsill, or doubled them up under him inside.

As a house, it was more like an idea of a house than a real one. It could have stood at either end of a scale of ideas of houses. It could have been a child's perfect playhouse, or an adult's ideal house—since everything that makes most houses nuisances had been done away with.

It was a shelter, but not for living in, for thinking in. It was, to the ordinary house, what the ceremonial thinking cap is to the ordinary hat.

Of course, according to the laws of nature, a beach should be able to keep itself clean, as cats do. We have all observed:

> *The moving waters at their priest-like task*
> *Of pure ablution round earth's human shore.*

But the tempo of modern life is too rapid. Our presses turn out too much paper covered with print, which somehow makes its way to our seas and their shores, for nature to take care of herself.

So Mr. Boomer, Edwin Boomer, might almost have been said to have joined the "priesthood."

Every night he walked back and forth for a distance of over a mile, in the dark, with his lantern and his stick, and a potato sack on his back to put the papers in—a picturesque sight, in some ways like a Rembrandt.

Edwin Boomer lived the most literary life possible. No poet, novelist, or critic, even one who bends over his desk for eight hours a day, could imagine the intensity of his concentration on the life of letters.

His head, in the small cloud of light made by his lantern, was constantly bent forward, while his eyes searched the sand, or studied the pages and fragments of paper that he found.

He read constantly. His shoulders were rounded, and he had been forced to start wearing glasses shortly after undertaking his duties.

Papers that did not look interesting at first glance he threw into his bag; those he wanted to study he stuffed into his pockets. Later he smoothed them out on the floor of the house.

Because of such necessity for discrimination, he had grown to be an excellent judge.

Sometimes he transfixed one worthless or unprinted paper after another on the nail, until it was full from what might be called the hilt to the point. Then it resembled one of those pieces of office equipment that used to be seen on the desks of careless businessmen and doctors. Sometimes he would put a match to this file of papers and walk along with it upraised like a torch, as if they were his paid bills, or like one of those fiery meat dishes called kebabs, served in Russian or Syrian restaurants.

Besides reading and such possibilities of fitful illumination, papers, particularly newspapers, had other uses. He could put them under his coat in the winter, to help keep out the cold wind from the sea. In the same season he could spread several layers of them over the floor of the house, for the same reason. Somewhere in his extensive reading he had learned that the ink used in printing newspapers makes them valuable for destroying odors; but he could think of no use to himself in that.

He was acquainted with all qualities of paper in all stages of soddenness and dryness. Wet newspaper became only slightly translucent. It stuck to his foot or hand, and rather than tearing, it slowly separated in shreds in a way he found rather sickening.

If really sea-soaked, it could be made into balls or other shapes. Once or twice when drunk (Boomer usually came to work that way several times a week), he had attempted a little rough modeling. But as soon as the busts and animals he made had dried out, he burned them, too.

Newspaper turned yellow quickly, even after a day's exposure. Sometimes he found one of the day before yesterday that had been dropped carelessly, half folded, half crumpled. Holding it up to the lantern, he noticed, even before the wars and murders, effects of yellowed corners on white pages, and outer pages contrasting with inner ones. Very old papers became almost the color of the sand.

On nights that Boomer was most drunk, the sea was of gasoline, terribly dangerous. He glanced at it fearfully over his shoulder between every sentence he read, and built his fire far back on the beach. It was brilliant, oily, and explosive. He was foolish enough then to think that it might ignite and destroy his only means of making a living.

On windy nights it was harder to clean up the beach, and at such times Boomer was more like a hunter than a collector.

But the flight of the papers was an interesting thing to watch. He had made many careful comparisons between them and the birds that occasionally flew within range of the lantern.

A bird, of course, inspired by a brain, by long tradition, by a desire that could often be understood to reach some place or obtain some thing, flew in a line, or a series of curves that were part of a line. One could tell the difference between its methodical flights to obtain something and its flights for show.

But the papers had no discernible goal, no brain, no feeling of race or group. They soared up, fell down, could not decide, hesitated, subsided, flew straight to their doom in the sea, or turned over in mid-air to collapse on the sand without another motion.

If any manner was their favorite, it seemed to be an oblique one, slipping sidewise.

They made more subtle use of air currents and yielded to them more whimsically than the often pigheaded birds. They were not proud of their tricks, either, but seemed unconscious of the bravery, the ignorance they displayed, and of Boomer, waiting to catch them on the sharpened nail.

The fold in the middle of large news sheets acted as a kind of spine, but the wings were not coordinated. Tabloids flew slightly better than full-sized sheets. Small rumpled scraps were most fantastic.

Some nights the air seemed full of them. To Boomer's drunken vision the letters appeared to fly from the pages. He raised his lantern and staff and ran waving his arms, headlines and sentences streaming around him, like a man shooing a flock of pigeons.

When he pinned them through with the nail, he thought of the Ancient Mariner and the Albatross, for, of course, he had run across that threatening poem many times.

He accomplished most on windless nights, when he might have several hours of early morning left for himself. He arranged himself cross-legged in the house and hung the lantern on a nail he had driven at the right height. The splintery walls glistened and the tiny place became quite warm.

His studies could be divided into three groups, and he himself classified them mentally in this way.

First, and most numerous: everything that seemed to be about himself, his occupation in life, and any instructions or warnings that referred to it.

Second: the stories about other people that caught his fancy, whose careers he followed from day to day in newspapers and fragments of books and letters; and whose further adventures he was always watching out for.

Third: the items he could not understand at all, that bewildered him completely but at the same time interested him so much that he saved them to read. These he tried, almost frantically, to fit into first one, then the other, of the two categories.

We give a few examples from each of the groups.

From the first: "The Exercitant will benefit all the more, the more he secludes himself from all friends and acquaintances and from all earthly solicitude, for example by moving from the house in which he dwelt, and taking another house or room, that there he may abide in all possible privacy . . . [obliterated] he comes to use his natural faculties more freely in diligently searching for that he so much desires."

That certainly was plain enough.

This was the type of warning that worried him: "The habit of perusing periodical works may properly be added to Averrhoe's catalogue of ANTI-MNEMONICS, or weakeners of the memory. Also 'eating of unripe fruit; gazing on the clouds and on movable things suspended in the air (that would apply); riding among a multitude of camels; frequent laughter (no); listening to a series of jests and anecdotes; the habit of reading tombstones in churchyards, etc.' " (And these last might.)

From the second category: "She slept about two hours and returned to her place in the hole, carrying with her an American flag, which she placed beside her. Her husband has brought her meals out to her and she announced that she intends to sit in the hole until the Public Social Service Company abandons the idea of setting a pole there."

Boomer wondered about this lady for two nights. On the third he found this, which seemed, to his way of looking at things, to clarify the situation a little further. It was part of a page from a book, whereas the first item was a bit of newspaper.

"Her ladyship's assumption was that she kept, at every moment of her life, every advantage—it made her beautifully soft, very nearly generous; so she didn't distinguish the little protuberant eyes of smaller social insects, often endowed with such range, from . . ."

It might be two nights more, or two weeks, however, before he would find the next step in this particular sequence.

Among the third group, of things that fascinated but puzzled,

Boomer saved such odds and ends as this (a small, untorn strip of pink paper):

"JOKE SPECS WITH SHIFTING EYES. Put on the spectacles and place the mouthpiece in the mouth. Blow in air intermittently; the eyes and eyebrows will then be raised and lowered. The movement can be effected quickly or slowly according to what joke effect it is desired to obtain. If the earpieces are too short in case of a large head, bend the curved portion behind the ear. Celluloid is inflammable! Consequently, do not bring your spectacles near a naked flame!!"

This would seem properly to belong to the set of warnings referring to himself. But if he was able to heed the last warning, there was much in the earlier instructions that he could not understand.

And this, written in pencil on letter paper, blurred but readable:

"I wasn't feeling well over my teeth, and I had three large ones taken out, for they made me nervous and sick sometime, and this is the reason I couldn't send in my lesson although I am thinking of being able to write like all the Authors, for I believe that is more in my mind than any other kind of work, for I am concentrating on the lessons, frequently, many times.

"Mr. Margolies, I am thinking of how those Authors write such long stories of 60,000 or 100,000 words in those magazines, and where do they get their imagination and the material.

"I would be very pleased to write such stories as those Writers."

Although Boomer had no such childish desire, he felt that the question posed was one having something to do with his own way of life; it might almost be addressed to him as well as to the unknown Mr. Margolies. But what was the answer? The more papers he picked up and the more he read, the less he felt he understood. In a sense he depended on "their imagination," and was even its slave, but at the same time he thought of it as a kind of disease.

We shall give one more of our friend's self-riddles. It was this, in muddy type on very old, brown paper (he made no distinction between the bewilderments of prose and those of poetry):

> *Much as a one-eyed room, hung all with night,*
>   *Only that side, which adverse to the eye*
> *Gives but one narrow passage to the light,*
>   *Is spread with some white shining tapestry,*
> *An hundred shapes that through the flit airs stray,*
>   *Rush boldly in, crowding that narrow way;*
> *And on that bright-faced wall obscurely dancing play.*

That sounded like something he had experienced. First his house seemed to him to be the "one-eyed room, hung all with night," and then it was his whole life at night on the shore. First the papers blowing in the air, then what was printed on them, were the "hundred shapes."

Should we explain that by the time he was ready to start reading Boomer was usually not very drunk? The alcohol had worn off. He still felt isolated and self-important, but unnaturally wide awake.

But what did these things mean?

Either because of the insect armies of type so constantly besieging his eyes, or because it was really so, the world, the whole world he saw, came before many years to seem printed, too.

Boomer held up the lantern and watched a sandpiper rushing distractedly this way and that.

It looked, to his strained eyesight, like a point of punctuation against the "rounded, rolling waves." It left fine prints with its feet. Its feathers were speckled; and especially on the narrow hems of the wings appeared marks that looked as if they might be letters, if only he could get close enough to read them.

Sometimes the people who frequented the beach in the daytime, whom he never saw, felt inclined to write in the sand. Boomer, on his part, thought that erasing these writings was probably included in his duties, too. Lowering the lantern, he carefully scuffed out "Francis Xavier School," "Lillian," "What the Hell."

The sand itself, if he picked some of it up and held it close to one eye, looked a little like printed paper, ground up or chewed.

But the best part of the long studious nights was when he had cleared up the allotted area and was ready to set fire to the paper jammed in the wire basket.

His forehead already felt hot, from drink or from reading so much, but he stood as near as he could to the feverish heat of the burning paper, and noticed eagerly each detail of the incineration.

The flame walked up a stretch of paper evenly, not hurriedly, and after a second the black paper turned under or over. It fell twisting into shapes that sometimes resembled beautiful wrought-iron work, but afterwards they dropped apart at a breath.

Large flakes of blackened paper, still sparkling red at the edges, flew into the sky. While his eyes could follow them he had never seen such clever, quivering maneuvers.

Then there were left frail sheets of ashes, as white as the original paper, and soft to the touch, or a bundle of gray feathers like a guinea hen's.

But the point was that everything had to be burned at last. All, all had to be burned, even bewildering scraps that he had carried with him for weeks or months. Burning paper was his occupation, by which he made his living, but over and above that, he could not allow his pockets to become too full, or his house to become littered.

Although he enjoyed the fire, Edwin Boomer did not enjoy its inevitability. Let us leave him in his house, at four one morning, his reading selected, the conflagration all over, the lantern shining clearly. It is an extremely picturesque scene, in some ways like a Rembrandt, but in many ways not.

1937

In Prison

❧

I can scarcely wait for the day of my imprisonment. It is then that my life, my real life, will begin. As Nathaniel Hawthorne says in *The Intelligence-Office*, "I want my place, my own place, my true place in the world, my proper sphere, my thing which Nature intended me to perform . . . and which I have vainly sought all my life-time." But I am not that nostalgic about it, nor have I searched in vain "all my life-time." I have known for many years in what direction lie my talents and my "proper sphere," and I have always eagerly desired to enter it. Once that day has arrived and the formalities are over, I shall know exactly how to set about those duties "Nature intended me to perform."

The reader, or my friends, particularly those who happen to be familiar with my way of life, may protest that for me any actual imprisonment is unnecessary, since I already live, in relationship to society, very much as if I were in a prison. This I cannot deny, but I must simply point out the philosophic difference that exists between Choice and Necessity. I may live now as if I were in prison, or I might even go and take lodgings near, or in, a prison and follow the prison routine faithfully in every detail—and still I should be a "minister without portfolio." The hotel existence I now lead might be compared in many respects to prison life, I believe: there are the corridors, the cellular rooms, the large, unrelated group of people with the different purposes in being there that animate every one of them; but it still displays great differences. And of course in any hotel, even the barest, it is impossible to overlook the facts of "decoration," the Turkey carpets, brass fire extinguishers, transom hooks, etc.—it is ridiculous to try to imagine oneself in prison in such surroundings! For example: the room I now occupy is papered with a not unattractive wallpaper, the pattern of which consists of silver stripes about an inch and a half wide running up and down, the same distance from each other. They are placed over, that is, they appear to be inside of, a free design of flowering vines which runs all over the wall against a faded brown background. Now at night, when the lamp is turned on, these silver stripes catch the light and glisten and seem to stand out a little, or rather, in a little, from the vines and flowers, apparently shutting them off from me. I could almost imagine myself, if it would do any good, in a large silver bird cage! But that's a parody, a fantasy on my real hopes and ambitions.

One must be *in;* that is the primary condition. And yet I have known of isolated villages, or island towns, in our Southern states where the prisoners are not really imprisoned at all! They are dressed in a distinctive uniform, usually the familiar picturesque suit of horizontal black and white stripes with a rimless cap of the same material, and sometimes, but not always, a leg iron. Then they are deliberately set at large every morning to work at assigned tasks in the town, or to pick up such odd jobs for themselves as they can. I myself have seen them, pumping water, cleaning streets, even helping housewives wash the windows or shake the carpets. One of the most effective scenes that I have ever seen, for color contrast, was a group of these libertine convicts, in their black and white stripes, spraying, or otherwise tending to, a large clump of tropical shrubbery on the lawn of a public building. There were several varieties of bushes and plants in the arrangement, each of which had either brilliantly colored or conspicuously marked leaves. One bush, I remember, had long knife-like leaves, twisting as they grew into loose spirals, the upper surface of the leaf magenta, the under an ocher yellow. Another had large, flat, glossy leaves, dark green, on which were scrawled magnificent arabesques in lines of chalk-yellow. These designs, contrasting with the bold stripes of the prison uniform, made an extraordinary, if somewhat florid, picture.

But the prisoners, if such they could be called—there must have hung over their lives the perpetual irksomeness of all half-measures, of "not knowing where one is at." They had one rule: to report back to the jail, as "headquarters," at nine o'clock, in order to be locked up for the night; and I was given to understand that it was a fairly frequent occurrence for one or two, who arrived a few minutes too late, to be locked out for the night!—when they would sometimes return to their homes, if they came from the same district, or would drop down and sleep on the very steps of the jail they were supposed to be secured in. But this shortsighted and shiftless conception of the meaning of prison could never satisfy me; I could never consent to submit to such terms of imprisonment,—no, never!

Perhaps my ideas on the subject may appear too exacting. It may seem ridiculous to you for me to be laying down the terms of my own imprisonment in this manner. But let me say that I have given this subject most of my thought and attention for several years, and believe that I am speaking not entirely from selfish motives. Books about imprisonment I like perhaps the best of all literature, and I have read a great many; although of course one is often disappointed in them in spite of the subject matter. Take *The Enormous Room*. How I envied the author of that book! But there was something artificial about it, something that puzzled me considerably until I realized that it was due to the fact that the author had had an inner conviction of his eventual release all during the period of his imprisonment—a flaw, or rather an air bubble, that was bound by its own nature to reach the surface and break. The same reason may account for the perpetual presence of the sense of humor that angered me so much. I believe that I like humor as well as the next person, as they say, but it has always seemed a great pity to me that so many intelligent people now believe that everything that can happen to them must be funny. This belief first undermines conversation and letter writing and makes them monotonous, and then penetrates deeper, to corrupt our powers of observation and comprehension—or so I believe.

The Count of Monte Cristo I once enjoyed very much, although now I doubt that I should be able to read it through, with its exposure of "an injustice," its romantic tunnel digging, treasure hunting, etc. However, since I feel that I may well be very much in its debt, and I do not wish to omit or slight any influence, even a childish one, I set the title down here. *The Ballad of Reading Gaol* was another of the writings on this subject which I never could abide—it seemed to me to bring in material that, although perhaps of great human interest, had nothing whatever to do with the subject at hand. "That little tent of blue, / Which prisoners call the sky," strikes me as absolute nonsense. I believe that even a keyhole of sky would be enough, in its blind, blue endlessness, to give someone, even someone who had never seen it before, an adequate idea of the sky; and as for calling it the "sky"—we all call it the sky, do we not; I see nothing pathetic whatever about that, as I am evidently supposed to. Rather give me Dostoevsky's *House of the Dead,* or *Prison Life in Siberia.* Even if there seems to have been some ambiguity about the status of prisoners there, at least one is in the hands of an authority who realizes the limitations and possibilities of his subject. As for the frequently published best-sellers by warders, executioners, turnkeys, etc., I have never read any of them, being determined to uphold my own point of view, and not wanting to introduce any elements of self-consciousness into my future behavior that I could possibly avoid.

I should like a cell about twelve or fifteen feet long by six feet wide. The door would be at one end, the window, placed rather high, at the other, and the iron bed along the side—I see it on the left, but of course it could perfectly well be on the right. I might or might not have a small table, or shelf, let down by ropes from the wall just under the window, and by it a chair. I should like the ceiling to be fairly high. The walls I have in mind are interestingly stained, peeled, or otherwise disfigured; gray or whitewashed, bluish, yellowish, even green—but I only hope they are of no other color. The prospect of unpainted boards with their possibilities of various grains can sometimes please me, or stone in slabs or irregular shapes. I run the awful risk of a red brick cell; however, whitewashed or painted bricks might be quite agreeable, particularly if they had not been given a fresh coat for some time and here and there the paint had fallen off, revealing, in an irregular but beveled frame (made by previous coats), the regularity of the brickwork beneath.

About the view from the window: I once went to see a room in the Asylum of the Mausoleum where the painter V—— had been confined for a year, and what chiefly impressed me about this room, and gave rise to my own thoughts on the subject, was the view. My traveling companion and I reached the Asylum in the late afternoon and were admitted to the grounds by a nun, but a family, living in a small house of their own, seemed to be in charge. At our calls they rushed out, four of them, eating their dinner and talking to us at the same time with their mouths full. They stood in a row, and at the end of it their little black-and-white kitten was busy scratching in the dirt. It was "an animated scene." The daughter, age eight, and a younger brother, each carrying and eating half a long loaf of bread, were to show us around. We first went through several long, dark, cellar-like halls, painted yellow, with the low blue doors of the cells along one side. The floors were of stone; the paint was peeling everywhere, but the general effect was rather solemnly pretty. The room we had come to see was on the ground floor. It might have been very sad if it had not been for the two little children who rushed back and forth, chewing their bites of white bread and trying to outdo each other in telling us what everything was. But I am wandering from my subject, which was the view from the window of this room: It opened directly onto the kitchen garden of the institution and beyond it stretched the open fields. A row of cypresses stood at the right. It was rapidly growing dark (and even as we stood there it grew too dark to find our way out if it had not been for the children) but I can still see as clearly as in a photograph the beautiful completeness of the view from that window: the shaven fields, the black cypress, and the group of swallows posed dipping in the gray sky—only the fields have retained their faded color.

As a view it may well have been ideal, but one must take all sorts of things into consideration, and consoling and inspirational as that scene may have been, I do not feel that what is suited to an asylum is necessarily suited to a prison. That is, because I expect to go to prison in full possession of my "faculties"—in fact, it is not until I am securely installed there that I expect fully to realize them—I feel that something a little less rustic, a little harsher, might be of more use to me personally. But it is a difficult question, and one that is probably best decided, as of course it must be, by chance alone.

What I should like best of all, I might as well confess, would be a view of a courtyard paved with stone. I have a fondness for stone courtyards that amounts almost to a passion. If I were not to be imprisoned I should at least attempt to make that part of my dream a reality; I should want to live in a farmhouse such as I have seen in foreign countries, a farmhouse with an absolutely bare stone platform attached to it, the stones laid in a simple pattern of squares or diamonds. Another pattern I admire is interlocking cobblestone fans, with a border of larger stones set around the edge. But from my cell window I should prefer, say, a lozenge design, outlined by long stones, the interior of the lozenges made of cobbles, and the pattern narrowing away from my window toward the distant wall of the prison yard. The rest of my scenery would be the responsibility of the weather alone, although I should rather face the east than the west since I much prefer sunrises to sunsets. Then, too, it is by looking toward the east that one obtains the most theatrical effects from a sunset, in my opinion. I refer to that fifteen minutes or half an hour of heavy gold in which any object can be made to look magically significant. If the reader can tell me of anything more beautiful than a stone courtyard lit obliquely in this way so that the shallowly rounded stones each cast a small shadow but the general surface is thickly sanded with gold, and a pole casts a long, long shadow and a limp wire an unearthly one—I beg him to tell me what it is.

I understand that most prisons are now supplied with libraries and that the prisoners are expected to read the Everyman's Library and other books of educational tendencies. I hope I am not being too reactionary when I say that my one desire is to be given one very dull book to read, the duller the better. A book, moreover, on a subject completely foreign to me; perhaps the second volume, if the first would familiarize me too well with the terms and purpose of the work. Then I shall be able to experience with a free conscience the pleasure, perverse, I suppose, of interpreting it not at all according to its intent. Because I share with Valéry's M. Teste the "knowledge that our thoughts are reflected back to us, too much so, through expressions made by others"; and I have resigned myself, or do I speak too frankly, to deriving what information and joy I can from this—lamentable but irremediable—state of affairs. From my detached rock-like book I shall be able to draw vast generalizations, abstractions of the grandest, most illuminating sort, like allegories or poems, and by posing fragments of it against the surroundings and conversations of my prison, I shall be able to form my own examples of surrealist art!—something I should never know how to do outside, where the sources are so bewildering. Perhaps it will be a book on the cure of a disease, or an industrial technique—but no, even to try to imagine the subject would be to spoil the sensation of wave-like freshness I hope to receive when it is first placed in my hands.

Writing on the Wall: I have formulated very definite ideas on this important aspect of prison life, and have already composed sentences and paragraphs (which I cannot give here) I hope to be able to inscribe on the walls of my cell. First, however, even before looking into the book mentioned above, I shall read very carefully (or try to read, since they may be partly obliterated, or in a foreign language) the inscriptions already there. Then I shall adapt my own compositions, in order that they may not conflict with those written by the prisoner before me. The voice of a new inmate will be noticeable, but there will be no contradictions or criticisms of what has already been laid down, rather a "commentary." I have thought of attempting a short, but immortal, poem, but I am afraid that is beyond me; I may rise to the occasion, however, once I am confronted with that stained, smeared, scribbled-on wall and feel the stub of pencil or rusty nail between my fingers. Perhaps I shall arrange my "works" in a series of neat inscriptions in a clear, Roman print; perhaps I shall write them diagonally, across a corner, or at the base of a wall and half on the floor, in an almost illegible scrawl. They will be brief, suggestive, anguished, but full of the lights of revelation. And no small part of the joy these writings will give me will be to think of the person coming after me—the legacy of thoughts I shall leave him, like an old bundle tossed carelessly into a corner!

Once I dreamed that I was in Hell. It was a low, Netherlands-like country, all the marsh grass a crude artificial green, lit by brilliant but almost horizontal sunlight. I was dressed in an unbecoming costume of gray cotton: trousers of an awkward length and a shirt hanging outside them, and my hair cut close. I suffered constantly from extreme dizziness, because the horizon (and this was how I knew I was in Hell) was at an angle of forty-five degrees. Although this useless tale may not seem to have much connection with my theme, I include it simply to illustrate the manner in which I expect my vision of the outside world to be miraculously changed when I first hear my cell door locked behind me, and I step to the window to take my first look out.

I shall manage to look just a little different in my uniform from the rest of the prisoners. I shall leave the top button of the shirt undone, or roll the long sleeves halfway between wrist and elbow—something just a little casual, a little Byronic. On the other hand, if that is already the general tone in the prison, I shall affect a severe, mechanical neatness. My carriage and facial expression will be influenced by the same motive. There is, however, no insincerity in any of this; it is my conception of my role in prison life. It is entirely a different thing from being a "rebel" outside the prison; it is to be unconventional, rebellious perhaps, but in shades and shadows.

By means of these beginnings, these slight differences, and the appeal (do not think I am boasting here, or overestimating the power of details, because I have seen it work over and over again) of my carefully subdued, reserved manner, I shall attract to myself one intimate friend, whom I shall influence deeply. This friend, already an important member of the prison society, will be of great assistance to me in establishing myself as an authority, recognized but unofficial, on the conduct of prison life. It will take years before I become an *influence,* and possibly—and this is what I dare to hope for, to find the prison in such a period of its evolution that it will be unavoidable to be thought of as an *evil influence* . . . Perhaps they will laugh at me, as they laughed at the Vicar of Wakefield; but of course, just at first, I should like nothing better!

Many years ago I discovered that I could "succeed" in one place, but not in all places, and never, never could I succeed "at large." In the world, for example, I am very much under the influence of dress, absurd as that may be. But in a place where all dress alike I have the gift of being able to develop a "style" of my own, something that is even admired and imitated by others. The longer my sentence, although I constantly find myself thinking of it as a life sentence, the more slowly shall I go about establishing myself, and the more certain are my chances of success. Ridiculous as it sounds, and is, I am looking forward to directing the prison dramatic association, or being on the baseball team!

But in the same way that I was led to protest against the ambiguity of the position of those prisoners who were in and out of prison at the same time (I have even seen their wives washing their striped trousers and hanging them on the line!) I should bitterly object to any change or break in my way of life. If, for example, I should become ill and have to go to the prison infirmary, or if shortly after my arrival I should be moved to a different cell—either of these accidents would seriously upset me, and I should have to begin my work all over again.

Quite naturally under these circumstances I have often thought of joining our army or navy. I have stood on the sidewalk an hour at a time, studying the posters of the recruiting offices: the oval portrait of a soldier or sailor surrounded by scenes representing his "life." But the sailor, I understand, may be shifted from ship to ship without so much as a by-your-leave; and then, too, I believe that there is something fundamentally uncongenial about the view of the sea to a person of my mentality. In the blithe photographs surrounding the gallant head of the soldier I have glimpsed him "at work" building roads, peeling potatoes, etc. Aside from the remote possibilities of active service, those pictures alone would be enough to deter me from entering his ranks.

You may say—people have said to me—you would have been happy in the more flourishing days of the religious order, and that, I imagine, is close to the truth. But even there I hesitate, and the difference between Choice and Necessity jumps up again to confound me. "Freedom is knowledge of necessity"; I believe nothing as ardently as I do that. And I assure you that to act in this way is the only logical step for me to take. I mean, of course, to be acted *upon* in this way is the only logical step for me to take.

1938

The Farmer's Children

ᘓ

Once, on a large farm ten miles from the nearest town, lived a hardworking farmer with his wife, their three little girls, and his children by a former marriage, two boys aged eleven and twelve. The first wife had been the daughter of a minister, a plain and simple woman who had named her sons Cato and Emerson; while the stepmother, being romantic and overgenerous, to her own children at least, had given them the names of Lea Leola, Rosina, and Gracie Bell. There was also the usual assortment of horses, cows, and poultry, and a hired man named Judd.

The farm had belonged to the children's father's grandfather, and although pieces of it had been sold from time to time, it was still very large, actually too large. The original farmhouse had been a mile away from the present one, on the "old" road. It had been struck by lightning and burned down ten years before, and Emerson and Cato's grandparents, who had lived in it, had moved in with their son and his first wife for the year or two they had lived on after the fire. The old home had been long and low, and an enormous willow tree, which had miraculously escaped the fire and still grew, had shaded one corner of the roof. The new home stood beside the macadamized "new" road and was high and box-like, painted yellow with a roof of glittering tin.

Besides the willow tree, the principal barn at the old home had also escaped the fire and it was still used for storing hay and as a shed in which were kept most of the farm implements. Because farm implements are so valuable, always costing more than the farmer can afford, and because the barn was so far from the house and could easily have been broken into, the hired man slept there every night, in a pile of hay.

Most of these facts later appeared in the newspapers. It also appeared that since Judd had come to be the hired man, three months ago, he and the children's father had formed a habit of taking overnight trips to town. They went on "business," something to do with selling another strip of land, but probably mostly to drink; and while they were away Emerson and Cato would take Judd's place in the old barn and watch over the reaper, the tedder, the hay rake, the manure spreader, the harrow, et cetera—all the weird and expensive machinery of jaws and teeth and arms and claws, of direct and reflex actions and odd gestures, apparently so intelligent, but, in this case, so completely helpless because it was still dragged by horses.

It was December and frightfully cold. The full moon was just coming up and the tin roof of the farmhouse and patches of the macadam road caught her light, while the farmyard was still almost in darkness. The children had been put outdoors by their mother, who was in a fit of temper because they got in her way while she was preparing supper. Bundled up in mackinaws, with icy hands, they played at raft and shipwreck. There was a pile of planks in a corner of the yard, with which their father had long been planning to repair some outhouse or other, and on it Lea Leola and Rosina sat stolidly, saved, while Cato, with a clothes pole, stood up and steered. Still on the sinking ship, a chicken coop across the yard, stood the baby, Gracie Bell, holding out her arms and looking apprehensively around her, just about to cry. But Emerson was swimming to her rescue. He walked slowly, placing his heel against his toes at every step, and swinging both arms round and round like a windmill.

"Be brave, Gracie Bell! I'm almost there!" he cried. He gasped loudly. "My strength is almost exhausted, but I'll save you!"

Cato was calling out, over and over, "Now the ship is sinking inch by inch! Now the ship is sinking inch by inch!"

Small and silvery, their voices echoed in the cold countryside. The moon freed herself from the last field and looked evenly across at the imaginary ocean tragedy taking place so far inland. Emerson lifted Gracie Bell in his arms. She clutched him tightly around the neck and burst into loud sobs, but he turned firmly back, treading water with tiny up-and-down steps. Gracie Bell shrieked and he repeated, "I'll save you, Gracie Bell. I'll save you, Gracie Bell," but did not change his pace.

The mother and stepmother suddenly opened the back door.

"Emerson!" she screamed. "Put that child down! Didn't I tell you the next time you made that child cry I'd beat you until you couldn't holler? Didn't I?"

"Oh, Ma, we was just . . ."

"What's the matter with you kids, anyway? Fight and scrap, fight and scrap, and yowl, yowl, yowl, from morning to night. And you two boys, you're too big," and so on. The ugly words poured out and the children stood about the yard like stage-struck actors. But, as their father said, "her bark was worse than her bite," and in a few minutes, as if silenced by the moon's bland reserve, she stopped and said in a slightly lower voice, "All right, you kids. What are you standing there waiting for? Come inside the house and get your supper."

The kitchen was hot, and the smell of fried potatoes and the warm yellow light of the oil lamp on the table gave an illusion of peacefulness. The two boys sat on one side, the two older girls sat on the other, and Gracie Bell on her mother's lap at the end. The father and Judd had gone to town, one reason why the mother had been unusually bad-tempered all afternoon. They ate in silence, except for the mother's endearments to Gracie Bell, whom she was helping to drink tea and condensed milk out of a white cup. They ate the fried potatoes with pieces of pork in them, slice after slice of white "store" bread and dishes of "preserves," and drank syrupy hot tea and milk. The oilcloth on the table was light molasses-colored, sprinkled with small yellow poppies; it glistened pleasantly, and the "preserves" glowed, dark red blobs surrounded by transparent ruby.

Tonight's the night for the crumbs, Cato was thinking, and from time to time he managed to slide four slices of bread under the edge of the oilcloth and then up under his sweater. His thoughts sounded loud and ominous to him and he looked cautiously at his sisters to see if they had noticed anything, but their pale, rather flat faces looked blankly back. Anyway, it was the night for crumbs and what else could he possibly do?

The other two times he and Emerson had spent the night in the old barn he had used bits of torn-up newspaper because he hadn't been able to find the white pebbles anywhere. He and his brother had walked home, still half asleep, in the gray-blue light just before sunrise, and he had been delighted to find the sprinkles of speckled paper here and there all along the way. He had dropped it out of his pocket a little at a time, scarcely daring to look back, and it had worked. But he had longed for the endless full moon of the tale, and the pebbles that would have shone "like silver coins." Emerson knew nothing of his plan—his system, rather—but it had worked without his help and in spite of all discrepancies.

The mother set Gracie Bell down and started to transfer dishes from the table to the sink.

"I suppose you boys forgot you've got to get over to the barn sometime tonight," she said ironically.

Emerson protested a little.

"Now you just put on your things and get started before it gets any later. Maybe sometime your pa will get them doors fixed or maybe he'll get a new barn. Go along, now." She lifted the tea kettle off the stove.

Cato couldn't find his knitted gloves. He thought they were on the shelf in the corner with the schoolbags. He looked methodically for them everywhere and then at last he became aware of Lea Leola's malicious smile.

"Ma! Lea Leola's got my gloves. She's hid them on me!"

"Lea Leola! Have you got his gloves?" Her mother advanced on her.

"Make her give them to me!"

Lea Leola said, "I ain't even seen his old gloves," and started to weep.

"Now, Cato, see what you've done! Shut up, Lea Leola, for God's sake, and you boys hurry up and get out of here. I've had enough trouble for one day."

At the door Emerson said. "It's cold, Ma."

"Well, Judd's got his blankets over there. Go on, go along and shut that door. You're letting the cold in."

Outside, it was almost as bright as day. The macadam road looked very gray and rang under their feet, which immediately grew numb with cold. The cold stuck quickly to the little hairs in their nostrils, which felt painfully stuffed with icy straws. But if they tried to warm their noses against the clumsy lapels of their mackinaws, the freezing moisture felt even worse, and they gave it up and merely pointed out their breath to each other as it whitened and then vanished. The moon was behind them. Cato looked over his shoulder and saw how the tin roof of the farmhouse shone, bluish, and how, above it, the stars looked blue, too, blue or yellow, and very small; you could hardly see most of them.

Emerson was talking quietly, enlarging on his favorite theme: how he could obtain a certain bicycle he had seen a while ago in the window of the hardware store in town. He went on and on but Cato didn't pay very much attention, first because he knew quite well already almost everything Emerson was saying or could say about the bicycle, and second because he was busy crumbing the four slices of bread which he had worked around into his pants pockets, two slices in each. It seemed to turn into lumps instead of crumbs and it was hard to pull off the little bits with his nails and flick them into the road from time to time from under the skirt of his mackinaw.

Emerson made no distinction between honest and dishonest methods of getting the bicycle. Sometimes he would discuss plans for deceiving the owner of the hardware store, who would somehow be maneuvered into sending it to him by mistake, and sometimes it was to be his reward for a deed of heroism. Sometimes he spoke of a glass-cutter. He had seen his father use one of these fascinating instruments. If he had one he could cut a large hole in the plate-glass window of the hardware store in the night. And then he spoke of working next summer as a hired man. He would work for the farmer who had the farm next to theirs; he saw himself performing prodigious feats of haying and milking.

"But Old Man Blackader only pays big boys four dollars a week," said Cato, sensibly, "and he wouldn't pay you that much."

"Well . . ."

Emerson swore and spat toward the side of the road, and they went on while the moon rose steadily higher and higher.

A humming noise ran along the telephone wires over their heads. They thought it might possibly be caused by all the people talking over them at the same time but it didn't actually sound like voices. The glass conductors that bore the wires shone pale green, and the poles were bleached silver by the moonlight, and from each one came a strange roaring, deeper than the hum of the wires. It sounded like a swarm of bees. They put their ears to the deep black cracks. Cato tried to peer into one and almost thought he could see the mass of black and iridescent bees inside.

"But they'd all be frozen—solid," Emerson said.

"No they wouldn't. They sleep all winter."

Emerson wanted to climb a pole. Cato said, "You might get a shock."

He helped him, however, and boosted up his thin haunches in both hands. But Emerson could just barely touch the lowest spike and wasn't strong enough to pull himself up.

At last they came to where their path turned off the road, and went through a corn field where the stalks still stood, motionless in the cold. Cato dropped quite a few crumbs to mark the turning. On the cornstalks the long, colorless leaves hung in tatters like streamers of old crepe paper, like the remains of booths that had stood along the midway of a county fair. The stalks were higher than their heads, like trees. Double lines of wire, with glinting barbs, were strung along both sides of the wheel tracks.

Emerson and Cato fought all day almost every day, but rarely at night. Now they were arguing amicably about how cold it was.

"It might snow even," Cato said.

"No," said Emerson, "it's too cold to snow."

"But when it gets awful cold it snows," said Cato.

"But when it gets real cold, awful cold like this, it can't snow."

"Why can't it?"

"Because it's too cold. Anyway, there isn't any up there."

They looked. Yes, except for the large white moon, the sky was as empty as could be.

Cato tried not to drop his crumbs in the dry turf between the wagon tracks, where they would not show. In the ruts he could see them a little, small and grayish. Of course there were no birds. But he couldn't seem to think it through—whether his plan was good for anything or not.

Back home in the yellow farmhouse the stepmother was getting ready for bed. She went to find an extra quilt to put over Lea Leola, Rosina, and Gracie Bell, sleeping in one bed in the next room. She spread it out and tucked it in without disturbing them. Then, in spite of the cold, she stood for a moment looking down uneasily at its pattern of large, branching hexagons, blanched, almost colorless, in the moonlight. That had always been such a pretty quilt! Her mother had made it. What was the name of that pattern? What was it it reminded her of? Out from the forms of a lost childish game, from between the pages of a lost schoolbook, the image fell upon her brain: a snowflake.

"Where is that damned old barn?" Emerson asked, and spat again.

It was a relief to get to it and to see the familiar willow tree and to tug at one side of the dragging barn door with hands that had no feeling left in them. At first it seemed dark inside but soon the moon lit it all quite well. At the left were the disused stalls for the cows and horses, the various machines stood down the middle and at the right, and the hay now hung vaguely overhead on each side. But it was too cold to smell the hay.

Where were Judd's blankets? They couldn't find them anywhere. After looking in all the stalls and on the wooden pegs that held the harness, Emerson dropped down on a pile of hay in front of the harrow, by the door.

Cato said, "Maybe it would be better up in the mow." He put his bare hands on a rung of the ladder.

Emerson said, "I'm too cold to climb the ladder," and giggled.

So Cato sat down in the pile of hay on the floor, too, and they started heaping it over their legs and bodies. It felt queer; it had no weight or substance in their hands. It was lighter than feathers and wouldn't seem to settle down over them; it just prickled a little.

Emerson said he was tired, and turning on his side, he swore a few more times, almost cautiously. Cato swore, too, and lay on his back, close to his brother.

The harrow was near his head and its flat, sharp-edged disks gleamed at him coldly. Just beyond it he could make out the hay rake. Its row of long, curved prongs caught the moonlight too, and from where he lay, almost on a level with them, the prongs made a steely, formal wave that came straight toward him over the floorboards. And around him in darkness and light were all the other machines: the manure spreader made a huge shadow; the reaper lifted a strong forearm lined with saw teeth, like that of a gigantic grasshopper; and the tedder's sharp little forks were suspended in one of the bright patches, some up, some down, as if it had just that minute stopped a cataleptic kicking.

Up over their heads, between the mows, every crack and hole in the old roof showed, and little flecks, like icy chips of moon, fell on them, on the clutter of implements and on the gray hay. Once in a while one of the shingles would crack, or one of the brittle twigs of the willow tree would snap sharply.

Cato thought with pleasure of the trail of crumbs he had left all the way from the house to here. "And there aren't any birds," he thought almost gleefully. He and Emerson would start home again as they had the previous times, just before sunrise, and he would see the crumbs leading straight back the way they had come, white and steadfast in the early light.

Then he began to think of his father and Judd, off in town. He pictured his father in a bright, electrically lit little restaurant, with blue walls, where it was very hot, eating a plate of dark red kidney beans. He had been there once and that was what he had been given to eat. For a while he thought, with disfavor, of his stepmother and stepsisters, and then his thoughts returned to his father; he loved him dearly.

Emerson muttered something about "that old Judd," and burrowed deeper into the hay. Their teeth were chattering. Cato tried to get his hands between his thighs, to warm them, but the hay got in the way. It felt like hoarfrost. It scratched and then melted against the skin of his numb hands. It gave him the same sensation as when he ate the acid grape jelly his stepmother made each fall and little sticks, little stiff crystal sticks, like ice, would prick and dissolve, also in the dark, against the roof of his mouth.

Through the half-open door the cornstalks in the corn field stood suspiciously straight and still. What went on among those leaf-hung stalks? Shouldn't they have been cut down, anyway? There stood the corn and there stood, or squatted, the machines. He turned his head to look at them. All that corn should be reaped. The reaper held out its arm stiffly. The hay-rack looked like the set coil of a big trap.

It hurt to move his feet. His feet felt like a horse's hooves, as if he had horseshoes on them. He touched one and yes, it was true, it felt just like a big horseshoe.

The harnesses were hanging on their pegs above him. Their little bits of metal glittered pale blue and yellow like the little tiny stars. If the harnesses should fall down on him he would have to be a horse and it would be so cold out in the field pulling the heavy harrow. The harnesses were heavy, too; he had tried the collars a few times and they were very heavy. It would take two horses; he would have to wake up Emerson, although Emerson was hard to wake when he got to sleep.

The disks of the harrow looked like the side—those shields hung over the side—of a Viking ship. The harrow was a ship that was going to go up to the moon with the shields all clanging on her sides; he must get up into the seat and steer. That queer seat of perforated iron that looked uncomfortable and yet when one got into it, gave one such a feeling of power and ease . . .

But how could it be going to the moon when the moon was coming right down on the hill? No, moons; there was a whole row of them. No, those must be the disks of the harrow. No, the moon had split into a sheaf of moons, slipping off each other sideways, off and off and off and off.

He turned to Emerson and called his name, but Emerson only moaned in his sleep. So he fitted his knees into the hollows at the back of his brother's and hugged him tightly around the waist.

At noon the next day their father found them in this position.

The story was in all the newspapers, on the front page of local ones, dwindling as it traveled over the countryside to short paragraphs on middle pages when it got as far as each coast. The farmer grieved wildly for a year; for some reason, one expression he gave to his feelings was to fire Judd.

1948

The Housekeeper

❦

My neighbor, old Mrs. Sennett, adjusted the slide of the stereo-
scope to her eyes, looked at the card with admiration, and then
read out loud to me, slowly, " 'Church in Marselaze. France.' "
Then, "Paris." "Paris," I decided, must be an addition of her
own. She handed the stereoscope over to me. I moved the card
a little farther away and examined the church and the small
figures of a man and woman in front of it. The woman was
dressed in a long skirt, a tiny white shirtwaist, and a dot-like
sailor hat, and, though standing at the foot of the church steps,
through the stereoscope she and the man appeared to be at least
fifty feet from the church.

"That's beautiful," I said, and handed the machine back to
Mrs. Sennett. We had exhausted all the funny cards, like the
one that showed a lady kissing the postman while her husband,
leaning out of a window, was about to hit the postman on the
head. Now we were reduced to things like the church and
"King of the Belgians' Conservatory," in which all the flowers
had been painted red by hand.

Outside, the rain continued to run down the screened win-
dows of Mrs. Sennett's little Cape Cod cottage, filling the
squares with cross-stitch effects that came and went. The long

weeds and grass that composed the front yard dripped against the blurred background of the bay, where the water was almost the color of the grass. Mrs. Sennett's five charges were vigorously playing house in the dining room. (In the wintertime, Mrs. Sennett was housekeeper for a Mr. Curley, in Boston, and during the summers the Curley children boarded with her on the Cape.)

My expression must have changed. "Are those children making too much noise?" Mrs. Sennett demanded, a sort of wave going over her that might mark the beginning of her getting up out of her chair. I shook my head no, and gave her a little push on the shoulder to keep her seated. Mrs. Sennett was almost stone-deaf and had been for a long time, but she could read lips. You could talk to her without making any sound yourself, if you wanted to, and she more than kept up her side of the conversation in a loud, rusty voice that dropped weirdly every now and then into a whisper. She adored talking.

Finally, we had looked at all the pictures and she put the little green trunk containing the stereoscope and the cards back on the under shelf of the table.

"You wouldn't think to look at me that I was of Spanish origin, would you?" she asked.

I assured her with my hands and eyebrows that I wouldn't, expressing, I hoped, a polite amount of doubt and eagerness to learn if she really were or not.

"Oh, yes," she said. "My mother was of pure Spanish blood. Do you know what my first name is?"

I shook my head.

"Carmen. That's Spanish. I was named after my mother."

I said "*Pret*-ty" as hard as I could. Mrs. Sennett was pleased and, looking down modestly, flicked a speck of dust off her large bosom. "Were you born in Spain, Mrs. Sennett?" I asked.

"No, not exactly. My father was on a ship and he brought my

mother back to England with him. I was born there. Where were you born?"

I told her in Worcester.

"Isn't that funny? The children's uncle is the boxing commissioner there. Mr. Curley, their father's brother."

I nodded my knowledge of Mr. Curley.

"But you'd never think to look at me that I'm half Spanish, would you?"

Indeed, to look at Mrs. Sennett made me think more of eighteenth-century England and its literary figures. Her hair must have been sadly thin, because she always wore, indoors and out, either a hat or a sort of turban, and sometimes she wore both. Today the turban was of black silk with a white design here and there. Because of the rainy weather she also wore a white silk handkerchief around her throat; it gave the appearance of a poetically slovenly stock. Mrs. Sennett's face was large and seemed, like the stereoscope cards, to be at two distances at the same time, as if fragments of a mask had been laid over a background face. The fragments were white, while the face around them was darker and the wrinkles looser. The rims of her eyes were dark; she looked very ill.

"They're Catholic, you know," she told me in her most grating whisper, lest she should offend the ears of the children in the dining room. "I'm not, but their father doesn't mind. He had eleven housekeepers inside two and a half years, after their mother died when Xavier was born, and now I've been with them almost five years. I was the only one who could stand the noise and of course it doesn't bother me any since I can't even hear it. Some Catholics would never trust their children to a Protestant, but their father's a broad-minded man. The children worry, though. I get them dressed up and off to Mass every Sunday and they're always tormenting me to come with them. Two Sundays ago, when they came back, Xavier was crying and crying. I kept asking him, 'What's the matter with you, Savey?' but I couldn't get anything out of him and finally Theresa said, 'He's crying because Francis told him you'd have to go to hell when you died.' "

Xavier had come to the door and was listening to the story. He was the youngest of the children. First came the twins, Francis and John, and after them, Mary and Theresa. They were all fair, pretty children. Mrs. Sennett dressed the boys in overalls and before starting off with them for the cottage every summer she had their heads shaved, so she wouldn't have to bother about haircuts.

Seeing Xavier now, she said, "You bad, noisy children!" He came over and leaned against her chair, and she scrubbed her large hands over his bristly head. Then she told him that she had company, and he went back to the dining room, where Theresa was now reading old funny papers out loud to all of them.

Mrs. Sennett and I continued talking. We told each other that we loved the bay, and we extended our affection to the ocean, too. She said she really didn't think she'd stay with the children another winter. Their father wanted her to, but it was too much for her. She wanted to stay right here in the cottage.

The afternoon was getting along, and I finally left because I knew that at four o'clock Mrs. Sennett's "sit down" was over and she started to get supper. At six o'clock, from my nearby cottage, I saw Theresa coming through the rain with a shawl over her head. She was bringing me a six-inch-square piece of spicecake, still hot from the oven and kept warm between two soup plates.

A few days later I learned from the twins, who brought over gifts of firewood and blackberries, that their father was coming the next morning, bringing their aunt and her husband and their cousin, also named Theresa, for a visit. Mrs. Sennett had promised to take them all on a picnic at the pond some pleasant day. They were going to cook outdoors and go swimming in fresh water, and they were going to take along cakes of Ivory soap, so that they could have baths at the same time. The men would walk to the pond, and a friend of Mrs. Sennett's in the village had promised to drive the rest of them there in his car. Mrs. Sennett rarely moved beyond her house and yard, and I could imagine what an undertaking the guests and the picnic would be for her.

I saw the guests arrive the next day, walking from the station with their bags, and I saw Mr. Curley, a tall, still young-looking man, greet Mrs. Sennett with a kiss. Then I saw no more of them for two days; I had a guest myself, and we were driving around the Cape most of the time. On the fourth day, Xavier arrived with a note, folded over and over. It was from Mrs. Sennett, written in blue ink, in a large, serene, ornamented hand, on linen-finish paper:

> *My Dear Neighbor,*
>
> *My Friend has disappointed me about the car. Tomorrow is the last day Mr. Curley has and the Children all wanted the Picnic so much. The Men can walk to the Pond but it is too far for the Children. I see your Friend has a car and I hate to ask this but could you possibly drive us to the Pond tomorrow morning? It is an awful load but I hate to have them miss the Picnic. We can all walk back if we just get there.*
>
> > *Very sincerely yours,*
> > *Carmen Sennett*

The next morning my guest and I put them all in the car. Everybody seemed to be sitting on Mrs. Sennett. They were in beautifully high spirits. Mrs. Sennett was quite hoarse from asking the aunt if the children were making too much noise and, if she said they were, telling them to stop.

We brought them back that evening—the women and children, at least. Xavier carried an empty gin bottle that Mrs. Sennett said his father had given him. She leaned over to the front seat and shouted in my ear, "*He likes his liquor. But he's a good man.*" The children's hair shone with cleanliness and John told me that they had left soapsuds all over the pond.

After the picnic, Mrs. Sennett's presents to me were numberless and I had to return empty dishes by the children several times a day. It was almost time for them to go back to school in South Boston. Mrs. Sennett insisted that she was not going; their father was coming down again to get them and she was just going to stay. He would have to get another housekeeper. She, Mrs. Sennett, was just going to stay right here and look at the bay all winter, and maybe her sister from Somerville would come to visit. She said this over and over to me, loudly, and her turbans and kerchiefs grew more and more distrait.

One evening, Mary came to call on me and we sat on an old table in the back yard to watch the sunset.

"Papa came today," she said, "and we've got to go back day after tomorrow."

"Is Mrs. Sennett going to stay here?"

"She said at supper she was. She said this time she really was, because she'd said that last year and came back, but now she means it."

I said, "Oh dear," scarcely knowing which side I was on.

"It was awful at supper. I cried and cried."

"Did Theresa cry?"

"Oh, we all cried. Papa cried, too. We always do."

"But don't you think Mrs. Sennett needs a rest?"

"Yes, but I think she'll come, though. Papa told her he'd cry every single night at supper if she didn't, and then we all *did*."

The next day I heard from Xavier that Mrs. Sennett was going back with them just to "help settle." She came over the following morning to say goodbye, supported by all five children. She was wearing her traveling hat of black satin and black straw, with sequins. High and somber, above her ravaged face, it had quite a Spanish-grandee air.

"This isn't really goodbye," she said. "I'll be back as soon as I get these bad, noisy children off my hands."

But the children hung on to her skirt and tugged at her sleeves, shaking their heads frantically, silently saying *"No! No! No!"* to her with their puckered-up mouths.

1948

Gwendolyn

My Aunt Mary was eighteen years old and away in "the States," in Boston, training to be a nurse. In the bottom bureau drawer in her room, well wrapped in soft pink tissue paper, lay her best doll. That winter, I had been sick with bronchitis for a long time, and my grandmother finally produced it for me to play with, to my amazement and delight, because I had never even known of its existence before. It was a girl doll, but my grandmother had forgotten her name.

She had a large wardrobe, which my Aunt Mary had made, packed in a toy steamer trunk of green tin embossed with all the proper boards, locks, and nailheads. The clothes were wonderful garments, beautifully sewn, looking old-fashioned even to me. There were long drawers trimmed with tiny lace, and a corset cover, and a corset with little bones. These were exciting, but best of all was the skating costume. There was a red velvet coat, and a turban and muff of some sort of moth-eaten brown fur, and, to make it almost unbearably thrilling, there was a pair of laced white glacé-kid boots, which had scalloped tops and a pair of too small, dull-edged, but very shiny skates loosely attached to their soles by my Aunt Mary with stitches of coarse white thread.

The looseness of the skates didn't bother me. It went very well with the doll's personality, which in turn was well suited to the role of companion to an invalid. She had lain in her drawer so long that the elastic in her joints had become weakened; when you held her up, her head fell gently to one side, and her outstretched hand would rest on yours for a moment and then slip wearily off. She made the family of dolls I usually played with seem rugged and childish: the Campbell Kid doll, with a childlike scar on her forehead where she had fallen against the fender; the two crudely felt-dressed Indians, Hiawatha and Nokomis; and the stocky "baby doll," always holding out his arms to be picked up.

My grandmother was very nice to me when I was sick. During this same illness, she had already given me her button basket to play with, and her scrap bag, and the crazy quilt was put over my bed in the afternoons. The button basket was large and squashed and must have weighed ten pounds, filled with every-thing from the metal snaps for men's overalls to a set of large cut-steel buttons with deer heads with green glass eyes on them. The scrap bag was interesting because in it I could find pieces of my grandmother's house dresses that she was wearing right then, and pieces of my grandfather's Sunday shirts. But the crazy quilt was the best entertainment. My grandmother had made it long before, when such quilts had been a fad in the little Nova Scotian village where we lived. She had collected small, irregularly shaped pieces of silk or velvet of all colors and got all her lady and gentleman friends to write their names on them in pencil—their names, and sometimes a date or word or two as well. Then she had gone over the writing in chain stitch with silks of different colors, and then put the whole thing together on maroon flannel, with feather-stitching joining the pieces. I could read well enough to make out the names of people I knew, and then my grandmother would sometimes tell me that that particular piece of silk came from Mrs. So-and-So's "going-away" dress, forty years ago, or that that was from a necktie of one of her brothers, since dead and buried in London, or that that was from India, brought back by another brother, who was a missionary.

When it grew dark—and this, of course, was very early—she would take me out of bed, wrap me in a blanket, and, holding me on her knees, rock me vigorously in the rocking chair. I think she enjoyed this exercise as much as I did, because she would sing me hymns, in her rather affectedly lugubrious voice, which suddenly thinned out to half its ordinary volume on the higher notes. She sang me "There is a green hill far away," "Will there be any stars in my crown?" and "In the sweet bye-and-bye." Then there were more specifically children's hymns, such as:

> *Little children, little children,*
> *Who love their Redeemer,*
> *Are the jewels, precious jewels,*
> *Bright gems for his crown . . .*

And then, perhaps because we were Baptists—nice watery ones— all the saints casting down their crowns (in what kind of a tantrum?) "around the glassy sea"; "Shall we gather at the river?"; and her favorite, "Happy day, happy day, when Jesus washed my sins away."

This is preliminary. The story of Gwendolyn did not begin until the following summer, when I was in my usual summer state of good health and had forgotten about the bronchitis, the realistic cat-and-kitten family in my chest, and the doctor's cold stethoscope.

Gwendolyn Appletree was the youngest child and only daughter of a large, widely spaced family that lived away out, four or five miles, on a lonely farm among the fir trees. She was a year or so older than I—that is, about eight—and her five or six brothers, I suppose in their teens, seemed like grown men to me. But Gwendolyn and I, although we didn't see each other very often, were friends, and to me she stood for everything that the slightly repellent but fascinating words "little girl" should mean. In the first place, her beautiful name. Its dactyl trisyllables could have gone on forever as far as I was concerned. And then, although older, she was as small as I was, and blond, and pink and white, exactly like a blossoming apple tree. And she was "delicate," which, in spite of the bronchitis, I was not. She had diabetes. I had been told this much and had some vague idea that it was because of "too much sugar," and that in itself made Gwendolyn even more attractive, as if she would prove to be solid candy if you bit her, and her pure-tinted complexion would taste exactly like the icing-sugar Easter eggs or birthday-candle holders, held to be inedible, except that I knew better.

I don't know what the treatment for diabetes was at that time—whether, for example, Gwendolyn was given insulin or not, but I rather think not. My grandparents, however, often spoke disapprovingly of the way her parents would not obey the doctor's orders and gave her whatever she wanted to eat, including two pieces of cake for tea, and of how, if they weren't more sensible, they would never keep her. Every once in a while, she would have a mysterious attack of some sort, "convulsions" or a "coma," but a day or two later I would see her driving with her father to the store right next door to our house, looking the same as ever and waving to me. Occasionally, she would be brought to spend the day or afternoon with me while her parents drove down the shore to visit relatives.

These were wonderful occasions. She would arrive carrying a doll or some other toy; her mother would bring a cake or a jar of preserves for my grandmother. Then I would have the opportunity of showing her all my possessions all over again. Quite often, what she brought was a set of small blocks that exactly fitted in a shallow cardboard box. These blocks were squares cut diagonally across, in clear reds, yellows, and blues, and we arranged them snugly together in geometric designs. Then, if we were careful, the whole thing could be lifted up and turned over, revealing a similar brilliant design in different colors on the other side. These designs were completely satisfying in their forthrightness, like the Union Jack. We played quietly together and did not quarrel.

Before her mother and father drove off in their buggy, Gwendolyn was embraced over and over, her face was washed one last time, her stockings were pulled up, her nose was wiped, she was hoisted up and down and swung around and around by her father and given some white pills by her mother. This sometimes went on so long that my grandfather would leave abruptly for the barn and my grandmother would busy herself at the sink and start singing a hymn under her breath, but it was nothing to the scenes of tenderness when they returned a few hours later. Then her parents almost ate her up, alternately, as if she really were made of sugar, as I half suspected. I watched these exciting scenes with envy until Mr. and Mrs. Appletree drove away, with Gwendolyn standing between them in her white dress, her pale-gold hair blowing, still being kissed from either side. Although I received many demonstrations of affection from my grandparents, they were nothing like this. My grandmother was disgusted. "They'll kiss that child to death if they're not careful," she said. "Oh, lallygagging, lallygagging!" said my grandfather, going on about his business.

I remember clearly three episodes of that summer in which Gwendolyn played the role of beautiful heroine—the role that grew and grew until finally it had grown far beyond the slight but convincing talents she had for acting it.

Once, my grandparents and I went to a church picnic. As I said, we were Baptists, but most of the village, including the Appletrees, were Presbyterians. However, on social occasions I think the two sects sometimes joined forces, or else we were broad-minded enough to go to a Presbyterian picnic—I'm not sure. Anyway, the three of us, dressed in our second-best, took a huge picnic supper and drove behind Nimble II to the picnic grounds beside the river. It was a beautiful spot; there were large spruce and pine trees right to the edge of the clear brown water and mossy terra-cotta-colored rocks; the ground was slippery with brown pine needles. Pans of beans and biscuits and scalloped potatoes were set out on long tables, and all our varieties of pickles and relishes (chowchows and piccalillis), conserves and preserves, cakes and pies, parkins and hermits— all glistening and gleaming in the late sunshine—and water for tea was being brought to the boil over two fires. My grand-mother settled herself on a log to talk to her friends, and I went wading in the river with mine. My cousin Billy was there, and Seth Hill, and the little McNeil twins, but Gwendolyn was missing. Later, I joined my family for supper, or as all Nova Scotians call their suppers, "tea." My grandmother spoke to one of the Appletree boys, filling his plate beside us, and asked him where his father and mother were, and how Gwendolyn was.

"Pretty poorly," he answered, with an imitative elderly-man shake of his head. "Ma thought we'd lost her yesterday morn-ing. I drove down and got the doctor. She's resting better today, though."

We went on drinking our tea and eating in silence, and after a while my grandfather started talking about something else. But just before we finished, when it was beginning to get gray, and a sweet, dank, fresh-water smell had suddenly started to come up off the river, a horse and buggy turned rapidly in to the picnic grounds and pulled up beside us. In it were Mr. and Mrs. Appletree, and Gwendolyn—standing between them, as usual—wearing one of her white dresses, with a little black-and-white-checked coat over it. A great fuss was made over them and her, and my grandfather lifted her down and held her on his knee, sitting on one of the rough benches beside the picnic tables. I leaned against him, but Gwendolyn wouldn't speak to me; she just smiled as if very pleased with everything. She looked prettier and more delicate than ever, and her cheeks were bright pink. Her mother made her a cup of weak tea, and I could see my grandmother's look as the sugar went into it. Gwendolyn had wanted to come so badly, her mother said, so they thought they'd bring her just for a little while.

Some time after this, Gwendolyn was brought to visit me again, but this time she was to spend the whole day and night and part of the next day. I was very excited, and consulted with my grandmother endlessly as to how we should pass the time— if I could jump with her in the barn or take her swimming in the river. No, both those sports were too strenuous for Gwendolyn, but we could play at filling bottles with colored water (made from the paints in my paintbox), my favorite game at the moment, and in the afternoon we could have a dolls' tea party.

Everything went off very well. After dinner, Gwendolyn went and lay on the sofa in the parlor, and my grandmother put a shawl over her. I wanted to pretend to play the piano to her, but I was made to stop and go outside by myself. After a while, Gwendolyn joined me in the flower garden and we had the tea party. After that, I showed her how to trap bumblebees in the foxgloves, but that was also put a stop to by my grandmother as too strenuous and dangerous. Our play was not without a touch of rustic corruption, either. I can't remember what happened, if anything, but I do remember being ordered out of the whitewashed privy in the barn after we had locked ourselves in and climbed on the seats and hung out the little window, with its beautiful view of the elm-studded "interval" in back of us. It was just getting dark; my grandmother was very stern with me and said we must never lock ourselves in there, but she was objectionably kind to Gwendolyn, who looked more angelic than ever.

After tea, we sat at the table with the oil lamp hanging over it for a while, playing with the wonderful blocks, and then it was bedtime. Gwendolyn was going to sleep in my bed with me. I was so overwrought with the novelty of this that it took me a long time to get ready for bed, but Gwendolyn was ready in a jiffy and lay on the far side of the bed with her eyes shut, trying to make me think she was asleep, with the lamplight shining on her blond, blond hair. I asked her if she didn't say her prayers before she got into bed and she said no, her mother let her say them in bed, "because I'm going to die."

At least, that was what I thought she said. I couldn't quite believe I had really heard her say it and I certainly couldn't ask her if she had said it. My heart pounding, I brushed my teeth with the icy well water, and spat in the china pot. Then I got down on my knees and said my own prayers, half aloud, completely mechanically, while the pounding went on and on. I couldn't seem to make myself get into my side of the bed, so I went around and picked up Gwendolyn's clothes. She had thrown them on the floor. I put them over the back of a chair— the blue-and-white-striped dress, the waist, the long brown stockings. Her drawers had lace around the legs, but they were very dirty. This fact shocked me so deeply that I recovered my voice and started asking her more questions.

"I'm asleep," said Gwendolyn, without opening her eyes.

But after my grandmother had turned out the lamp, Gwendolyn began to talk to me again. We told each other which colors we liked best together, and I remember the feeling of profound originality I experienced when I insisted, although it had just occurred to me, that I had always liked black and brown together best. I saw them floating in little patches of velvet, like the crazy quilt, or smooth little rectangles of enamel, like the paint-sample cards I was always begging for at the general store.

Two days after this visit, Gwendolyn did die. One of her brothers came in to tell my grandmother—and I was there in the kitchen when he told her—with more of the elderly-man headshakes and some sad and ancient phrases. My grandmother wept and wiped her eyes with her apron, answering him with phrases equally sad and ancient. The funeral was to be two days later, but I was not going to be allowed to go.

My grandfather went, but not my grandmother. I wasn't even supposed to know what was taking place, but since the Presbyterian church was right across the village green from our house, and I could hear the buggies driving up over the gravel, and then the bell beginning to ring, I knew quite well, and my heart began to pound again, apparently as loudly as the bell was ringing. I was sent out to play in the yard at the far side of the house, away from the church. But through one of the kitchen windows—the kitchen was an ell that had windows on both sides—I could see my curious grandmother drawing up her rocking chair, as she did every Sunday morning, just behind a window on the other side of the ell, to watch the Presbyterians going to church. This was the unacknowledged practice of the Baptists who lived within sight of the church, and later, when they met at their own afternoon service, they would innocently say to each other things like "They had a good turnout this morning" and "Is Mrs. Peppard still laid up? I missed her this morning."

But today it was quite different, and when I peeked in at my grandmother at one side of the ell, she was crying and crying between her own peeks at the mourners out the other side. She had a handkerchief already very wet, and was rocking gently.

It was too much for me. I sneaked back into the house by the side door and into the shut-up parlor, where I could look across at the church, too. There were long lace curtains at the window and the foxgloves and bees were just outside, but I had a perfectly clear, although lace-patterned, view of everything. The church was quite large—a Gothic structure made of white clapboards, with non-flying buttresses, and a tall wooden steeple—and I was as familiar with it as I was with my grandmother. I used to play hide-and-seek among the buttresses with my friends. The buggy sheds, now all filled, were at the back, and around the large grass plot were white wooden pillars with double chains slung slackly between them, on which my cousin Billy, who lived right next door to the church, and I liked to clamber and swing.

At last, everyone seemed to have gone inside, and an inner door shut. No, two men in black stood talking together in the open outside doorway. The bell suddenly stopped ringing and the two men vanished, and I was afraid of being in the parlor alone, but couldn't leave now. Hours seemed to go by. There was some singing, but I didn't recognize the hymns, either because I was too nervous or because, as they sometimes did, the Presbyterians sang hymns unfamiliar to me.

I had seen many funerals like this before, of course, and I loved to go with my grandfather when he went to the graveyard with a scythe and a sickle to cut the grass on our family's graves.

The graveyard belonging to the village was surely one of the prettiest in the world. It was on the bank of the river, two miles below us, but where the bank was high. It lay small and green and white, with its firs and cedars and gravestones balancing against the dreaming lavender-red Bay of Fundy. The headstones were mostly rather thin, coarse white marble slabs, frequently leaning slightly, but there was a scattering of small urns and obelisks and broken columns. A few plots were lightly chained in, like the Presbyterian church, or fenced in with wood or iron, like little gardens, and wild rosebushes grew in the grass. Blueberries grew there, too, but I didn't eat them, because I felt I "never knew," as people said, but once when I went there, my grandmother had given me a teacup without a handle and requested me to bring her back some teaberries, which "grew good" on the graves, and I had.

And so I used to play while my grandfather, wearing a straw hat, scythed away, and talked to me haphazardly about the people lying there. I was, of course, particularly interested in the children's graves, their names, what ages they had died at—whether they were older than I or younger. The favorite memorial for small children was a low rectangle of the same coarse white marble as the larger stones, but with a little lamb recumbent on top. I adored these lambs, and counted them and caressed them and sat on them. Some were almost covered by dry, bright-gold lichen, some with green and gold and gray mixed together, some were almost lost among the long grass and roses and blueberries and teaberries.

But now, suddenly, as I watched through the window, something happened at the church across the way. Something that could not possibly have happened, so that I must, in reality, have seen something like it and imagined the rest; or my concentration on the one thing was so intense that I could see nothing else.

The two men in black appeared again, carrying Gwendolyn's small white coffin between them. Then—this was the impossibility—they put it down just outside the church door, one end on the grass and the other lifted up a little, to lean at a slight angle against the wall. Then they disappeared inside again. For a minute, I stared straight through my lace curtain at Gwendolyn's coffin, with Gwendolyn shut invisibly inside it forever, there, completely alone on the grass by the church door.

Then I ran howling to the back door, out among the startled white hens, with my grandmother, still weeping, after me.

If I care to, I can bring back the exact sensation of that moment today, but then, it is also one of those that from time to time are terrifyingly thrust upon us. I was familiar with it and recognized it; I had already experienced it once, shortly before the bronchitis attack of the previous winter. One evening, we were all sitting around the table with the lamp hanging above it; my grandfather was dozing in the Morris chair, my grandmother was crocheting, and my Aunt Mary, who had not yet gone away to Boston, was reading *Maclean's Magazine*. I was drawing pictures when suddenly I remembered something, a present that had been given to me months before and that I had forgotten all about. It was a strawberry basket half filled with new marbles—clay ones, in the usual mottled shades of red, brown, purple, and green. However, in among them were several of a sort I had never seen before: fine, unglazed, cream-colored clay, with purple and pink lines around them. One or two of the larger ones of this sort even had little sprigs of flowers on them. But the most beautiful of all, I thought, was a really big one, probably an inch and a half in diameter, of a roughly shiny glazed pink, like crockery. It moved me almost to tears to look at it; it "went right through me."

Anyway, I started thinking about these marbles—wondering where they had been all this time, where I had put them, if they had got lost—until at last it became unbearable and I had to go and find them. I went out to the kitchen in the dark and groped around on the floor of a cupboard where I kept some of my belongings. I felt the edges of riffled old books and sharp mechanical toys, and then, at the back, I did feel the strawberry basket. I dragged it out and carried it into the sitting room.

My relatives paid no attention. I stared into the basket and took out a few of the marbles. But what could have happened? They were covered with dirt and dust, nails were lying mixed in with them, bits of string, cobwebs, old horse chestnuts blue with mildew, their polish gone. The big pink marble was there, but I hardly recognized it, all covered with dirt. (Later, when my grandmother washed it off, it was as good as new, of course.) The broad lamp flame started to blur; my aunt's fair hair started to blur; I put my head down on top of the marbles and cried aloud. My grandfather woke up with a jerk and said, "Heavens, what ails the child now?" Everyone tried to comfort me—for what, they had no idea.

A month or so after the funeral—it was still summer—my grandparents went away for the day to visit Cousin Sophy, "over the mountain." I was supposed to stay with another aunt, the mother of my cousin Billy, and to play with him while they were gone. But we soon left his yard and wandered back to mine, which was larger and more interesting, and where we felt the additional charm of being all alone and unwatched. Various diversions, quarrels, and reconciliations made up the long, sunny afternoon. We sucked water from jelly glasses through chive straws until we reeked of them, and fought for the possession of insects in matchboxes. To tease me, Billy deliberately stepped on one of the boxes and crushed its inhabitant flat. When we had made up after this violence, we sat and talked for a while, desultorily, about death in general, and going to heaven, but we were growing a little bored and reckless, and finally I did something really bad: I went in the house and upstairs to my Aunt Mary's bedroom and brought down the tissue-paper-wrapped, retired doll. Billy had never seen her before and was as impressed with her as I had been.

We handled her carefully. We took off her hat and shoes and stockings, and examined every stitch of her underclothes. Then we played vaguely at "operating" on her stomach, but we were rather too much in awe of her for that to be a success. Then we had the idea of adorning her with flowers. There was a clump of Johnny-jump-ups that I thought belonged to me; we picked them and made a wreath for the nameless doll. We laid her out in the garden path and outlined her body with Johnny-jump-ups and babies'-breath and put a pink cosmos in one limp hand. She looked perfectly beautiful. The game was more exciting than "operation." I don't know which one of us said it first, but one of us did, with wild joy—that it was Gwendolyn's funeral, and that the doll's real name, all this time, was Gwendolyn.

But then my grandparents drove into the yard and found us, and my grandmother was furious that I had dared to touch Aunt Mary's doll. Billy was sent straight home and I don't remember now what awful thing happened to me.

1953

Memories of Uncle Neddy

❧

It's raining in Rio de Janeiro, raining, raining, raining. This
morning the papers said it is the rainiest rainy season in seventy-
six years. It is also hot and sticky. The sea—I'm writing in a
penthouse apartment, eleven floors up, facing southeast over the
sea—the sea is blurred with rain, almost hidden by the mixture
of rain and fog, that rarity here. Just close enough inshore to
be visible, an empty-looking freighter lunges heavily south. The
mosaic sidewalks are streaming; the beach is dark, wet, beaten
smooth; the tide line is marked by strands of dark seaweed,
another rarity. And how it rains! It is seeping in under the
french doors and around the window frames. Every so often a
weak breeze seeps in, too, and with it a whiff of decay: some-
thing or other spoiled, fruit or meat. Or perhaps it's a whiff of
mildew from my old books and old papers, even from the shirt
I have on, since in this weather even clothes mildew quickly.
If the rain keeps up much longer the radio will stop working
again and the hi-fi will rust beyond repair. At flood tide the sea
may cross the avenue and start rising slowly up the base of the
apartment building, as it's been known to do.

And Uncle Neddy, that is, my Uncle Edward, is *here.* Into this wildly foreign and, to him, exotic setting, Uncle Neddy has just come back, from the framer's. He leans slightly, silently backwards against the damp-stained pale-yellow wall, looking quite cheerfully into the eyes of whoever happens to look at him —including the cat's, who investigated him just now. Only of course it isn't really Uncle Neddy, not as he was, or not as I knew him. This is "little Edward," before he became an uncle, before he became a lover, husband, father, or grandfather, a tin-smith, a drunkard, or a famous fly-fisherman—any of the various things he turned out to be.

Except for the fact that they give me asthma, I am very fond of molds and mildews. I love the dry-looking, gray-green dust, like bloom on fruit, to begin with, that suddenly appears here on the soles of shoes in the closet, on the backs of all the black books, or the darkest ones, in the bookcase. And I love the black shadow, like the finest soot, that suddenly shows up, slyly, on white bread, or white walls. The molds on food go wild in just a day or two, and in a hot, wet spell like this, a tiny jungle, green, chartreuse, and magenta, may start up in a corner of the bathroom. That gray-green bloom, or that shadow of fine soot, is just enough to serve as a hint of morbidity, attractive morbid-ity—although perhaps mortality is a better word. The gray-green suggests life, the sooty shadow—although living, too —death and dying. And now that Uncle Neddy has turned up again, the latter, the black, has suddenly become associated with him. Because, after all these years, I realize only now that he represented "the devil" for me, not a violent, active Devil, but a gentle black one, a devil of weakness, acquiescence, tentatively black, like the sooty mildew. He died, or his final incarnation died, aged seventy-six, some years ago, and two or three years before that I saw him for the last time. I don't know how he held out so long. He looked already quite dead then, dead and covered with shadow, like the mold, as if his years of life had finally determined to obscure him. (He had looked, too, then, like a dried-out wick, in the smoke-blackened chimney of an oil lamp.)

But here he is again now, young and clean, about twelve years old, with nothing between us but a glaze of old-fashioned varnishing. His widow, Aunt Hat, sent him to me, shipped him thousands of miles from Nova Scotia, along with one of his younger sisters, my mother, in one big crate. Why on earth did Aunt Hat send me the portrait of her late husband? My mother's might have been expected, but Uncle Neddy's came as a complete surprise; and now I can't stop thinking about him. His married life was long-drawn-out and awful; that was common knowledge. Can his presence here be Aunt Hat's revenge? Her last word in their fifty-odd-year battle? And an incredible last straw for him? Or is he here now because he was one of a pair and Aunt Hat was a fiend for order? Because she couldn't bear to break up a set of anything? He looks perfectly calm, polite— quite a pleasant child, in fact—almost as if he were glad to be here, away from it all.

(The frames these ancestor-children arrived in were a foot wide, painted and repainted with glittery, gritty gilt paint. They were meant to hang against dark wallpaper in a haircloth-and-mahogany northern parlor and brighten it up. I have taken the liberty of changing them to narrow, carefully dulled, gold ones, "modern." Now the portraits are reduced to the scale suitable for hanging in apartments.)

Uncle Neddy stands on an imaginary dark red carpet, against a dun-colored wall. His right arm rests on the back of a small chair. This chair is a holy wonder; it must have been the painter's "property" chair—at least, I never saw anything like it in my grandmother's house. It consists of two hard-looking maroon-colored pads, both hung with thick, foot-long, maroon fringes; the lower one makes the seat, the upper one, floating in the airless air, and on which Uncle Neddy's arm rests, the back. Uncle Neddy wears a black suit, velveteen, I think; the jacket has pockets and is gathered to a yoke. He has a narrow white collar and white cuffs and a double black bow of what appears to be grosgrain ribbon is tied under the jacket collar. Perhaps his face is more oblivious than calm. Its not actually belonging to the suit or the chair gives it an extraneous look. It could almost have drifted in from another place, or another year, and settled into the painting. Plump (he was never in the slightest plump, that I can remember), his hair parted neatly on the left, his cheeks as pink as a girl's, or a doll's. He looks rather more like his sisters than like Uncle Neddy—the later versions of him, certainly. His tight trousers come to just below the knee and I can make out three ornamental buttons on each side. His weight rests on the left leg; his right leg is crossed in front of it and the toe of his right boot barely touches the other boot and the red carpet. The boots are very small, buttoned. In spite of his peaceful expression, they probably hurt him. I remember his telling me about the copper-toed boots he wore as a child, but these have no copper toes and must be his "good" boots. His body looks neatly stuffed. His eyes are a bright hazel and in the left one—right, to me—the painter has carefully placed a highlight of dry white paint, like a crumb. He never looked so clean and glossy, so peaceful and godly, so presentable, again— or certainly not as I remember him.

But of course he did have a streak of godliness somewhere, or else of a hypocrisy so common then, so unrecognized, that it fooled everyone including himself. How often did my grand-mother tell me that as a small boy my Uncle Neddy had read the Bible, Old and New Testaments, straight through three times? Even as a child, I never quite believed this, but she was so utterly convinced that perhaps it really was true. It was the thing for children to do. Little Edward had also been a great text-memorizer and hymn-singer, and this much I did believe because when I knew him he often quoted texts, and not the well-known ones that everybody quoted, either; and he sang in the church choir. He also said grace before meals. Rather, he read grace. His memory for texts apparently didn't go that far. He had a little black book, printed in black on yellowish paper, with "artistic" red initial letters at the top and middle of each page, that gave two graces for every day in the year. This he held just under the edge of the table, and with his head down read the grace for that day and meal to his family, in a small, muffled voice. The little book was so worn with use that the pages were loose. Occasionally a few would fall out onto the floor and have to be retrieved when grace was over, while my little cousin Billy (Uncle Neddy's youngest child, a year or two younger than I was) and I, if I happened to be present, rolled our eyes at each other and giggled. My grandparents rather disapproved of their son for using a book. After all, my grandfather thriftily said the same grace every time, year in, year out, at all our regular meals. "Oh Lord," it began, "we have reasons to thank Thee"—but this sounded like "raisins," to me. (But then, at this time I also confused "as we forgive our debtors" with "taters," a word I'd heard used humorously for "potatoes.") However, if we had company to dinner or "tea," my grandfather was perfectly capable of producing a longer, more grateful one, or even making up one of his own to suit the occasion.

Until age or drink had spoiled it, Uncle Neddy had a very nice baritone voice, and Sundays when he was well enough to go to church he appeared in the back row of the choir. On those days he wore a navy-blue suit and a hard collar, a dark blue satin tie with a red stripe, and a stickpin with a small, dead diamond in it, much like the white highlight in his left eye that I am contemplating right now.

But I want to try to be chronological about this little boy who doesn't look much like a little boy. His semi-disembodied head seems too big for his body; and his body seems older, far less alive, than the round, healthy, painted face which is so very much in the present it seems to be taking an interest in it, even here, so very far away from where it saw such a very different world for so long.

The first dramatic episode of his life that I know about was when his foot got scalded. He told me the story more than once, usually as a warning to keep away from something hot. It concerned his boots, not these in the painting but his first pair of copper-toed boots, real little boots, no buttons or laces. Out of curiosity, he stood too near someone who was dipping boiling water out of the big boiler on the back of the kitchen stove and somehow a dipperful fell straight into a boot top. The boot was pulled off immediately, and then his sock. "And the skin came with it," Uncle Neddy always said, proud and morbid, while an icicle suddenly probed the bottom of my stomach. The family doctor came, and for a long time poor Uncle Neddy couldn't walk. His mother and sisters—he was the only son, the second child—all said he had been a very stoical boy; on that occasion he had only given one scream. Later on, he had performed prodigies of stoicism in respect to the Nova Scotian winter cold. He couldn't endure being bundled up and would run out of the house and all the way to school, with the thermometer at ten, or twenty, below, without his overcoat. He would condescend to wear mittens and a muffler, but no more, and his ears had been frostbitten over and over again, and once one was frozen.

After these feats of endurance, his life, except for the Bible-reading, is unknown to me for a long time. No—it was Uncle Neddy who dug all the wax off the face of my mother's big wax doll from France, with his fingernails, and chewed it like chewing gum. The delicacy of the doll's complexion depended on this wax; without it, she was red-faced and common. Uncle Neddy and my mother were playing upstairs; when my mother protested, he pushed her downstairs. Then when she pretended to faint and lay there at the foot of the stairs with her eyes shut, in great remorse he ran and got a quart dipper full of icy well water and threw it over her, crying out that he had killed his little sister.

And although she has been dead for over forty years, his little sister is here now, too, beside him. *Her* imaginary carpet is laid out geometrically in dark red, green, and blue, or is it supposed to be tiles? and her wall is darker than his. She leans on a fairly normal round table, draped in a long red tablecloth, and her left leg is crossed over her right one. She must be about nine. She wears a small bustle and a gold brooch, but her black hair is cut short all over, with a fringe over her eyes, and she looks almost more like a boy than he does.

The paintings are unsigned and undated, probably the work of an itinerant portrait painter. Perhaps he worked from tintypes, because in the family album the little girl's dress appears again. Or did she have only the one dress, for dress-up? In the painting it is dark blue, white-sprigged, with the bustle and other additions purple, and two white frills making a sort of "bertha." (In the tintype the French wax doll appears, too, seated on her lap, big and stiff, her feet sticking out in small white boots beneath her petticoats, showing fat legs in striped stockings. She stares composedly at the camera under a raffish blond wig, in need of combing. The tintype man has tinted the cheeks of both the doll and my mother a clear pink. Of course, this must have been before the doll had lost her waxen complexion under Uncle Neddy's fingernails.)

Or perhaps the painter did the faces—clearer and brighter

than the rest of the picture, and in Uncle Neddy's case slightly out of proportion, surely—from "life," the clothes from tintypes, and the rest from his imagination. He may have arrived in the village with his canvases already filled in, the unrecognizable carpets, the round table and improbable chair, ready and waiting to be stood on and leaned on. Did Uncle Neddy insist, "I want to be painted with the chair"? Did the two children fight, more than seventy years ago, over which one would have which background?

Well, Uncle Neddy grew up; he skated a great deal, winters (without bundling up), went through all the grades of the village school, and very early (I heard much later) began to fall in love and to—alas for Neddy—"chase women." I even heard, overheard, rather, that there had been prolonged family worry about a "widow." He must have begun drinking about this time, too, although that was never mentioned until years later when he became, on occasion, a public disgrace. It was hard to know what to do with him; he showed all the classical symptoms of being "wild." In vain family prayers morning and night, the childhood Bible-reading, choir practice, Sunday School ("Sabbath School," my grandfather called it), church itself, Friday prayer meetings, and the annual revivals at which Uncle Neddy went forward and repented of all. At one of these, Uncle Neddy even took the "pledge," the temperance pledge that he could still recite to me years later, although he had broken it heaven only knew how many times by then:

> *Trusting in help from heaven above*
> *We pledge ourselves to works of love,*
> *Resolving that we will not make*
> *Or sell or buy or give or take*
> *Rum, Brandy, Whiskey, Cordials fine,*
> *Gin, Cider, Porter, Ale or Wine.*

Tobacco, too, we will not use
And trust that we may always choose
A place among the wise and good
And speak and act as Christians should.

This was called the "Pledge of the Iron Age Band of Hope." The "Band of Hope" was an inspirational society for younger members of the church, but why "Iron Age"? Uncle Neddy didn't know and I never found out. It became vaguely associated in my mind with his profession. Because, after all these moral incentives, Uncle Neddy inevitably, immediately, began to show signs of being "wild" all over again and finally he was apprenticed to a tinsmith, to learn a trade—tinsmithing and installing and repairing wood-burning furnaces. And then, still very young, he married Aunt Hat. I got the impression later (I was a little pitcher with big ears) that perhaps he "had" to marry her, but I may be doing him an injustice.

Redheaded, rawboned, green-eyed, handsome, Aunt Hat came from Galway Mines, a sort of ghost town twenty miles off, where iron mining and smelting were still carried on in a reduced and primitive way. It had once been more flourishing, but I remember boarded-up houses, boarded-up stores with rotting wooden sidewalks in front of them, and the many deep black or dark red holes that disfigured the hills. Also a mountainous slag heap, dead, gray, and glistening. Long before I was born, one of these slag heaps, built up for years, I don't know why, right beside or on the river that farther downstream ran through our village, had given way and there had been a flood. I heard this story many times because my grandparents' house was on the lower side of the village, near the river, and it had been flooded. A warning had been given, but in the excitement of rescuing the older children, the clock, the cow and horse, my grandmother forgot the latest baby (later my aunt), and my grandfather had dashed back into the house to find her floating peacefully in her wooden cradle, bobbing over the kitchen floor. (But after this the poor baby had erysipelas.)

If Uncle Neddy was a "devil," a feeble, smoky-black one, Aunt Hat was a red, real one—redheaded, freckled, red-knuckled, strong, all fierce fire and flame. There *was* something of the Old Nick about her. They complemented each other; they were devils together. Rumor had it that the only other redhead for miles around was the parish priest at Galway Mines—the only Catholic community in the county. True or not, the village gossips drew their strictly Protestant and cruel conclusions.

My own recollections begin now, things I saw or heard: Uncle Neddy is a tinsmith, a married man, the father of three living and one or two dead children. He has a big shop across the green from my grandparents' house, in the only part of my grandfather's former tannery not torn down. (The local tanning trade had come to an end before I was born, when chemicals replaced tanbark.) From the entrance, with double doors, the shop starts out fairly bright; a large section is devoted to "store" galvanized pails and enameled pots and pans, two or three or more black kitchen ranges with nickel trimmings, farming implements, and fishing rods—the last because fishing was Uncle Neddy's passion. But the farther in one goes, the darker and more gloomy it becomes; the floor is covered with acrid-smelling, glinting, black dust and the workbench stretching across the far end is black, with glints of silver. Night descends as one walks back, then daylight grows as one reaches the dirty windows above the workbench. This night sky of Uncle Neddy's is hung with the things he makes himself: milk pails, their bottoms shining like moons; flashing tin mugs in different sizes; watering pots like comets, in among big dull lengths of stove pipe with wrinkled blue joints like elephants' legs dangling overhead.

When he was at work, Uncle Neddy always wore a black leather cap, or perhaps it was so shiny with wear it looked like leather, and black, black overalls. He chewed tobacco. The plugs of chewing tobacco had a little red tin apple pressed into one corner; these he took off and gave to me. He loved children and was very good with them. When he kissed me, he smelled violently of "Apple" chewing tobacco and his sooty chin was very scratchy—perhaps he shaved only on Sundays. Frequently he smelled of something else violent, too, and I remember a black or dark brown bottle, unlabeled, kept in the murk under the workbench, being lifted out for a hasty swig.

The shop was full of fascinating things to look at, but surely most of their charm lay in the fact that, besides being brand-new, they were all out of place. Who would expect to see comfortable-looking kitchen stoves, with names like "Magee Ideal" and "Magic Home" on their oven doors, standing leaning sidewise, in a shop? Stone-cold, too, with empty, brand-new teakettles hanging from the rafters over them and the stove-lid lifters hanging up in a bunch, like dried herbs? Or pots and pans, enameled brown or a marbleized blue-and-white, sitting on the floor? Or dozens of tin mugs, the kind we used every day of our lives and that Uncle Neddy actually made, hanging overhead, brilliantly new and clean, not dull and brown, the way they got at home? And kitchen pumps, sticky red or green, and the taller, thinner variety of pump for the barnyard, lying on the floor? Besides all these things there were fascinating black machines attached to the workbench and worked by hand. One was for rolling the blue-black sheet iron into stovepipes; one made turned-over edges on strips of tin so that they wouldn't cut the fingers, and there were others of more mysterious functions, all black and sinister. There were blowtorches and a sort of miniature forge, little anvils, heavy shears in all sizes, wooden mallets, boxes of stubby, gray-blue, flat-headed rivets and, best of all, solder. It came in thick silver rods, with a trade name stamped along them. What I liked best was to watch Uncle Neddy heat the end of a rod to the melting point and dribble it quickly to join a wide ribbon of tin and make a mug, sometimes a child-size mug, then solder on a strip already folded under on both sides in the folding machine for the handle. When they were cold, drops of solder that fell to the dirty floor could be picked up, pure silver, cool and heavy, and saved. Under the bench were piles of bright scraps of tin with sharp edges, curved shapes, triangles, pieces with holes in them, as if they'd been cut from paper, and prettiest of all, thin tin shavings, curled up tight, like springs. Occasionally, Uncle Neddy would let me help him hold a stick of solder and dribble it around the bottom of a pail. This was thrilling, but oh, to be able to write one's name with it, in silver letters! As he worked, bent over, clipping, hammering, soldering, he chewed tobacco and spat long black spits under the bench. He was like a black snail, a rather quick but cautious snail, leaving a silvery, shiny trail of solder.

Probably the paying part of his business was installing furnaces, but that didn't interest Billy and me, although Billy was sometimes allowed to go along. They went off, with a helper, down the shore, to places like Lower Economy, the red wagon loaded with furnace parts and stovepipes, pulled by Nimble, our horse.

While Uncle Neddy worked away, chewing and spitting and drinking, with an occasional customer to talk to (there were two kitchen chairs in the front of the shop where men sometimes sat and talked, about fishing, mostly), or with a child or two to keep him company, his wife was cleaning house. Scrub, scrub and polish, polish, she went, all day long, in the house, next door but up higher, on a grass-covered slope. The house was shingled, painted bright red, the only red house in the village, and although it seemed big enough for Uncle Neddy's family, it was never quite finished; another veranda, a spare room, were always in the process of being added on, or shingled, but never quite completed, or painted. A narrow veranda led from the street to a side door, the only one used, and chickweed grew profusely underneath it, down the slope. My grandmother would send me across the street to pick some for her canaries and Aunt Hat would come out, lean over, and ask me crossly what I was doing, or just bang a dust mop on the railing, over my head. Her sharp-jawed, freckled face and green eyes behind gold-rimmed glasses peered over at me, upside down. She had her good days and her bad days, as my grandmother said, but mostly they seemed to be bad and on those she did everything more vigorously and violently. Sometimes she would order me home, where I meant to go, anyway, and with my innocent handful of chickweed, I ran.

Her three living children—there were two girls, older than Billy and I—all had beautiful curly hair. The girls were old enough to comb their own hair, but when Billy's curls were being made, really made, for Sunday School, his shrieks could be heard all the way across the green to our house. Then Billy would arrive to go to Sunday School with me, his face smeared with tears, the beautiful red-brown curls in perfect tubes, with drops of water (Aunt Hat wet the curls and turned them over her finger with a hard brush) falling from the end of each onto the white, ruffled collar of his Sunday blouse. Mondays, Aunt Hat energetically scrubbed the family's clothes, summers, down below, out back. On good days she occasionally burst quite loudly into song as she scrubbed and rinsed:

> *Oh, the moon shines tonight on pretty Red Wing,*
> *The breeze is sighing,*
> *The night bird's crying.*

Oh, far beneath the sky her warrior's sleeping
While Red Wing's weeping
Her heart awa-a-y . . .

This song is still associated in my mind not with a disconsolate Indian maiden and red wings but with a red house, red hair, strong yellow laundry soap, and galvanized scrubbing boards (also sold in Uncle Neddy's shop; I forgot them). On other weekdays, Aunt Hat, as I have said, cleaned house: it was probably the cleanest house in the county. The kitchen linoleum dazzled; the straw matting in the upstairs bedrooms looked like new and so did the hooked rugs; the "cozy corner" in the parlor, with a red upholstered seat and frilled red pillows standing on their corners, was never disarranged; every china ornament on the mantelpiece over the airtight stove was in the same place and dustless, and Aunt Hat always seemed to have a broom or a long-handled brush in her hand, ready to take a swipe either at her household effects or at any child, dog, or cat that came her way. Her temper, like her features, seemed constantly at a high temperature, but on bad days it rose many degrees and she "took it out," as the village said behind her back, in cleaning house. They also said she was "a great hand at housework" or "a demon for housework"; sometimes, "She's a Tartar, that one!" It was also remarked on that in a village where every sunny window was filled with houseplants and the ladies constantly exchanged "slips" of this and that desirable one, Aunt Hat had "no luck" with plants; in fact, nothing would grow for her at all.

Yes, she was a Tartar; it came out in her very freckles. She sunburned easily. When we went on a picnic, one hour in the northern sun and the V of her neck was flaming. Uncle Neddy would say, almost as if he were proud of it, "Hat's neck looks as if I'd taken a flatiron to it!" Wearing a straw hat and a gray cardigan instead of his black work clothes, even in the sunlight he still looked dark. But instead of being like a dark snail, he was a thin, dark salamander, enjoying, for a moment, his wife's fieriness.

His married life was miserable, we all knew that. My girl cousins whispered to me about the horrible, endless fights that went on, nights, under the low, slanting ceiling of their parents' bedroom, papered all over with small, pained-looking rosebuds, like pursed mouths. When things got too bad he would come to see "Mother" and they would shut themselves in the front parlor, or even in the pantry, standing up, for a talk. At our house, my grandmother was the one who did all the complaining; my grandfather never complained. When she said things about her daughter-in-law that he felt were too harsh, he merely murmured, "Yes, temper . . . temper . . . too bad," or maybe it was "too sad." (To Billy and me, when we quarreled, he said, "Birds in their little nests agree," a quotation I have never been able to place and even then didn't altogether agree with, from my observation of birds in their little nests.) There were days and weeks when these visits from a bedeviled-looking Uncle Neddy occurred often; dramas of which I knew nothing were going on; once in a while I made out that they concerned money, "deeds," or "papers." When Uncle Neddy had finally gone back to his shop, my grandmother would collapse into her kitchen rocking chair and announce: "*She* makes the balls and he fires them . . ." Then she would start rocking, groaning and rocking, wiping her eyes with the edge of her apron, uttering from time to time the mysterious remark that was a sort of chorus in our lives: "Nobody knows . . . *nobody knows* . . ." I often wondered what my grandmother knew that none of the rest of us knew and if she alone knew it, or if it was a total mystery that really nobody knew except perhaps God. I even asked her, "*What* do you know, Gammie, that we don't know?

Why don't you tell us? Tell me!" She only laughed, dabbing at her tears. She laughed as easily as she cried, and one very often turned into the other (a trait her children and grand-children inherited). Then, "Go on with you!" she said. "Scat!"

From the rocking chair by the window, she had a good view of all the green, the people on their way to the general store just around the corner, or on Sundays, to the tall white Presby-terian church opposite, and, diagonally to the right, of Uncle Neddy's shop and the red house. She disapproved of the way Aunt Hat fed her family. Often, around time for "tea," Billy or one of the girls could be seen running across to the store, and a few minutes later running back with a loaf of bread or some-thing in a paper bag. My grandmother was furious: "Store bread! Store bread! Nothing but store bread!" Or, "More canned things, I'll bet! More *soda crackers* . . ." I knew from direct observation that when he was far too big for the family high chair, Billy was squeezed into it and given what was called "pap" for *his* "tea." This was a soup plate full of the soda crackers, swimming in milk, limp and adhesive, with a lot of sugar to make them go down. The "pap" would be topped off by two pieces of marble cake, or parkins, for dessert. Aunt Hat did bake those, if not bread, and her parkins were good, but, as if out of spite, hard enough to break the teeth.

Sometimes I inadvertently brought on my grandmother's tears myself, by repeating things Billy told me. Perhaps he, too, was firing the balls made on the other side of the green, or pebbles, suited to the verbal slingshot of his tender years. "Is it true that Nimble [the one horse—later there were two horses, the second unfortunately named Maud, the name, straight from Tennyson, of one of my aunts]—is it true that Nimble belongs to Uncle Neddy? Billy says he does. And that Nelly and Martha Washington do, too?" (The cow and her calf; I had named the calf myself.)

My grandmother grew indignant. "I *gave* your Uncle Edward that horse on his tenth wedding anniversary! Not only that, but he sold him back to me two years afterwards and he still keeps saying I haven't finished paying him yet! When I have! And he uses that horse all the time, much more than we do!"

"Oh pshaw, mother," said my grandfather. "That's an old story now."

"Oh yes," said my grandmother. "Nimble, and the buffalo robe, and the dinner service, and *pew rent*—they're all old stories now. *You'd* never remember anything. But *I* won't forget. *I* won't forget." And she set the rocking chair rocking as if it were, as it probably was, a memory machine.

I have a few more memories of Uncle Neddy at this period in his life when the tinsmith business was still going on, and the furnace business, flourishing or not, I don't know, but before the obvious decline had set in and before I went away to Boston and saw him at less and less frequent intervals. One memory, brief but poignant, like a childhood nightmare that haunts one for years, or all one's life, the details are so clear and so awful, is of a certain Christmas. Or maybe it was a Christmas Eve, because it takes place after the lamps were lit—but of course it grew dark very early in the winter. There was a large Christmas tree, smelling overpoweringly of fir, in the parlor. It was rather sparsely decorated with colored paper chains, strings of tinsel and popcorn, and a very few glass balls or other shiny ornaments: a countrified, homemade tree, chopped down and brought fresh from the snow-covered "commons." But there were a few little silver and gold baskets, full of candies, woven from strips of metal by "the blind children," and clips holding twisted wax candles that after many warnings were finally lit. One of my aunts played "Holy Night" on the piano and the candles flickered in time to our singing.

This was all very nice, but still I remember it as "the Black

Christmas." My other grandparents, in the States, had sent a large box of presents. It contained woolen caps and mufflers for Billy and me, and I didn't like them at all. His set was dark blue but mine was *gray* and I hated it at sight. There were also mittens and socks, and some of these were red or blue, and the high black rubber boots I'd wanted, but my pair was much too big. Laid out under the tree, even by flickering candlelight, everything looked shapeless and sad, and I wanted to cry. And then Santa Claus came in, an ordinary brown potato sack over his shoulder, with the other presents sagging in it. He was terrifying. He couldn't have been dressed in black, but that was my impression, and I did start to cry. He had artificial snow sprinkled on his shoulders, and a pointed red cap, but the beard! It wasn't white and woolly at all, it was made of rope, a mass of frayed-out rope. This dreadful figure cavorted around the room, making jokes in a loud, deep, false voice. The face that showed above the rope beard looked, to me, like a Negro's. I shrieked. Then this Santa from the depths of a coal mine put down his sack that could have been filled with coal, and hugged and kissed me. Through my sobs, I recognized, by touch and smell and his suddenly everyday voice, that it was only Uncle Neddy.

This Christmas, so like a nightmare, affected me so that shortly afterwards I had a real nightmare about Uncle Neddy, or at least about his shop. In it, I crossed the road and was about to go into the shop when the door was blocked by a huge horse, coming out. The horse filled the doorway, towering high over me and showing all her big yellow teeth in a grin. She whinnied, shrill and deafening; I felt the hot wind coming out of her big nostrils; it almost blew me backwards. I had the presence of mind to say to the horse, "You are a nightmare!" and of course she was, and so I woke up. But awake, I still felt uncomfortable for a long time about Uncle Neddy's possibly having been inside, his escape cut off by that fearful animal.

I said that Uncle Neddy was a great fisherman; it was the thing he did best of all, perhaps the only thing he did perfectly. (For all I know, his tinware, beautiful and shiny as it was, may have been badly made.) He could catch trout where no one else could and sometimes he would go off before daybreak and arrive at our house at seven o'clock with a string of rose-speckled trout for his mother's breakfast. He could cast into the narrowest brooks and impossibly difficult spots and bring out trout after trout. He tied beautiful flies, for himself and friends, and later for customers by mail.

> *Our uncle, innocent of books,*
> *Was rich in lore of fields and brooks . . .*

Whittier wrote of his, and it was true of mine.

But he was not altogether innocent of books. There had been all that childhood Bible-reading that had left the supply of texts from which he still quoted. And also, in his parlor, on a shelf above the "cozy corner" and in a small bookcase, there was an oddly assorted collection of books. I wasn't familiar with them the way I was, with the outsides, at least, of every single book on the shelves in the upstairs hall at my grandmother's (*Inglesby's Legends*; *Home Medicine*; *Emerson's Essays*; and so on), but this was only because of Aunt Hat. Every time I managed to be alone in the parlor with Uncle Neddy's books, she soon found me and shooed me off home. But I did get to look at them, or some of them, usually the same ones over and over. It was obvious that Uncle Neddy had been strongly affected by the sinking of the *Titanic*; in his modest library there were three different books about this catastrophe, and in the dining room, facing his place at the table, hung a chromograph of the ship going down: the iceberg, the rising steam, people struggling in the water, everything, in full color. When I was left alone in the parlor, an ear cocked for Aunt Hat, I could scarcely wait to take out the *Titanic* books—one very big and heavy, red, with gilt trimmings—and look at the terrifying pictures one more time. There were also *The Tower of London*; a book about Queen Victoria's Diamond Jubilee; *Advice to Young Men* ("Avoid lonely walks . . ."); and several of a religious nature. Also some little fat books about a character named "Dolly Dimples" that looked nice, and were pleasant to hold, but proved boring to read. But the *Titanic* books with their pictures, some of them actual photographs, were the best.

The other chief attraction in Uncle Neddy's parlor was an Edison phonograph, very old, that still worked. It had a flaring, brown-and-gold horn and played thick black cylinders. My girl cousins were allowed to play it. I remember only two out of the box of cylinders: a brief Sousa march that could have marched people about fifty yards, and "Cohen on the Telephone," which I loved. I knew that it was supposed to be funny, and laughed, although I hadn't any idea who or what a Cohen was or what I was laughing at, and I doubt that Uncle Neddy entirely understood it, either.

I suppose that Uncle Neddy's situation in life, his fortune and prospects, could never have been considered happy, even in his small world, but I was very young, and except for an occasional overheard, or eavesdropped-on remark and those private conversations in the parlor or pantry that always upset my grandmother, nothing untoward came to my knowledge, consciously that is, for years. Then even I began to hear more about Uncle Neddy's drinking, and the shop began its long deterioration. There was no place to buy liquor in the village;

the nearest government liquor store was in a town fifteen miles away. At first this meant a daylong drive behind Nimble or Maud; sometimes an overnight stay at the house of a relative, niece or cousin, of my grandfather's. Probably when Uncle Neddy went to town he brought back a supply of rum, the usual drink, heavy, dark, and strong. All I knew of alcohol at that time was the homemade wines the ladies sometimes served each other, or the hot toddy my grandfather sometimes made himself on freezing winter nights. But finally phrases like "not himself," "taken too much," "three seas over," sank into my consciousness and I looked at my poor uncle with new eyes, expectantly. There was one occasion when he had to be taken away from the home funeral of Mrs. Captain McDonald, an old woman everyone was very fond of. What at first passed for Uncle Neddy's natural if demonstrative grief had got "out of hand." My grandmother moaned about this; in fact, she moaned so loudly in her bedroom across the hall from mine that I could hear almost every word. "He'll disgrace us all; you'll see. I've *never* . . . There's *never* been a drunkard in *my* family . . . *None* of my brothers . . ." This time my grandfather remained quite silent.

Then Uncle Neddy bought a Model T Ford. There were very few cars in the village then; the family who had driven the coach to the railroad station, four miles off, for years and years, had been the first to acquire one, and there were only two or three more. Uncle Neddy got his Ford somehow, and the younger daughter, fifteen or so, with long curls just like Mary Pickford's, drove it hell-for-leather, expertly. Perhaps she drove her father the fifteen miles to town, in no time, to buy rum— anyway, he got it, and when he didn't have it, there was another unbelievable overheard remark, that he drank *vanilla*.

Meanwhile, the shop was changing. First, there were many more things for sale and less and less work seemed to be done at the old black-and-silver glinting workbench. There were many household effects that came ready-made: can openers, meat grinders, mixing spoons, gray-mottled enamel "sets" of saucepans. There were more fishing rods and then gorgeous barbed fish lures, displayed on cardboard stands. The stoves were now all, or almost all, white enamel, and there were white-enamel kitchen sinks, and faucets, and electric water pumps. The chewing tobacco with the little tin apple in the corner was still on sale, but next to it one day there were chocolate bars: Moirs and Cadbury's, with nuts, without nuts, or in little sections with a different cream in each. These were magnetic, of course, but they cost five cents, or ten cents, and Billy and I had rarely had more than a penny to buy anything in our lives. Uncle Neddy was as kind to us, to any children, as always. He would take a whole ten-cent bar, divide it into its little squares, and share it out. A punchboard appeared, two or three of them. For ten cents one could punch out a little rolled-up paper with a number on it and, with luck, the number would win a whole big box of chocolates or a tin of biscuits. It was still a fascinating place to go, but not nearly as fascinating as when Uncle Neddy had been making tin mugs and soldering.

Then I went away to live in the States and came back just for the summers. Perhaps two or three years went by, I'm not sure, but one summer a gasoline pump appeared in front of the shop. Cars stopped to be filled up; not very often, but there were more of them, although the road was still dirt and gravel, "crowned" in the middle. Billy and I competed with each other as to which one had seen the most and the biggest trucks. If a truck stopped for gasoline, we rushed to examine it: red or blue paint, decorated with white lines or gold lines, with arrowheads, what load it was carrying, and where it was going. Sometimes Uncle Neddy poured water into its radiator from one of his own watering cans while it stood steaming and trembling. Another summer, and the road had been covered with tar. The red house still had an unpainted wing, its "new" shingles already gray. Another summer the Governor General drove through and stopped to make a speech in front of Uncle Neddy's shop. Another little girl, not me, curtsied and presented a large bouquet of flowers to his wife, Lady Bing.

Although there are more, these are all the memories I want to keep on remembering—I couldn't forget them if I tried, probably—and remembering clearly, as if they had just happened or were still happening. My grandfather dies. My grandmother goes to live with a daughter in Quebec. I go away to school, then to college. I come back at longer and longer intervals to Uncle Neddy's village. Once I go fishing with him and he deplores my casting, but, as always, very gently. He grows older—older, thinner, bent, and more unshaven, the sooty bristles mixed with silver. His voice grows weaker, too, and higher-pitched. He has stomach ulcers. He is operated on, but won't stop, can't stop drinking—or so I am told. It has taken the form of periodic bouts and an aunt tells me (I'm old enough to be confided in) that "Everyone knows" and that "It will kill him." However, when he dies it is of something quite different.

The last time I saw him he was very weak and very bent. The eyes of the man who used to lean down to hug and kiss me were now on a level with mine. When I kissed him, the smell was only half the same: rum—he no longer chewed tobacco. I knew, and he said it, that he was "not long for this world." Aunt Hat had aged, too. The red hair had faded to pink, but her jaw, her freckles, and her disposition were exactly the same. She no longer shooed me out of the house. Now she expressed her feelings by pretending not to see the presents from the States, clamping her jaw tight, and swatting at flies. Some days she refused to speak; others, she spoke—disparagingly, of whatever subject came up. The filling station was owned and manned by others.

I don't believe that Uncle Neddy ever went anywhere in his life except possibly two or three times as far as Boston after his daughters had moved there and married, and I'm not sure of that. And now he is here, on the other side of the Equator, with his little sister, looking like the good boy in an Horatio Alger story: poor, neat, healthy, polite, and by some lucky accident—preventing a banker from having his pocket picked, or catching a runaway horse—about to start out being a "success" in life, and perhaps taking his little sister along with him. He is overdressed for this climate and his cheeks are so pink he must be sweating in his velveteen suit.

I am going to hang them here side by side, above the antique (Brazilian antique) chest of drawers. In spite of the heat and dampness, they look calmly on and on, at the invisible Tropic of Capricorn, at the extravagant rain still blotting out the southern ocean. I must watch out for the mildew that inevitably forms on old canvases in the rainy season, and wipe them off often. It will be the gray or pale-green variety that appears overnight on dark surfaces, like breath on a mirror. Uncle Neddy will continue to exchange his direct, bright-hazel, child's looks, now, with those of strangers—dark-eyed Latins he never knew, who never would have understood him, whom he would have thought of, if he had ever thought of them at all, as "foreigners." How late, Uncle Neddy, how late to have started on your travels!

1977

In the Village

ℰ

A scream, the echo of a scream, hangs over that Nova Scotian village. No one hears it; it hangs there forever, a slight stain in those pure blue skies, skies that travelers compare to those of Switzerland, too dark, too blue, so that they seem to keep on darkening a little more around the horizon—or is it around the rims of the eyes?—the color of the cloud of bloom on the elm trees, the violet on the fields of oats; something darkening over the woods and waters as well as the sky. The scream hangs like that, unheard, in memory—in the past, in the present, and those years between. It was not even loud to begin with, perhaps. It just came there to live, forever—not loud, just alive forever. Its pitch would be the pitch of my village. Flick the lightning rod on top of the church steeple with your fingernail and you will hear it.

She stood in the large front bedroom with sloping walls on either side, papered in wide white and dim-gold stripes. Later, it was she who gave the scream.

The village dressmaker was fitting a new dress. It was her first in almost two years and she had decided to come out of black, so the dress was purple. She was very thin. She wasn't at all sure whether she was going to like the dress or not and she kept lifting the folds of the skirt, still unpinned and dragging on the floor around her, in her thin white hands, and looking down at the cloth.

"Is it a good shade for me? Is it too bright? I don't know. I haven't worn colors for so long now . . . How long? Should it be black? Do you think I should keep on wearing black?"

Drummers sometimes came around selling gilded red or green books, unlovely books, filled with bright new illustrations of the Bible stories. The people in the pictures wore clothes like the purple dress, or like the way it looked then.

It was a hot summer afternoon. Her mother and her two sisters were there. The older sister had brought her home, from Boston, not long before, and was staying on, to help. Because in Boston she had not got any better, in months and months— or had it been a year? In spite of the doctors, in spite of the frightening expenses, she had not got any better.

First, she had come home, with her child. Then she had gone away again, alone, and left the child. Then she had come home. Then she had gone away again, with her sister; and now she was home again.

Unaccustomed to having her back, the child stood now in the doorway, watching. The dressmaker was crawling around and around on her knees eating pins as Nebuchadnezzar had crawled eating grass. The wallpaper glinted and the elm trees outside hung heavy and green, and the straw matting smelled like the ghost of hay.

Clang.

Clang.

Oh, beautiful sounds, from the blacksmith's shop at the end of the garden! Its gray roof, with patches of moss, could be seen above the lilac bushes. Nate was there—Nate, wearing a long black leather apron over his trousers and bare chest, sweating hard, a black leather cap on top of dry, thick, black-and-gray curls, a black sooty face; iron filings, whiskers, and gold teeth, all together, and a smell of red-hot metal and horses' hoofs.

Clang.

The pure note: pure and angelic.

The dress was all wrong. She screamed.

The child vanishes.

Later they sit, the mother and the three sisters, in the shade on the back porch, sipping sour, diluted ruby: raspberry vinegar. The dressmaker refuses to join them and leaves, holding the dress to her heart. The child is visiting the blacksmith.

In the blacksmith's shop things hang up in the shadows and shadows hang up in the things, and there are black and glistening piles of dust in each corner. A tub of night-black water stands by the forge. The horseshoes sail through the dark like bloody little moons and follow each other like bloody little moons to drown in the black water, hissing, protesting.

Outside, along the matted eaves, painstakingly, sweetly, wasps go over and over a honeysuckle vine.

Inside, the bellows creak. Nate does wonders with both hands; with one hand. The attendant horse stamps his foot and nods his head as if agreeing to a peace treaty.

Nod.

And nod.

A Newfoundland dog looks up at him and they almost touch noses, but not quite, because at the last moment the horse decides against it and turns away.

Outside in the grass lie scattered big, pale granite discs, like millstones, for making wheel rims on. This afternoon they are too hot to touch.

Now it is settling down, the scream.

Now the dressmaker is at home, basting, but in tears. It is the most beautiful material she has worked on in years. It has been sent to the woman from Boston, a present from her mother-in-law, and heaven knows how much it cost.

Before my older aunt had brought her back, I had watched my grandmother and younger aunt unpacking her clothes, her "things." In trunks and barrels and boxes they had finally come, from Boston, where she and I had once lived. So many things in the village came from Boston, and even I had once come from there. But I remembered only being here, with my grandmother.

The clothes were black, or white, or black-and-white.

"Here's a mourning hat," says my grandmother, holding up something large, sheer, and black, with large black roses on it; at least I guess they are roses, even if black.

"There's that mourning coat she got the first winter," says my aunt.

But always I think they are saying "morning." Why, in the morning, did one put on black? How early in the morning did one begin? Before the sun came up?

"Oh, here are some housedresses!"

They are nicer. Clean and starched, stiffly folded. One with black polka dots. One of fine black-and-white stripes with black grosgrain bows. A third with a black velvet bow and on the bow a pin of pearls in a little wreath.

"Look. She forgot to take it off."

A white hat. A white embroidered parasol. Black shoes with buckles glistening like the dust in the blacksmith's shop. A silver mesh bag. A silver calling-card case on a little chain. Another bag of silver mesh, gathered to a tight, round neck of strips of silver that will open out, like the hatrack in the front hall. A silver-framed photograph, quickly turned over. Handkerchiefs with narrow black hems—"morning handkerchiefs." In bright sunlight, over breakfast tables, they flutter.

A bottle of perfume has leaked and made awful brown stains.

Oh, marvelous scent, from somewhere else! It doesn't smell like that here; but there, somewhere, it does, still.

A big bundle of postcards. The curdled elastic around them breaks. I gather them together on the floor.

Some people wrote with pale-blue ink, and some with brown, and some with black, but mostly blue. The stamps have been torn off many of them. Some are plain, or photographs, but some have lines of metallic crystals on them—how beautiful!— silver, gold, red, and green, or all four mixed together, crumbling off, sticking in the lines on my palms. All the cards like this I spread on the floor to study. The crystals outline the buildings on the cards in a way buildings never are outlined but should be—if there were a way of making the crystals stick. But probably not; they would fall to the ground, never to be seen again. Some cards, instead of lines around the buildings, have words written in their skies with the same stuff, crumbling, dazzling and crumbling, raining down a little on little people who sometimes stand about below: pictures of Pentecost? What are the messages? I cannot tell, but they are falling on those specks of hands, on the hats, on the toes of their shoes, in their paths—wherever it is they are.

Postcards come from another world, the world of the grandparents who send things, the world of sad brown perfume, and morning. (The gray postcards of the village for sale in the village store are so unilluminating that they scarcely count. After all, one steps outside and immediately sees the same thing: the village, where we live, full-size, and in color.)

Two barrels of china. White with a gold band. Broken bits. A thick white teacup with a small red-and-blue butterfly on it, painfully desirable. A teacup with little pale-blue windows in it.

"See the grains of rice?" says my grandmother, showing me the cup against the light.

Could you poke the grains out? No, it seems they aren't really there any more. They were put there just for a while and then they left something or other behind. What odd things people do with grains of rice, so innocent and small! My aunt says that she has heard they write the Lord's Prayer on them. And make them make those little pale-blue lights.

More broken china. My grandmother says it breaks her heart. "Why couldn't they have got it packed better? Heaven knows what it cost."

"Where'll we put it all? The china closet isn't nearly big enough."

"It'll just have to stay in the barrels."

"Mother, you might as well use it."

"*No*," says my grandmother.

"Where's the silver, Mother?"

"In the vault in Boston."

Vault. Awful word. I run the tip of my finger over the rough, jeweled lines on the postcards, over and over. They hold things up to each other and exclaim, and talk, and exclaim, over and over.

"There's that cake basket."

"Mrs. Miles . . ."

"Mrs. Miles's sponge cake . . ."

"She was very fond of her."

Another photograph—"Oh, that *Negro* girl! That friend."

"She went to be a medical missionary. She had a letter from her, last winter. From Africa."

"They were great friends."

They show me the picture. She, too, is black-and-white, with glasses on a chain. A morning friend.

And the smell, the wonderful smell of the dark-brown stains. Is it roses?

A tablecloth.

"She did beautiful work," says my grandmother.

"But look—it isn't finished."

Two pale, smooth wooden hoops are pressed together in the linen. There is a case of little ivory embroidery tools.

I abscond with a little ivory stick with a sharp point. To keep it forever I bury it under the bleeding heart by the crab-apple tree, but it is never found again.

Nate sings and pumps the bellows with one hand. I try to help, but he really does it all, from behind me, and laughs when the coals blow red and wild.

"Make me a ring! Make me a ring, Nate!"

Instantly it is made; it is mine.

It is too big and still hot, and blue and shiny. The horseshoe nail has a flat oblong head, pressing hot against my knuckle.

Two men stand watching, chewing or spitting tobacco, matches, horseshoe nails—anything, apparently, but with such presence; they are perfectly at home. The horse is the real guest, however. His harness hangs loose like a man's suspenders; they say pleasant things to him; one of his legs is doubled up in an improbable, affectedly polite way, and the bottom of his hoof is laid bare, but he doesn't seem to mind. Manure piles up behind him, suddenly, neatly. He, too, is very much at home. He is enormous. His rump is like a brown, glossy globe of the whole brown world. His ears are secret entrances to the under-world. His nose is supposed to feel like velvet and does, with ink spots under milk all over its pink. Clear bright-green bits of stiffened froth, like glass, are stuck around his mouth. He wears medals on his chest, too, and one on his forehead, and simpler decorations—red and blue celluloid rings overlapping each other on leather straps. On each temple is a clear glass bulge, like an eyeball, but in them are the heads of two other little horses (his dreams?), brightly colored, real and raised, untouchable, alas, against backgrounds of silver blue. His trophies hang around him, and the cloud of his odor is a chariot in itself.

At the end, all four feet are brushed with tar, and shine, and he expresses his satisfaction, rolling it from his nostrils like noisy smoke, as he backs into the shafts of his wagon.

The purple dress is to be fitted again this afternoon but I take a note to Miss Gurley to say the fitting will have to be postponed. Miss Gurley seems upset.

"Oh dear. And how is—" And she breaks off.

Her house is littered with scraps of cloth and tissue-paper patterns, yellow, pinked, with holes in the shapes of *A, B, C,* and *D* in them, and numbers; and threads everywhere like a fine vegetation. She has a bosom full of needles with threads ready to pull out and make nests with. She sleeps in her thimble. A gray kitten once lay on the treadle of her sewing machine, where she rocked it as she sewed, like a baby in a cradle, but it got hanged on the belt. Or did she make that up? But another gray-and-white one lies now by the arm of the machine, in imminent danger of being sewn into a turban. There is a table covered with laces and braids, embroidery silks, and cards of buttons of all colors—big ones for winter coats, small pearls, little glass ones delicious to suck.

She has made the very dress I have on, "for twenty-five cents." My grandmother said my other grandmother would certainly be surprised at that.

The purple stuff lies on a table; long white threads hang all about it. Oh, look away before it moves by itself, or makes a sound; before it echoes, echoes, what it has heard!

Mysteriously enough, poor Miss Gurley—I know she is poor —gives me a five-cent piece. She leans over and drops it in the pocket of the red-and-white dress that she has made herself. It is very tiny, very shiny. King George's beard is like a little silver flame. Because they look like herring- or maybe salmon-scales, five-cent pieces are called "fish scales." One heard of people's rings being found inside fish, or their long-lost jackknives. What if one could scrape a salmon and find a little picture of King George on every scale?

I put my five-cent piece in my mouth for greater safety on the way home, and swallowed it. Months later, as far as I know, it is still in me, transmuting all its precious metal into my growing teeth and hair.

Back home, I am not allowed to go upstairs. I hear my aunts running back and forth, and something like a tin washbasin falls bump in the carpeted upstairs hall.

My grandmother is sitting in the kitchen stirring potato mash for tomorrow's bread and crying into it. She gives me a spoonful and it tastes wonderful but wrong. In it I think I taste my grandmother's tears; then I kiss her and taste them on her cheek.

She says it is time for her to get fixed up, and I say I want to help her brush her hair. So I do, standing swaying on the lower rung of the back of her rocking chair.

The rocking chair has been painted and repainted so many times that it is as smooth as cream—blue, white, and gray all showing through. My grandmother's hair is silver and in it she keeps a great many celluloid combs, at the back and sides, streaked gray and silver to match. The one at the back has longer teeth than the others and a row of sunken silver dots across the top, beneath a row of little balls. I pretend to play a tune on it; then I pretend to play a tune on each of the others before we stick them in, so my grandmother's hair is full of music. She laughs. I am so pleased with myself that I do not feel obliged to mention the five-cent piece. I drink a rusty, icy drink out of the biggest dipper; still, nothing much happens.

We are waiting for a scream. But it is not screamed again, and the red sun sets in silence.

Every morning I take the cow to the pasture we rent from Mr. Chisolm. She, Nelly, could probably go by herself just as well, but I like marching through the village with a big stick, directing her.

This morning it is brilliant and cool. My grandmother and I are alone again in the kitchen. We are talking. She says it is cool enough to keep the oven going, to bake the bread, to roast a leg of lamb.

"Will you remember to go down to the brook? Take Nelly around by the brook and pick me a big bunch of mint. I thought I'd make some mint sauce."

"For the leg of lamb?"

"You finish your porridge."

"I think I've had enough now . . ."

"Hurry up and finish that porridge."

There is talking on the stairs.

"No, now wait," my grandmother says to me. "Wait a minute."

My two aunts come into the kitchen. She is with them, wearing the white cotton dress with black polka dots and the flat black velvet bow at the neck. She comes and feeds me the rest of the porridge herself, smiling at me.

"Stand up now and let's see how tall you are," she tells me.

"Almost to your elbow," they say. "See how much she's grown."

"Almost."

"It's her hair."

Hands are on my head, pushing me down; I slide out from under them. Nelly is waiting for me in the yard, holding her nose just under in the watering trough. My stick waits against the door frame, clad in bark.

Nelly looks up at me, drooling glass strings. She starts off around the corner of the house without a flicker of expression.

Switch. Switch. How annoying she is!

But she is a Jersey and we think she is very pretty. "From in front," my aunts sometimes add.

She stops to snatch at the long, untrimmed grass around the gatepost.

"Nelly!"

Whack! I hit her hipbone.

On she goes without even looking around. Flop, flop, down over the dirt sidewalk into the road, across the village green in front of the Presbyterian church. The grass is gray with dew; the church is dazzling. It is high-shouldered and secretive; it leans backwards a little.

Ahead, the road is lined with dark, thin old elms; grass grows long and blue in the ditches. Behind the elms the meadows run along, peacefully, greenly.

We pass Mrs. Peppard's house. We pass Mrs. McNeil's house. We pass Mrs. Geddes's house. We pass Hills' store.

The store is high, and a faded gray-blue, with tall windows, built on a long, high stoop of gray-blue cement with an iron hitching rail along it. Today, in one window there are big cardboard easels, shaped like houses—complete houses and houses with the roofs lifted off to show glimpses of the rooms inside, all in different colors—with cans of paint in pyramids in the middle. But they are an old story. In the other window is something new: shoes, single shoes, summer shoes, each sitting on top of its own box with its mate beneath it, inside, in the dark. Surprisingly, some of them appear to be exactly the colors and texture of pink and blue blackboard chalks, but I can't stop to examine them now. In one door, great overalls hang high in the air on hangers. Miss Ruth Hill looks out the other door and waves. We pass Mrs. Captain Mahon's house.

Nelly tenses and starts walking faster, making over to the right. Every morning and evening we go through this. We are approaching Miss Spencer's house. Miss Spencer is the milliner the way Miss Gurley is the dressmaker. She has a very small white house with the doorstep right on the sidewalk. One front window has lace curtains with a pale-yellow window shade pulled all the way down, inside them; the other one has a shelf across it on which are displayed four summer hats. Out of the corner of my eye I can see that there is a yellow chip straw with little wads of flamingo-colored feathers around the crown, but again there is no time to examine anything.

On each side of Miss Spencer's door is a large old lilac bush. Every time we go by, Nelly determines to brush off all her flies on these bushes—brush them off forever, in one fell swoop. Then Miss Spencer is apt to come to the door and stand there, shaking with anger, between the two bushes still shaking from Nelly's careening passage, and yell at me, sometimes waving a hat in my direction as well.

Nelly, leaning to the right, breaks into a cow trot. I run up with my stick.

Whack!

"Nelly!"

Whack!

Just this once she gives in and we rush safely by.

Then begins a long, pleasant stretch beneath the elms. The Presbyterian manse has a black iron fence with openwork four-sided pillars, like tall, thin bird cages, bird cages for storks. Dr. Gillespie, the minister, appears just as we come along, and rides slowly toward us on his bicycle.

"Good day." He even tips his hat.

"Good day."

He wears the most interesting hat in the village: a man's regular stiff straw sailor, only it is black. Is there a possibility that he paints it at home, with something like stove polish? Because once I had seen one of my aunts painting a straw-colored hat navy blue.

Nelly, oblivious, makes cow flops. Smack. Smack. Smack. Smack.

It is fascinating. I cannot take my eyes off her. Then I step around them: fine dark-green and lacy and watery at the edges.

We pass the McLeans', whom I know very well. Mr. McLean is just coming out of his new barn with the tin hip roof and with him is Jock, their old shepherd dog, long-haired, black and white and yellow. He runs up barking deep, cracked, soft barks in the quiet morning. I hesitate.

Mr. McLean bellows, "Jock! You! Come back here! Are you trying to frighten her?"

To me he says, "He's twice as old as you are."

Finally I pat the big round warm head.

We talk a little. I ask the exact number of Jock's years but Mr. McLean has forgotten.

"He hasn't hardly a tooth in his head and he's got rheumatism. I hope we'll get him through next winter. He still wants to go to the woods with me and it's hard for him in the snow. We'll be lost without him."

Mr. McLean speaks to me behind one hand, not to hurt Jock's feelings: *"Deaf as a post."*

Like anybody deaf, Jock puts his head to one side.

"He used to be the best dog at finding cows for miles around. People used to come from away down the shore to borrow him to find their cows for them. And he'd always find them. The first year we had to leave him behind when we went up to the mountain to get the cows I thought it would kill him. Well, when his teeth started going he couldn't do much with the cows any more. Effie used to say, 'I don't know how we'd run the farm without him.' "

Loaded down with too much black and yellow and white fur, Jock smiles, showing how few teeth he has. He has yellow caterpillars for eyebrows.

Nelly has gone on ahead. She is almost up the hill to Chisolms' when I catch up with her. We turn in to their steep, long drive, through a steep, bare yard crowded with unhappy apple trees. From the top, though, from the Chisolms' back yard, one always stops to look at the view.

There are the tops of all the elm trees in the village and there, beyond them, the long green marshes, so fresh, so salt. Then the Minas Basin, with the tide halfway in or out, the wet red mud glazed with sky blue until it meets the creeping lavender-red water. In the middle of the view, like one hand of a clock pointing straight up, is the steeple of the Presbyterian church. We are in the "Maritimes" but all that means is that we live by the sea.

Mrs. Chisolm's pale frantic face is watching me out the kitchen window as she washes the breakfast dishes. We wave, but I hurry by because she may come out and ask questions. But her questions are not as bad perhaps as those of her husband, Mr. Chisolm, who wears a beard. One evening he had met me in the pasture and asked me how my soul was. Then he held me firmly by both hands while he said a prayer, with his head bowed, Nelly right beside us chewing her cud all the time. I had felt a soul, heavy in my chest, all the way home.

I let Nelly through the set of bars to the pasture where the brook is, to get the mint. We both take drinks and I pick a big bunch of mint, eating a little, scratchy and powerful. Nelly looks over her shoulder and comes back to try it, thinking, as cows do, it might be something especially for her. Her face is close to mine and I hold her by one horn to admire her eyes again. Her nose is blue and as shiny as something in the rain. At such close quarters my feelings for her are mixed. She gives my bare arm a lick, scratchy and powerful, too, almost upsetting me into the brook; then she goes off to join a black-and-white friend she has here, mooing to her to wait until she catches up.

For a while I entertain the idea of not going home today at all, of staying safely here in the pasture all day, playing in the brook and climbing on the squishy, moss-covered hummocks in the swampy part. But an immense, sibilant, glistening loneliness suddenly faces me, and the cows are moving off to the shade of the fir trees, their bells chiming softly, individually.

On the way home there are the four hats in Miss Spencer's window to study, and the summer shoes in Hills'. There is the same shoe in white, in black patent leather, and in the chalky, sugary, unearthly pinks and blues. It has straps that button around the ankle and above, four of them, about an inch wide and an inch apart, reaching away up.

In those unlovely gilded red and green books, filled with illustrations of the Bible stories, the Roman centurions wear them, too, or something very like them.

Surely they are my size. Surely, this summer, pink or blue, my grandmother will buy me a pair!

Miss Ruth Hill gives me a Moirs chocolate out of the glass case. She talks to me: "How is she? We've always been friends.

We played together from the time we were babies. We sat together in school. Right from primer class on. After she went away, she always wrote to me—even after she got sick the first time."

Then she tells a funny story about when they were little.

That afternoon, Miss Gurley comes and we go upstairs to watch the purple dress being fitted again. My grandmother holds me against her knees. My younger aunt is helping Miss Gurley, handing her the scissors when she asks. Miss Gurley is cheerful and talkative today.

The dress is smaller now; there are narrow, even folds down the skirt; the sleeves fit tightly, with little wrinkles over the thin white hands. Everyone is very pleased with it; everyone talks and laughs.

"There. You see? It's so becoming."

"I've never seen you in anything more becoming."

"And it's so nice to see you in color for a change."

And the purple is real, like a flower against the gold-and-white wallpaper.

On the bureau is a present that has just come, from an uncle in Boston whom I do not remember. It is a gleaming little bundle of flat, triangular satin pillows—sachets, tied together with a white satin ribbon, with an imitation rosebud on top of the bow. Each is a different faint color; if you take them apart, each has a different faint scent. But tied together the way they came, they make one confused, powdery odor.

The mirror has been lifted off the bureau and put on the floor against the wall.

She walks slowly up and down and looks at the skirt in it.

"I think that's about right," says Miss Gurley, down on her knees and looking into the mirror, too, but as if the skirt were miles and miles away.

But, twitching the purple skirt with her thin white hands, she says desperately, "I don't know what they're wearing any more. I have no *idea!*" It turns to a sort of wail.

"Now, now," soothes Miss Gurley. "I do think that's about right. Don't you?" She appeals to my grandmother and me.

Light, musical, constant sounds are coming from Nate's shop. It sounds as though he were making a wheel rim.

She sees me in the mirror and turns on me: "Stop sucking your thumb!"

Then in a moment she turns to me again and demands, "Do you know what I want?"

"No."

"I want some humbugs. I'm dying for some humbugs. I don't think I've had any humbugs for years and years and years. If I give you some pennies, will you go to Mealy's and buy me a bag?"

To be sent on an errand! Everything is all right.

Humbugs are a kind of candy, although not a kind I am particularly fond of. They are brown, like brook water, but hard, and shaped like little twisted pillows. They last a long time, but lack the spit-producing brilliance of cherry or strawberry.

Mealy runs a little shop where she sells candy and bananas and oranges and all kinds of things she crochets. At Christmas, she sells toys, but only at Christmas. Her real name is Amelia. She also takes care of the telephone switchboard for the village, in her dining room.

Somebody finds a black pocketbook in the bureau. She counts out five big pennies into my hand, in a column, then one more.

"That one's for you. So you won't eat up all my humbugs on the way home."

Further instructions:

"Don't run all the way."

"Don't stop on the bridge."

I do run, by Nate's shop, glimpsing him inside, pumping away with one hand. We wave. The beautiful big Newfoundland dog is there again and comes out, bounding along with me a ways.

I do not stop on the bridge but slow down long enough to find out the years on the pennies. King George is much bigger than on a five-cent piece, brown as an Indian in copper, but he wears the same clothes; on a penny, one can make out the little ermine trimmings on his coat.

Mealy has a bell that rings when you go in so that she'll hear you if she's at the switchboard. The shop is a step down, dark, with a counter along one side. The ceiling is low and the floor has settled well over to the counter side. Mealy is broad and fat and it looks as though she and the counter and the showcase, stuffed dimly with things every which way, were settling down together out of sight.

Five pennies buys a great many humbugs. I must not take too long to decide what I want for myself. I must get back quickly, quickly, while Miss Gurley is there and everyone is upstairs and the dress is still on. Without taking time to think, quickly I point at the brightest thing. It is a ball, glistening solidly with crystals of pink and yellow sugar, hung, impractically, on an elastic, like a real elastic ball. I know I don't even care for the inside of it, which is soft, but I wind most of the elastic around my arm, to keep the ball off the ground, at least, and start hopefully back.

But one night, in the middle of the night, there is a fire. The church bell wakes me up. It is in the room with me; red flames are burning the wallpaper beside the bed. I suppose I shriek.

The door opens. My younger aunt comes in. There is a lamp lit in the hall and everyone is talking at once.

"Don't cry!" my aunt almost shouts to me. "It's just a fire. Way up the road. It isn't going to hurt you. Don't *cry!*"

"Will! Will!" My grandmother is calling my grandfather. "Do you have to go?"

"No, don't go, Dad!"

"It looks like McLean's place." My grandfather sounds muffled.

"Oh, not their new barn!" My grandmother.

"You can't tell from here." He must have his head out the window.

"*She's* calling for you, Mother." My older aunt: "I'll go."

"No. *I'll* go." My younger aunt.

"Light that other lamp, girl."

My older aunt comes to my door. "It's way off. It's nowhere near us. The men will take care of it. Now you go to sleep." But she leaves my door open.

"Leave her door open," calls my grandmother just then. "Oh, why do they have to ring the bell like that? It's enough to terrify anybody. Will, be *careful.*"

Sitting up in bed, I see my grandfather starting down the stairs, tucking his nightshirt into his trousers as he goes.

"Don't make so much noise!" My older aunt and my grandmother seem to be quarreling.

"Noise! I can't hear myself think, with that bell!"

"I bet Spurgeon's ringing it!" They both laugh.

"It must have been heat lightning," says my grandmother, now apparently in her bedroom, as if it were all over.

"*She's* all right, Mother." My younger aunt comes back. "I don't think she's scared. You can't see the glare so much on that side of the house."

Then my younger aunt comes into my room and gets in bed with me. She says to go to sleep, it's way up the road. The men have to go; my grandfather has gone. It's probably somebody's barn full of hay, from heat lightning. It's been such a hot summer there's been a lot of it. The church bell stops and her voice is suddenly loud in my ear over my shoulder. The last echo of the bell lasts for a long time.

Wagons rattle by.

"Now they're going down to the river to fill the barrels," my aunt is murmuring against my back.

The red flame dies down on the wall, then flares again.

Wagons rattle by in the dark. Men are swearing at the horses.

"Now they're coming back with the water. Go to sleep."

More wagons; men's voices. I suppose I go to sleep.

I wake up and it is the same night, the night of the fire. My aunt is getting out of bed, hurrying away. It is still dark and silent now, after the fire. No, not silent; my grandmother is crying somewhere, not in her room. It is getting gray. I hear one wagon, rumbling far off, perhaps crossing the bridge.

But now I am caught in a skein of voices, my aunts' and my grandmother's, saying the same things over and over, sometimes loudly, sometimes in whispers:

"Hurry. For heaven's sake, *shut the door!*"

"Sh!"

"Oh, we can't go on like this, we . . ."

"It's too dangerous. Remember that . . ."

"Sh! Don't let her . . ."

A door slams.

A door opens. The voices begin again.

I am struggling to free myself.

Wait. Wait. No one is going to scream.

Slowly, slowly it gets daylight. A different red reddens the wallpaper. Now the house is silent. I get up and dress by myself and go downstairs. My grandfather is in the kitchen alone, drinking his tea. He has made the oatmeal himself, too. He gives me some and tells me about the fire very cheerfully.

It had not been the McLeans' new barn after all, but someone else's barn, off the road. All the hay was lost but they had managed somehow to save part of the barn.

But neither of us is really listening to what he is saying; we are listening for sounds from upstairs. But everything is quiet.

On the way home from taking Nelly to the pasture I go to see where the barn was. There are people still standing around, some of them the men who got up in the night to go to the river. Everyone seems quite cheerful there, too, but the smell of burned hay is awful, sickening.

Now the front bedroom is empty. My older aunt has gone back to Boston and my other aunt is making plans to go there after a while, too.

There has been a new pig. He was very cute to begin with, and skidded across the kitchen linoleum while everyone laughed. He grew and grew. Perhaps it is all the same summer, because it is unusually hot and something unusual for a pig happens to him: he gets sunburned. He really gets sunburned, bright pink, but the strangest thing of all, the curled-up end of his tail gets so sunburned it is brown and scorched. My grandmother trims it with the scissors and it doesn't hurt him.

Sometime later this pig is butchered. My grandmother, my aunt, and I shut ourselves in the parlor. My aunt plays a piece on the piano called "Out in the Fields." She plays it and plays it; then she switches to Mendelssohn's "War March of the Priests."

The front room is empty. Nobody sleeps there. Clothes are hung there.

Every week my grandmother sends off a package. In it she puts cake and fruit, a jar of preserves, Moirs chocolates.

Monday afternoon every week.

Fruit, cake, Jordan almonds, a handkerchief with a tatted edge.

Fruit. Cake. Wild-strawberry jam. A New Testament.

A little bottle of scent from Hills' store, with a purple silk tassel fastened to the stopper.

Fruit. Cake. "Selections from Tennyson."

A calendar, with a quotation from Longfellow for every day.

Fruit. Cake. Moirs chocolates.

I watch her pack them in the pantry. Sometimes she sends me to the store to get things at the last minute.

The address of the sanatorium is in my grandmother's handwriting, in purple indelible pencil, on smoothed-out wrapping paper. It will never come off.

I take the package to the post office. Going by Nate's, I walk far out in the road and hold the package on the side away from him.

He calls to me. "Come here! I want to show you something."

But I pretend I don't hear him. But at any other time I still go there just the same.

The post office is very small. It sits on the side of the road like a package once delivered by the post office. The government has painted its clapboards tan, with a red trim. The earth in front of it is worn hard. Its face is scarred and scribbled on, carved with initials. In the evening, when the Canadian Pacific mail is due, a row of big boys leans against it, but in the daytime there is nothing to be afraid of. There is no one in front, and inside it is empty. There is no one except the postmaster, Mr. Johnson, to look at my grandmother's purple handwriting.

The post office tilts a little, like Mealy's shop, and inside it looks as chewed as a horse's manger. Mr. Johnson looks out through the little window in the middle of the bank of glass-fronted boxes, like an animal looking out over its manger. But he is dignified by the thick, beveled-edged glass boxes with their solemn, upright gold-and-black-shaded numbers.

Ours is 21. Although there is nothing in it, Mr. Johnson automatically cocks his eye at it from behind when he sees me.

21.

"Well, well. Here we are again. Good day, good day," he says.

"Good day, Mr. Johnson."

I have to go outside again to hand him the package through the ordinary window, into his part of the post office, because it is too big for the little official one. He is very old, and nice. He has two fingers missing on his right hand where they were caught in a threshing machine. He wears a navy-blue cap with a black leather visor, like a ship's officer, and a shirt with feathery brown stripes, and a big gold collar button.

"Let me see. Let me see. Let me see. Hm," he says to himself, weighing the package on the scales, jiggling the bar with the two remaining fingers and thumb.

"Yes. Yes. Your grandmother is very faithful."

Every Monday afternoon I go past the blacksmith's shop with the package under my arm, hiding the address of the sanatorium with my arm and my other hand.

Going over the bridge, I stop and stare down into the river. All the little trout that have been too smart to get caught—for how long now?—are there, rushing in flank movements, foolish assaults and retreats, against and away from the old sunken fender of Malcolm McNeil's Ford. It has lain there for ages and is supposed to be a disgrace to us all. So are the tin cans that glint there, brown and gold.

From above, the trout look as transparent as the water, but if one did catch one, it would be opaque enough, with a little slick moon-white belly with a pair of tiny, pleated, rose-pink fins on it. The leaning willows soak their narrow yellowed leaves.

Clang.

Clang.

Nate is shaping a horseshoe.

Oh, beautiful pure sound!

It turns everything else to silence.

But still, once in a while, the river gives an unexpected gurgle. "*Slp*," it says, out of glassy-ridged brown knots sliding along the surface.

Clang.

And everything except the river holds its breath.

Now there is no scream. Once there was one and it settled slowly down to earth one hot summer afternoon; or did it float up, into that dark, too dark, blue sky? But surely it has gone away, forever.

It sounds like a bell buoy out at sea.

It is the elements speaking: earth, air, fire, water.

All those other things—clothes, crumbling postcards, broken china; things damaged and lost, sickened or destroyed; even the frail almost-lost scream—are they too frail for us to hear their voices long, too mortal?

Nate!

Oh, beautiful sound, strike again!

1953

Notes

THE BAPTISM. First published in *Life and Letters Today* 16 (Spring 1937), pp. 71–8. Reprinted in *The Best Short Stories 1938 and the Yearbook of the American Short Story*, ed. Edward J. O'Brien, 1938, p. 393; also listed with a three-star rating in the Honor Roll of *The Yearbook*.

THE COUNTRY MOUSE. Published here for the first time. Probably written in 1961.

THE DIARY OF "HELENA MORLEY": THE BOOK & ITS AUTHOR. First published by Farrar, Straus and Giroux in 1957. Written between 1953 and 1956.

EFFORTS OF AFFECTION: A MEMOIR OF MARIANNE MOORE. First published in *Vanity Fair*, May 1983, pp. 44–60. Written between 1969 and 1979.

THE FARMER'S CHILDREN. First published in *Harper's Bazaar*, February 1948, p. 160. Reprinted in *The Best American Short Stories*, ed. Martha Foley, 1949, pp. 39–47.

GREGORIO VALDES. First published as "Gregorio Valdes, 1879–1939," in *Partisan Review* 6 (Summer 1939), pp. 91–7.

GWENDOLYN. First published in *The New Yorker*, June 27, 1953, pp. 26–31.

THE HOUSEKEEPER. First published in *The New Yorker*, September 11, 1948, pp. 56–61, and signed "Sarah Foster."

IN PRISON. First published in *Partisan Review* 4 (March 1938), pp. 3–10. Reprinted in *The Partisan Reader*, eds. William Phillips and Philip Rahv, 1946, pp. 20–7; and in *The Poet's Story*, ed. Howard Moss, 1973.

IN THE VILLAGE. First published in *The New Yorker*, December 19, 1953, pp. 26–34. Reprinted in *Stories from The New Yorker, 1950–1960*, 1960, pp. 290–308. Also reprinted between sections I ("Brazil") and II ("Elsewhere") of the American edition of *Questions of Travel*, 1965.

MEMORIES OF UNCLE NEDDY. First published in *The Southern Review* 13 (Fall 1977), pp. 786–803.

MERCEDES HOSPITAL. Published here for the first time. Written in 1941.

PRIMER CLASS. Published here for the first time. Probably written in 1960.

THE SEA & ITS SHORE. First published in *Life and Letters Today* 17 (Winter 1937), pp. 103–8. Reprinted in *New Letters in America*, eds. Horace Gregory and Eleanor Clark, 1937, pp. 19–25.

TO THE BOTEQUIM & BACK. Published here for the first time. Probably written in 1970.

A TRIP TO VIGIA. First published in *The New Yorker*, June 6, 1983, pp. 34–8. Probably written in 1967.

THE U.S.A. SCHOOL OF WRITING. First published in *The New Yorker*, July 18, 1983, pp. 32–8. Probably written in 1966.